The Inner Life of
Krishnamurti

To Giancarlo,
   with a heart full of gratitude
for your participation at a
memorable event.

   May reading this work inspire
transformations in your life.

   Many blessings,

   [signature]

13 JAN 01

Krishnamurti, Hawaii
P. O. Box 22492
Honolulu, Hawaii 96823

The Inner Life of Krishnamurti

Private Passion and Perennial Wisdom

Aryel Sanat

A publication supported by
THE KERN FOUNDATION

Quest Books
Theosophical Publishing House
Wheaton, Illinois ◆ Chennai (Madras), India

Copyright 1999 by Aryel Sanat

First Quest Edition 1999

All rights reserved. No part of this book may be
reproduced in any manner without written permission
except for quotations embodied in critical articles
or reviews. For additional information write to

The Theosophical Publishing House
P.O. Box 270
Wheaton, IL 60189-0270

A publication of the Theosophical Publishing House,
a department of the Theosophical Society in America

Library of Congress Cataloging-in Publication Data

Sanat, Aryel.
   The inner life of Krishnamurti: private passion and perennial
      wisdom / Aryel Sanat. — 1st Quest ed.
   p.   cm.
   Includes bibliographical references and index.
   ISBN 0-8356-0781-X
   1. Krishnamurti, J. (Jiddu), 1895-1986.   2. Philosophers—
   India.   I. Title.

   B5134.K75 S26   1999
   181'.4—dc21
   [B]
                                                99-052028
                                                CIP

   4   3   2   1   *   99   00   01   02   03   04   05

Printed in the United States of America

Contents

To Connie Sue

ACKNOWLEDGMENTS

OVER THE MANY YEARS IT HAS TAKEN TO PUT into writing what follows, numerous people have contributed in very different ways toward the end result, and I thank them all.

In theosophical and New Age circles, the following people have been of particular help to me: N. Sri Ram, Helen Zahara, Fritz L. Kunz, Emily Sellon, Manuel Metauten, Joy Mills, Abelardo del Real, Geoffrey Hodson, Carlos Menéndez, Dora Kunz, Capel (Mac) McCutcheon, Radha Burnier, René Revert, Marcelo Yanes, Ed Abdill, Marcial Cruz, Bing Escudero, Francisco León Fesser, Clarence (Pete) R. Pedersen, John Algeo, and Florence Kanga.

For a better practical understanding of Gurdjieff, whose teachings will be detected here and there in the text, I thank Professor Jacob Needleman and Kathy Riordan Speeth.

I owe a great deal to numerous people with whom I have participated in Krishnamurti discussions over the last thirty years. While it would not be possible to mention them all, the most critical of these contributions came from David Bohm, Fritz Wilhelm, Alan Kishbaugh, David Shainberg, María Teresa St. John, Michael Nitschke, Alain Naudé, Armando Verea, Telegar Satish, Galadriel Frond, Elizabeth and Bob Russell, Carlos Román, Rohit Vaidya, Arun Prabhu, C. P. Prakash, Ruth Geier Conner, Richard Purple, Steve Sante, Bill Byrne, Kirti R. Vashee, Elliot Ryan, and Michael Krohnen. I further thank Michael for what is, to my mind, the best book to date about Krishnamurti's life, *The Kitchen Chronicles: 1,001 Lunches with J. Krishnamurti*. His friendship over more than two decades has been a source of inspiration throughout.

The most life-transforming of these explorations were

with Krishnamurti himself.

I also thank Tarthang Tulku and his staff at the Nyingma Institute in Berkeley, Roshi Seikan Hasegawa and the staff of the Rock Creek Buddhist Temple of America near Washington, D. C., and Rolando Amador for practical insights into Vajrayana and Zen Buddhism.

I will be forever grateful to the Rev. Armando Velasco Farnés, who helped put into sharp relief for me what the real teachings of Christianity are and their intimate relationship to the perennial philosophy—a theme that appears in various forms in my work.

Michael Sellon helped bring out my innate passion for art and aesthetics and introduced me to the very intimate and important relationship between all art forms and the foundations of the perennial philosophy referred to in the early chapters. For that, and for a friendship that was pivotal in my understanding and development, I will always be grateful to him.

I thank Professors R. M. Lemos, Howard Pospesel, Edward Schuh, Leonard Carrier, David Cooper, Charley D. Hardwick, David F. T. Rodier and Charles S. J. White. They contributed much through their friendship and/or teaching to my philosophical formation, which is a major factor in some elements in this book. Discussions with Professor Renée Weber were also of great value.

I thank Toni Packer for her excellent discussions of Krishnamurti's teachings and their inescapable connection with Zen in *The Work of this Moment*. I similarly express my gratitude to Sylvia Cranston for her indispensable anthology of the sources for the New Age, *Reincarnation: The Phoenix Fire Mystery*, which she coedited with Joseph Head, and for her definitive biography of H. P. Blavatsky, *HPB: The Extraordinary Life and Influence of Helena Blavatsky, Founder of the Modern Theosophical Movement*. I also thank Joseph E. Ross for his revealing historical account of one of the first New Age colonies in California, *Krotona of Old Hollywood 1866-1913*.

Special mention must also be made of Michael Mendizza's remarkable aesthetic and historical achievement in his video film,

Krishnamurti: With a Silent Mind, produced by Evelyne Blau. I thank them both for this unusually exquisite film, and for their kindness.

Without John White's faith in this project and dogged determination in seeing it through publication, it would not have been published. Words will never convey the depth of my gratitude.

Connie Sue Sanabria, Pete Pedersen, Florence Kanga, Hillary Rodrigues, Cornelis (Neil) J. Bakker, James Burnell Robinson, Paula Mango, Mary Zimbalist, and T. Parchure made valuable suggestions toward the completion of the final version.

Like the process of smelting out ore impurities, Carolyn Bond's superb editing skills forced me to write a much better book than I would have on my own. Thank you, Carolyn.

I am of course solely responsible for any imperfections remaining after so many valuable critiques and assessments from everyone mentioned.

Without the multidimensional support and tender care of Connie Sue Sanabria, this book would not be a reality. To her I further owe a deeper understanding of *what is* than any book or discussion can—or has—conferred.

There is a kind of help that is very difficult to acknowledge because it comes from the silence, where personal credit has very little significance. Nevertheless, from this end, one cannot help but feel a depth of gratitude.

Introduction

J. Krishnamurti is, perhaps, the quintessential iconoclast of the twentieth century. Though he steadfastly denied identification with any particular philosophy, religion, or school of psychology, his transformative insights and observations have deeply influenced many people, and indeed, the century itself. Though some have tried to write his story, nobody is likely ever to succeed in telling all there is to tell. The complete Krishnamurti story may never be known. What I have tried to do in what follows is investigate a few unexplored pieces of the puzzle implied by his life and work—particularly his esoteric life, a subject that has been kept under wraps until now.

Part of the reason for the silence surrounding Krishnamurti's inner life is that most of those who have been interested in his life and work—including writers on those subjects—have perceived him as opposed, without exception, to anything related to esoteric doctrines. Indeed, in many of his talks and writings, Krishnamurti insisted emphatically that occult mystifications were frivolous or dangerous ways of dissipating energy. He often said such energy should be directed to the task of understanding oneself and *what is*, without any of the screens provided by one's conditioning. He stressed repeatedly that if humanity is to have a spiritually meaningful future—or perhaps any future at all—the radical mutation that such understanding implies must take place.

Further, throughout more than six decades of teaching, Krishnamurti earned a reputation for scathing exposés of the shallowness and danger implied in all belief systems, particularly those based on psychic or occult teachings. In light of this public stance, people familiar with Krishnamurti's work may find it surprising that his private life was rich in esoteric happenings from early childhood until his death. There is no question but that the insights and observations of Krishnamurti's work are ultimately what matter, as he himself emphasized and as is underlined in the following discussion. Nevertheless, the fact that his personal life was so saturated with the esoteric is intriguing, particularly since he was in public so vigorously opposed to occult teachings.

Even more important, however, is the fact that an understanding of Krishnamurti's inner life is essential to a clear grasp of the deeper aspects of what he taught. Krishnamurti himself suggested this, as the explorations in Parts II and III reveal. Anyone sympathetic to Krishnamurti's insights and observations is thus placed in an unenviable position: Rejection of his esoteric life as the product of some vision, delusion, or hallucination means accepting a break in the integrity of what he said in his talks and books.

Yet most authors who have written about Krishnamurti explain away the esoteric elements present in his life by attributing them to hallucinations, delusions, visions, or inventions on the part of the witnesses—and often of Krishnamurti himself. However, these attempts to insist on a separation between Krishnamurti and esoteric teachings may be based on a misunderstanding of the nature and purpose of the esoteric. Because of deeply entrenched prejudices regarding what esoterism is and what Krishnamurti said regarding it, I begin Part I with a look at the perennial philosophy and its tenets, especially as they relate to Krishnamurti's life and work.

Probably the most intriguing aspect of my assessment of Krishnamurti's esoteric life has to do with the question of whether and in what way the teachers called "Masters" by him and by the theosophists who took care of him as a young man are "real." While the esoteric tradition often speaks of Masters in the context of myths, they are also said to be men and women who have been the custodians and exponents of the perennial philosophy. It is generally believed that Krishnamurti denied the existence of these Masters and denied being the vehicle for the manifestation of the Lord Maitreya, as his theosophical mentors had proclaimed. Parts II and III document fully that Krishnamurti denied neither. In fact, at the heart of this account is the revelation that the Masters and the Lord Maitreya were realities to Krishnamurti, apparently every single day of his life since he first encountered them in his youth.

Part III also considers some of the deeper, philosophical implications of Krishnamurti's spiritual experiences, particularly as they relate to the future of humanity. Though Krishnamurti had no system, no method, no metaphysics—he was most emphatically not a philosopher in the narrow, academic sense—his work, I contend, represents the best and deepest that twentieth-century philosophy has achieved. Like Socrates, he was a pure investigator into *that which is*. Interestingly, Socrates' explorations were often limited by his identification with Greek culture, whereas Krishnamurti had no such identifications—with their presuppositions—at any level.

For many students of the New Age movement as well as for Krishnamurti scholars—not to mention academics in general—the revelations made in these pages are likely to be quite controversial. My research has attempted to examine the evidence—what Krishnamurti said about these questions, what those who witnessed his life and doings reported, and what well-documented accounts of events reveal about his insights and experiences—with the aim of clarifying the true nature of his esoteric life. What you will find in what follows is largely the result of extensive and intensive discussions, spanning several decades, with people holding very diverse—even mutually exclusive—perspectives regarding Krishnamurti and his approach to issues.

It is beyond the scope of this book to present a comprehensive biography of Krishnamurti. It is possible to follow much of what is said here without previous acquaintance with his life. However, the reader is forewarned that familiarity with what has been published about Krishnamurti's life and work will provide useful background for understanding the issues discussed. Quite apart from the strange happenings in his life—and as the very extensive bibliography cited suggests—there is an immense amount of published material that is germane to this discussion. Among the most useful primary sources are Pupul Jayakar's *Krishnamurti: A Biography* and Mary Lutyens' four volumes of memoirs of Krishnamurti. Other books on Krishnamurti's life and work, some useful and others flawed in various ways, are referred to in the endnotes for readers who wish to explore further the themes I discuss.

However, as Krishnamurti was a revolutionary in the deepest sense of that word, it will most emphatically not do to settle for someone else's explanations or interpretations of either his life or what he said. If you want to give yourself an opportunity to understand Krishnamurti, you must go to the source itself. As a place to start, I would strongly recommend Krishnamurti's *The First and Last Freedom* and his three-volume *Commentaries on Living*.

When he was a boy, Krishnamurti was usually called "Krishna." Later, many called him "Krishnaji," which in India is considered both endearing and respectful. In the last two decades of his life he often went by "K." All these names are used in the text.

The reader will notice that the word *theosophy* is sometimes capitalized, but more often is not. This acknowledges the distinction between Theosophy as a system of thought—and therefore capitalized—and a transformative, nondiscursive, psychological engagement in theosophy, which is in lower case. The system of thought called Theosophy is a recent, conceptual outgrowth of the ancient initiatory states of awareness identified as theosophy. It serves the useful purpose of making theosophy more accessible to those for whom analytical thinking still has an appeal. In itself, however, transformative theosophy shuns all conditioning and therefore all thought, including systems of thought.

Throughout this study a style of tentativeness, manifested in expressions such as "perhaps," "it seems that," "apparently," is sometimes employed. This is because research into questions such as those concerning Krishnamurti's inner life, to be a true investigation, means one necessarily does not know one's way. Making assertions only masks the facts and deflects us from them. To find the facts of any matter means putting aside any presuppositions. This is particularly true in this investigation. Beginning without presuppositions is, in fact, the foundation of phenomenological research. Setting aside one's preconceptions, insight may be possible, although there is still no guarantee. In fact, the psychological state that takes place in the process of the investigation may be more significant than the knowledge arrived at as its consequence.

One final word. What follows is the result of more than thirty years of research. Even though I have conducted that research in a spirit of letting truth lead me by the hand—wherever it might go—errors of various sorts may have crept in. Errors of fact, if any can be found, ought to be easily correctable by helpful critiques, for which I would be most thankful. I have already benefited from such critiques, as is reflected in some of the names mentioned in the acknowledgments. More difficult to pinpoint with accuracy—but perhaps more important in their potential consequences—are any errors I may have made in the assessment of the material discussed. I should therefore make it very clear that I have no "ax to grind" for or against anyone, either Krishnamurti or any other person or organization mentioned. Anyone looking for a gospel in the following pages will be disappointed: This book is essentially an inquiry into the facts concerning Krishnamurti's inner life, not a promotion for any idea or group.

I am not a "devotee" of Krishnamurti, if by that expression is meant deifying him or his teachings, or assuming that he can do—or say—no wrong. In spite of the nature of much of the material in this book, I believe that, while exceptional, Krishnamurti was a human being and as such was subject to failings common to all humanity. Nor do I identify with, or have a predilection for, any particular school, organization, or teaching.

You may take what follows as part of an ongoing, friendly dialogue on who J. Krishnamurti was. I ask the reader, as is often recommended in courts of law, to suspend judgment until the whole case has been heard. Krishnamurti's inner life is a very strange story, not the least because he largely kept it a secret for more than five decades. It is a story with critical implications for our understanding of both his life and his work. But equally important, it is essential for our understanding of theosophy, Buddhism, the teachings of Gurdjieff, the perennial philosophy—in fact, the contemporary spiritual milieu in its entirety.

With that preamble, let us begin.

PART ONE

THE FOUNTAINHEAD

CHAPTER ONE

The Perennial Philosophy

J. KRISHNAMURTI ARRIVED FOR THE FIRST TIME in California's Ojai Valley in the summer of 1922, when he was twenty-seven. Shortly afterwards, he went through mysterious experiences of a psychological, psychic, and spiritual nature, which included physical signs and manifestations. These happenings have been identified by some with the transformations of "higher yoga." At the time, Krishnamurti referred to what was happening to him as "the process," an expression that has subsequently been used by everyone who has spoken or written of these experiences, though he also sometimes used yogic terminology to refer to them.

In her memoir of K, Pupul Jayakar described the events this way:

> In August 1922 Krishnamurti was to be plunged into the intense spiritual awakening that changed the course of his life. In the Indian tradition, the yogi who delves into the labyrinth of consciousness awakens exploding kundalini energies and entirely new fields of psychic phenomena, journeying into unknown areas of the mind. A yogi who touches these primordial energies and undergoes mystic initiation is recognized as being vulnerable to immense dangers; the body and mind face perils that could lead to insanity or death.

The yogi learns the secret doctrines and experiences the awakening of dormant energy under the instruction of the guru. Once the yogi becomes an adept, these transformations of consciousness on the playground of consciousness are revealed in a mystical drama. The body and mind must undergo a supremely dangerous journey. The adept is surrounded and protected by his disciples; secrecy and a protective silence pervade the atmosphere.[1]

There are several points worth looking at carefully in Pupul Jayakar's comments. However, in order to understand her remarks, it is important that we explore the background and context in which Krishnamurti's experiences took place, a task which takes us into the body of teachings generally referred to as the perennial philosophy. A look at these teachings and their historical background will help us put Krishnamurti's life and experiences in proper perspective.

K's Teachers

While Jayakar's remarks are made in general about any yogi, she gives the impression that K had a guru who was in charge of all the proceedings connected with the process. When the process took place, however, references made by K and other witnesses in this regard were not to one guru, but to several teachers. K and others called these teachers, who included Gautama Buddha and the Lord (or Buddha) Maitreya, the "Masters." These teachers were said by K and others to have been the same who inspired the foundation of the Theosophical Society, a worldwide organization founded by Madame H. P. Blavatsky and Colonel Henry S. Olcott in 1875, devoted to the brotherhood of humanity and the study of comparative religion, philosophy, and science. The Society is said by many to be the springboard for what has come to be called the New Age movement and for numerous other cultural developments of the twentieth century. I call this grand phenomenon "the perennial renaissance," for reasons that will become clear below.

Some students of K have stated that these teachers were visions, or even hallucinations. The explanations offered in many books about Krishnamurti concerning his teachers are unfortunately puzzling in that they contradict everything he himself said on the subject. For instance, in *Krishnamurti: The Man, The Mystery, and The Message,* Stuart Holroyd seems certain that K must have been wrong in what he perceived regarding these teachers. Holroyd says about K's more explicit pronouncements:

> One cannot but wonder whether there was not, perhaps at a subconscious level, an element of role-playing and even self-deception in the way that Krishnamurti was speaking at this time.[2]

For her part, Pupul Jayakar characterizes Krishnamurti's connection with these teachers as "visions," without providing evidence for her opinion:

> [K] beheld visions of the Buddha, Maitreya, and the other Masters of the occult hierarchy.[3]

Given the fact that K himself never described his encounters as "visions" and that his whole life was about *not* being deceived, opinions to the contrary would seem to require a great deal more than unsupported assertions. A better course, I suggest, and one that I plan to follow, is to look at the evidence concerning how K himself viewed these experiences and how witnesses described the events in question.

In subsequent manifestations of the process that took place in the late 1940s, in the presence of Pupul Jayakar and her sister, Nandini Mehta, K always spoke in the plural when referring to those who were in charge of the psychic proceedings. Who, we must ask, were those "teachers," and what part did they play in his life in particular and in the inception of the perennial renaissance in general?

It seems clear from what K himself stated at various times that his teachers were the same as those identified by Madame Blavatsky and others as connected to the dissemination of the perennial philosophy and the founding of the theosophical movement. If we accept that K was stating the simple truth about who his teachers were, a great deal can be explained about his experiences that otherwise remains mysterious. More importantly, pivotal elements of what K taught can be clarified by recognizing their connection to the perennial perspective. All of this makes it critical for anyone who wishes to understand K's life and work to have as good an understanding as possible of who these teachers were according to K and to those who first brought their teachings to public attention.

The Physical Reality of the Masters

Helena Petrovna Blavatsky (1831-1891; referred to as HPB) said in numerous works that she started the theosophical movement at the behest of her teachers, who she said were the living exponents and custodians of the very ancient perennial philosophy. After Blavatsky, many other esoteric writers have attributed spiritual teachings to these same teachers. Some have referred to them as "Ascended Masters," "the Great White Brotherhood," and similar appellations. Though their work is independent of the Theosophical Society and its founders, Elizabeth Clare Prophet and Alice Bailey, for example, stated that their books were inspired by these teachers.

More recently, a new crop of writers, mostly scholars of early theosophical history, have attempted to assess the reality of the Masters. Many begin with the assumption that these teachers were Blavatsky's imaginative creation. Alternately, they claim that, if the Masters were real in any way, they were people

Blavatsky met in the ordinary course of her life and about whom she exaggerated. Perhaps the best known of these recent studies is K. Paul Johnson's *The Masters Revealed*.[4] Johnson and others who claim that the Masters are fictional are entitled to their opinions. When dealing with the question of Blavatsky's teachers, however, a large body of evidence and quite a number of reputable witnesses can document the physical reality of these teachers.

For instance, Colonel Henry Steel Olcott (1832-1907; first president of the Theosophical Society) wrote a six-volume history of the early years of the movement, in which he gave numerous instances of the physical reality of the Masters.[5] Olcott's evidence is of special interest for a number of reasons. To begin with, he was himself an eyewitness: He reports having met the Masters on several occasions, both alone and in the presence of others, including, on a few occasions, HPB. Of equal importance, his background as a lawyer and journalist enhanced his innate abilities as a researcher and impartial observer. Further, before his association with HPB, he had been one of the most respected psychic investigators in the world and had exposed numerous frauds. In fact, it was in this capacity and as a journalist for the New York *Sun* that he first met HPB.[6] Olcott had earned his rank during the American Civil War investigating graft and fraud in the military and was so highly respected that he was put in charge of the investigation of President Lincoln's assassination.

Given Olcott's background, reputation, and careful research methods, his evidence must be considered specifically and taken seriously. He made notes immediately after each physical encounter with the Masters. If there were others present, Olcott secured from them affidavits to the effect that they had indeed been part of an experience in which a Master was physically present. And he always made sure he had witnesses attesting to these affidavits. Again, Olcott's evidence is not limited to one or two meetings; he reports witnessed encounters, with supporting affidavits, that span the period from 1874 to 1907.

The Masters sometimes left a physical item behind after these encounters, some of which—including letters and a turban a Master was wearing—can be examined to this day. Later researchers, such as Geoffrey Barborka, have also investigated and documented the physical presence of the Masters in the early years of the movement. Barborka provides testimonials of numerous eyewitnesses who attest to the Masters' physical reality.[7]

According to documented reports, the Masters communicated physically not only with HPB and Olcott but with at least two dozen other people, most of whom were disciples. Among these others, the most important from the perspective of the present investigation were Annie Besant (1847-1933; who became second president of the Theosophical Society in 1907) and Charles Webster Leadbeater (1847-1934). Their first meetings with the Masters occurred while HPB and Olcott were still living, and their relationship with the Masters continued until Leadbeater (CWL) and Besant (AB) died (in 1934 and 1933, respectively). The early years of the Theosophical Society—its most influential period, when CWL and AB were still vigorous presences—ended in the mid to late 1920s. It was precisely at that point that these same teachers began to be a presence in Krishnamurti's lifetime of teaching. No one has given evidence that they communicated with others once K began his work as a teacher. Thus Krishnamurti was himself one of many witnesses to the existence of these teachers. In fact, he may turn out to be their most significant witness.

According to Blavatsky, the Masters were neither "spirits of light" nor "goblins damn'd," as she wrote in *The Key to Theosophy*.[8] Rather, she said—and her colleagues and other witnesses concurred—that her teachers were men who happened to be wiser, more insightful, and more compassionate than the common run of humanity. (Some of these teachers are said to be women, but no feminine teachers were known to be openly involved in Blavatsky's work.) Many of them—though not all—had presumably acquired yogic abilities. These abilities made it possible for them to communicate with people in ways that might be considered "magical" or "supernatural" by someone unacquainted with deeper aspects of yoga and similar esoteric schools. Anyone wishing to speak of these Masters—whether in the context of writing or speaking about K or in any other context— should read Blavatsky's own words about them:

> [The Masters] are *living men*, born as we are born, and doomed to die like every other mortal. . . . We call them "Masters" because they are our teachers; and because from them we have derived all the Theosophical truths, however inadequately some of us may have expressed, and others understood, them. They are men of great learning, whom we term initiates, and still greater holiness of life. They are not ascetics in the ordinary sense, though they certainly remain apart from the turmoil and strife of your western world.[9]

One of Blavatsky's eminent students, Gottfried de Purucker, asserted the living presence of these teachers:

> No one who has read history can be oblivious of the fact that its annals are bright at certain epochs with the amazing splendor of certain human beings, who during the periods of their lifetimes, have swayed the destinies, not merely of nations, but of whole continents. The names of some of these men are household words in all civilized countries, and the most negligent student of history cannot have done otherwise than have stood amazed at the mark that they made in the world, while they lived—yes, and perhaps have left behind them results surpassing in almost immeasurable degree the remarkable achievements of their own respective lifetimes.
>
> A few of these are the Buddha and

Shankaracharya in India; Lao-Tse and Confucius in China; Jesus the great Syrian Sage in his own epoch and land; Apollonius of Tyana, Pythagoras, Orpheus, Olen, Musaeus, Pamphos, and Philammon, in Greece; and many, many more in other lands. . . .

One point of great importance should be noted: that a careful scrutiny of the teachings of these Great Men, the Seers and Sages of past times, shows us that in the various and varying forms in which their respective Messages were cast, there is always to be found an identical systematized Doctrine, identical in substance in all cases, though frequently varying in outward form: a fact proving the existence all over the world of what Theosophy very rightly points to as the existence of a Universal Religion of mankind—a Religion-Philosophy-Science based on Nature herself, and by no means nor at any time resting solely on the teachings of any one individual, however great he may have been. It is also foolish, downright absurd, for any thoughtful man or woman to deny the existence of these great outstanding figures of world-history, for there they are; and the more we know about them, the more fully do we begin to understand something of their sublime nature and powers. . . .

We introduced these great men in order to illustrate the thesis that the human race has produced these monuments of surpassing genius in the past; and there is not the slightest reasonable or logical argument that could be alleged by anybody in support of the very lame and halting notion that no such men live now, or could live in the future. The burden of all the evidence at hand runs quite to the contrary. It would be a riddle virtually unsolvable, if one were to suppose that because such men have existed in the past, they could not exist again or that—and this comes to the same thing—what the human race has once produced, it could never again produce.[10]

Nietzsche

One of the best contributions to understanding what a Master is may come not from the New Age milieu but from Friedrich Nietzsche (1844-1900). Explaining Nietzsche's course of thought will also illumine an important dimension of this study—specifically, the necessity for transformation, which is central to the work of both HPB and K.

Nietzsche was deeply concerned that humanity had come to a point where the old nostrums of conventional religion would no longer serve adequately to rein in the darker side of the human psyche. Speaking primarily of Christianity and Judaism but insisting this was a universal phenomenon, he predicted that the moralities and religions the world knew in the nineteenth century would lead to nihilism—to loss of any sense of morality worthy of the name, to loss of any sense of communion with something good, true, and beautiful. The old ways had run their course. A new morality, a new way of being, was called for if the darkest dangers of nihilism were to be avoided.

However, what could such a new morality be based on? It could not be based on metaphysics. Immanuel Kant (1724-1804) and Ludwig Feuerbach (1804-1872) had led the way in showing why the claims of metaphysics and conventional religion have absolutely no foundation. It is humans who create what they believe is reality, Kant would say; it is humans who create what they believe is religion, Feuerbach would say.

Nietzsche predicted that as the public became increasingly educated, their disappointment in the old systems would lead first to cynicism and then to some form of psychological and social chaos. Psychologically, there would be more depression and more dependence on some form of narcotic—religion having once been the great narcotic; once it failed, use of chemical narcotics would be widespread. Socially, there would be more enmity and self-centeredness, based on resentment and pettiness. To see how accurate a prophet Nietzsche was, all we have to do is look around at the world today.

According to Nietzsche, humanity would find itself at a major crossroads just after the nineteenth century. Either humans would discover a new way to be, or they would be overtaken by disaster. As he saw it, these were the only choices. Whichever each one of us chooses, that is what we choose for the entire human race. We and we alone are responsible for what happens in our daily lives and for what happens globally. There are no longer scriptures and authorities to appeal to as there were in the past.

If metaphysics, conventional religion, and morality are cast aside, what could be the foundation for a new humanity, a new era? Even by Nietzsche's time, the limitations of the analytical mind for dealing effectively with ethical, aesthetic, and religious questions—the deeper problems of humanity—were already recognized. If anything, the twentieth century has turned that nineteenth-century insight, which then had the makings of a mere skirmish, into a rout.

What is required, in fact, is not a new system of some kind; what is required is *transformation*. Humans must put behind them the resentment, fear, hope, and pettiness that always accompany reliance on the analytical mind—that is, on concepts—for solving deeper issues. A new human being must come into existence who is not a follower and a believer but, in Nietzsche's words, an *Übermensch*—literally, a superman.

Nietzsche's characterization of this superman comes intriguingly close to what HPB said about the Masters. The superman is "beyond good and evil," that is, the superman does not live according to conventional systems of morality with their very limited sense of "right" and "wrong." Christ and the Buddha would be examples: they did not follow the conventions of their societies but set the laws of morality themselves by their own goodness. The superman also has no hope or fear, since both of

these are based on the assumption that one is a time-bound entity, and the superman lives beyond time. As Philip Novak put it:

> The Superman is one: whose self-mastery yields an
> abundance of the power to create; who exercises the
> master privilege of the free spirit—living *experi-*
> *mentally*; who bids farewell to the reverences of
> youth and who stands apart from the views and val-
> ues of the herd; who reverences enemies as allies;
> who knows how to forget and recuperate from the
> blows of life; who shakes off with a single shrug the
> vermin that eat deeply into others; whose overflow-
> ing plenitude and gratitude cleanse both body and
> spirit of all guilt and all *ressentiment*; who perceives
> that "body" and "spirit" are two names for a single
> mystery; who calls humankind to return in love to
> its true home, the Earth; whose every muscle quiv-
> ers with a proud consciousness of truly free will and
> a sovereign individuality that 'no longer flows out
> into a God'; who realizes that creative individuality
> is indeed the Earth's goal and humanity's hope; who,
> without metaphysical consolations, affirms life not
> only in its joy but in all its horror and who, thereby,
> conquers nihilism. . . . This 'anti-nihilist; this victor
> over God and nothingness—*he must come one day.'*
>
> The Superman is shaped in the school of
> self-overcoming whose curriculum requires both
> courage and discipline, and above all, the ability to
> distinguish between an asceticism that denies life
> and one that stands in its service. The school of self-
> overcoming gives birth to the creative will.[11]

There are important differences between the notions of the
superman and the Masters. However, everything Nietzsche has to
say about the superman is applicable to everything HPB said

about the Masters. Krishnamurti's numerous remarks about transformation point in the same direction. That is, HPB, Nietzsche, and K were addressing the same issue but from different perspectives. Therefore, considering all three simultaneously enriches our understanding of who the Masters are and what transformation is.

Incidentally, this explains the high regard in which Nietzsche was held in theosophical and related circles even while he was living. Rudolf Steiner, who was then a Theosophist, met Nietzsche and wrote a series of articles as well as a book about him.[12] Given the revolutionary nature of Nietzsche's work and the fact that the rest of the world largely ignored him for about a century, such interest on the part of the Theosophists is clearly more than a passing curiosity. In 1920 Krishnaji read Nietzsche's *Thus Spake Zarathustra*—a major source for the notion of the superman—a book that "impressed him," according to Mary Lutyens.[13]

The Perennial Renaissance

What Nietzsche said was so similar on important points to theosophical teachings, and like HPB, he was so much ahead of his time, it is hard not to see his work as integral to the grand perennial effort of our era. Contemporary with Nietzsche, there were other revolutionary thinkers in various fields who seem to have been similarly inspired and, like Nietzsche, were perhaps peripherally but not directly connected with theosophical work. For these reasons, it seems appropriate to speak of the grand historical phenomenon of our times as the perennial renaissance rather than as the theosophical movement. The theosophical movement is unquestionably the center around which much of the perennial work turned, but the perennial renaissance is clearly more comprehensive and more pervasive. As one of HPB's perennial teachers said in a letter addressed to an English Theosophist:

> Europe is a large place but the world is bigger yet.
> . . . There is more to this movement than you have
> yet had an inkling of, and the work of the T. S. is
> linked in with similar work that is secretly going on
> in all parts of the world. Even in the T. S. there is a
> division managed by a Greek Brother [Master]
> about which not a person in the Society has a suspi-
> cion excepting the old woman [HPB] and Olcott; and
> even he only knows it is progressing, and occasion-
> ally executes an order I send him in connection with
> it.[14]

The presence of numerous circles of theosophical influence
throughout the world is amply documented, for instance, by
James Webb in his book *The Occult Establishment.* This is all the
more interesting given Webb's lack of sympathy with
Theosophy.[15]

Asian Renaissance

The work of Blavatsky's teachers was instrumental in
bringing about major shifts in several Asian cultures, which experienced significant transformations as a result and which have in
turn had a great impact on subsequent developments in religion,
philosophy, and social life all over the world.[16] Though this influence is well documented, it is unfortunately not generally known.

An example of this influence would be the developments
that took place in the Hindu Renaissance in the twentieth century. Mahatma Gandhi is widely acknowledged as a pivotal figure in
this movement, but it is rarely recognized that what started him
on his path toward reform and revolution was his contact with
HPB and her disciples. In his *Autobiography* he explains how he
left India for England, yearning to become as British as he could
and leave behind what he then perceived to be the superstitions of
his country. In London, however, he met Blavatsky and a group of
theosophists, who showed him the enormous value of the Hindu

scriptures—something he had not conceived of before. His main tutors were Bertram and Archibald Keightley, editors of HPB's magnum opus, *The Secret Doctrine*.[17]

It is true that one person does not a revolution make. Other important figures, including Rabindranath Tagore, Sri Bhagavan Das, Jawaharlal Nehru, and Sarvepalli Radhakrishnan, contributed to the twentieth-century Hindu Renaissance. What is not widely known is that they were all members of the Theosophical Society. Bhagavan Das and Radhakrishnan in particular were following in the footsteps of HPB's teachers in their expositions of Indian culture and philosophy.

Another major landmark in the Hindu Renaissance was the establishment of the Central Hindu College in Benares (Varanasi) in 1898 as the first educational institution in India where a high level of respect for Indian scriptures and philosophy joined hands with rigorous European scholarly methods. What is not widely acknowledged is that the College was founded by Annie Besant. She continued to support it until her death in 1933.

The Perennial Philosophy

The perennial philosophy, or theosophy, does not belong to any single culture or regional tradition. It is not strictly Asian, as has been suggested by some writers, just as it is not European, African, or Mayan. It transcends all of these specific traditions. Moreover, a wider and truer understanding of the perennial philosophy is more likely to be had by not holding fast to traditional, regional interpretations.

For instance, a fundamental perennial teaching is that there is a state of awareness of insight and compassion. Christians refer to the all-comprehensive reality that is this state of awareness by the name "Christ." Buddhists might call it "Avalokiteshvara," while people in other religions and cultures give it yet other names. From the perennial perspective, the names and the cultural trappings that go with them are of little importance; what is important is daily communion with this insight-compassion.

Many Christians, however, become caught in the cultural trappings surrounding insight-compassion and insist that it is only accessible through the name and form of Christ as our Lord and Savior. Communion with universal insight and compassion is thus turned into acceptance of certain beliefs. This is used by some Christians to justify segregating themselves from those who do not share in the world of beliefs identified as Christian. In this way the universal, perennial teaching is turned into something incompatible with it—it becomes particular and limited. This happens, of course, not only in Christianity but in all religions and cultures.

Aldous Huxley, in the 1940s, was the first to use the expression "perennial philosophy" in the sense it has come to have.[18] However, he was following the lead of Blavatsky in using the phrase to refer to that body of ancient teachings. Blavatsky alternately spoke of "occult philosophy," "the Hermetic teachings," "*gupta vidya*," "occultism," "the ancient wisdom," "esoteric teachings," "the secret doctrine," and "theosophy," among a number of other appellations, by which she meant the same body of teachings that Huxley was talking about when he spoke of the perennial philosophy.

It should be explained that the word *occultism* (and its cognates), which was employed extensively by HPB and her early students, was used by her strictly as a synonym for the perennial philosophy. In her writings, that family of words never has the connotations of evil and the supernatural that they have come to have in the writings of other authors. It is important to keep this in mind whenever references are made to K's "occult" or "esoteric" life, in order to avoid confusion. In her work *The Key to Theosophy*, which was written in the form of questions and answers on various subjects related to the perennial philosophy, HPB commented:

The "Wisdom-Religion" was one in antiquity; and the sameness of primitive religious philosophy is proven to us by the identical doctrines taught to the Initiates during the MYSTERIES, an institution once universally diffused. "All the old worships indicate the existence of a single Theosophy anterior to them. The key that is to open one must open all; otherwise it cannot be the right key."

. . . So it is in our day. We can show the line of descent of every Christian religion, as of every, even the smallest, sect. The latter are the minor twigs or shoots grown on the larger branches; but shoots and branches spring from the same trunk— the WISDOM-RELIGION. To prove this was the aim of Ammonius [Saccas], who endeavoured to induce Gentiles and Christians, Jews and Idolaters, to lay aside their contentions and strifes, remembering only that they were all in possession of the same truth under various vestments, and were all the children of a common mother. This is the aim of Theosophy likewise.[19]

Blavatsky also said that the "wisdom-religion," or perennial philosophy, had been taught secretly for millennia in all major cultures of the world. Anyone interested in becoming acquainted with its teachings and practices, she said, would have to be initiated into its "mysteries." The word *mystery* comes from the Greek *mysterion*, meaning "secret rite" or "divine secret." This word in turn is related to *mystes*, "one initiated into the mysteries." Krishnamurti's process, as well as several initiations he underwent prior to the process, were said by him and by his theosophical mentors to be part of that ancient tradition.

Why, we might ask, did such initiations and the teachings they conveyed need to be secret? The word *occult*, which means "hidden," was applied to these experiences and teachings largely because they were traditionally veiled in secrecy. To understand this necessity, it is best to quote Blavatsky at length, since she provides the background for our discussion of the perennial philosophy:

> The WISDOM-RELIGION was ever one, and being the last word of possible human knowledge, was, therefore, carefully preserved. It preceded by long ages the Alexandrian Theosophists [Saccas and his disciples], reached the modern, and will survive every other religion and philosophy.
>
> . . . [It was preserved] among Initiates of every country; among profound seekers after truth—their disciples; and in those parts of the world where such topics have always been most valued and pursued: in India, Central Asia, and Persia.
>
> . . . The best proof you can have of the fact [of its esoterism] is that every ancient religious, or rather philosophical, cult consisted of an esoteric or secret teaching, and an exoteric (outward public) worship. Furthermore, it is a well-known fact that the MYSTERIES of the ancients comprised with every nation the "greater" (secret) and "Lesser" (public) MYSTERIES—e.g., in the celebrated solemnities called the *Eleusinia,* in Greece.
>
> From the Hierophants of Samothrace, Egypt, and the initiated Brahmins of the India of old, down to the later Hebrew Rabbis, all preserved, for fear of profanation, their real *bona fide* beliefs secret. The Jewish Rabbis called their secular religious series the Mercavah (the exterior body), "the vehicle," or, *the covering which contains the hidden soul*—i.e., their highest secret knowledge.
>
> Not one of the ancient nations ever imparted through its priests its real philosophical secrets to the masses, but allotted to the latter only

ßks. Northern Buddhism has its "greater" and
ßsser" vehicle, known as the *Mahayana*, the
ßic, and the *Hinayana*, the exoteric, Schools.
ßan you blame them for such secrecy; for sure-
ßy, ßou would not think of feeding your flock of
sheep on learned dissertations on botany instead of
on grass?

Pythagoras called his *Gnosis* "the knowledge of things that are . . ." and preserved that
knowledge for his pledged disciples only: for those
who could digest such mental food and feel satisfied;
and he pledged them to silence and secrecy.

Occult alphabets and secret ciphers are the
development of the old Egyptian *hieratic* writings,
the secret of which was, in the days of old, in the
possession only of the Hierogrammatists, or initiated Egyptian priests. Ammonius Saccas, as his biog-
raphers tell us, bound his pupils by oath not to
divulge his higher doctrines except to those who had
already been instructed in preliminary knowledge,
and who were also bound by a pledge.

Finally, do we not find the same even in
early Christianity, among the Gnostics, and even in
the teachings of Christ? Did he not speak to the
multitudes in parables which had a two-fold meaning, and explain his reasons only to his disciples?
"To you," he says, "it is given to know the mysteries of the kingdom of heaven; but unto them that are
without, all these things are done in parables: (Mark
iv, 11)." The Essenes of Judea and Carmel made similar distinctions, dividing their adherents into neo-
phytes, brethren, and the *perfect*, or those initiated.
Examples might be brought from every country to
this effect.[20]

Blavatsky was the first person in history to make widely known to the public the existence of the perennial philosophy, and to propagate some of its main teachings. According to her, a new era, in which what used to be hidden would become widely available, was to begin at this time. If she was right about this, it might explain, for instance, the otherwise surprising popularity of formerly secret, esoteric spiritual paths, such as Zen and Tibetan Buddhism. Those schools had been hermetically sealed to outsiders since their inception—until the perennial renaissance brought them out into public notice. Blavatsky's presence and teachings were said to represent the first salvo of that "new dispensation" or "new age." Subsequently, numerous scholars and authors have made statements (usually without giving credit to HPB) confirming and expanding upon what she said on the subject. For instance, Ken Wilber, one of the leading contemporary exponents of transpersonal psychology, wrote:

> The perennial philosophy is the worldview that has been embraced by the vast majority of the world's greatest spiritual teachers, philosophers, thinkers, and even scientists. It's called "perennial" or "universal" because it shows up in virtually all cultures across the globe and across the ages. We find it in India, Mexico, China, Japan, Mesopotamia, Egypt, Tibet, Germany, Greece. . . .
>
> And wherever we find it, it has essentially similar features, it is in essential agreement the world over. We moderns, who can hardly agree on anything, find this rather hard to believe. But as Alan Watts summarized the available evidence . . ."Thus we are hardly aware of the extreme peculiarity of our own position, and find it difficult to recognize the plain fact that there has otherwise been a single philosophical consensus of universal extent. It has been held by [men and women] who

report the same insights and teach the same essential doctrine whether living today or six thousand years ago, whether from New Mexico in the Far West or from Japan in the Far East."

This is really quite remarkable. I think, fundamentally, it's a testament to the universal nature of these truths, to the universal experience of a collective humanity that has everywhere agreed to certain profound truths about the human condition and about its access to the Divine. That's one way to describe the *philosophia perennis*.[21]

It is of critical importance to keep in mind the perennial foundations of K's inner life. Yet all hitherto available biographical materials make no reference to these foundations, leaving their readers to puzzle over the source of K's work. Even when discussing the Theosophical Society and its leaders, these authors will either assume that no perennial teachers were involved in the movement's foundation, thus contradicting HPB's testimony, or claim that such teachers were the invention of Theosophical Society leaders. The equally unsupported assertions are often made that, when K stated that the perennial teachers were in charge of the process, he was either having visions, or was deluded. Yet all of these interpretations contradict what K said consistently over a period of nearly eighty years—from 1909 to 1986— about his relationship with the Masters.

Teachers

K's own perspective on the issue of gurus was radical and unequivocal: his acid attacks on the following of gurus or anyone else are well known. People who have been touched by his expositions tend to share his concern about authorities. Therefore it is understandable that when they hear of or read about the teachers of the perennial philosophy, they immediately dismiss the notion without further research.

However, an important distinction is to be made between, on the one hand, the dangers of slavishly and gullibly following a guru, as evidenced in many New Age as well as establishment circles and, on the other hand, following the voice of wisdom no matter what its source. Making this distinction might dispel some of the confusion regarding spiritual teachers in general. It is also worth noting that K himself was certainly a teacher, recognized himself as such, and spoke on numerous occasions about the importance of teachers. For K, however, a teacher of deeper matters has no knowledge to offer and cannot liberate anyone; rather, such a teacher performs the vital task of pointing in the right direction. This may consist largely of showing what does not work, what is false. As K put it:

> Can you, if you are the *guru* of so and so, dispel his darkness, dispel the darkness for another? Knowing that he is unhappy, confused, has not enough brain matter, has not enough love, or sorrow, can you dispel that? Or has he to work tremendously on himself? You may point out, you may say, "Look, go through that door," but he has to do the work entirely from the beginning to the end. . . . You are the *guru* and you point out the door. You have finished your job. Your function as the *guru* is then finished. You do not become important. I do not put garlands around your head. I have to do all the work. You have not dispelled the darkness of ignorance. You have, rather, pointed out to me that, "You are the door through which you yourself have to go."[22]

Dismissing *any* authority in deeper matters does not preclude the existence of and necessity for teachers. Pythagoras, the Buddha, Socrates, Jesus, Nagarjuna—and Krishnamurti—were all teachers of deeper matters. They gave out the perennial teaching in a manner appropriate to their respective circumstances.

Poignantly, when one reads biographical materials on these and other historical teachers, one almost always finds that they were helped by secret schools and teachers. Often one must turn to original sources in order to find this. Krishnamurti himself is certainly no exception in this regard, as he did make references to his own secret teachers and their school, as will be shown later.

A Perennial Renaissance

A non sequitur follows from the notion that there were no perennial teachers connected with the founding of the theosophical movement. Theosophy is significantly responsible for the revolution in thought and culture that has taken place in the twentieth century. It can be seen as a major force behind a plethora of cultural phenomena we take for granted today, including: a renaissance in Asian culture; a renewed interest in Cabalistic studies; major developments in psychology, exemplified in the work of Freud, Jung, and others; movements for education and social reform, such as the feminist movement, the Boy Scouts, and the biodynamic farming of Rudolph Steiner; and educational advances such as Summerhill, and the Waldorf, Montessori, and Krishnamurti schools. It also provided the philosophical and aesthetic foundations for the nonobjective art of the twentieth century, as well as such literary movements as the Irish literary renaissance and *modernismo* in Latin-American literature. Even practices such as cremation and vegetarianism were introduced and broadcast in non-Asian countries through the perennial renaissance, spearheaded by the theosophical movement. The teachers of the perennial philosophy are described as practitioners of insight and compassion, passionately intent on furthering transformations in human experience. If such teachers exist, yet were not behind this powerful and influential movement, would that not be an oversight of colossal proportions on their part?

Moreover, anyone who claims there were no perennial teachers behind the theosophical movement is forced to give HPB the credit for single-handedly precipitating the amazing revolution that has come about because of it. History certainly provides examples of a single person being largely responsible for a major social or cultural transformation. Martin Luther is one such person who comes to mind. However, in the case of Luther, there were social and political forces conspiring to make the Reformation a possibility. The rise of capitalism, the emergence of humanism, the discovery of the Americas by Europeans, corruption in the Vatican, and the fact that Germanic and Anglo-Saxon monarchs were about to break away from the abuses of popish Rome are some of the more prominent ones.

In Blavatsky's case, however, there were no readily visible helpers—whether political, economic, or religious—to promote her work. Instead, she was persecuted by those who either envied or misunderstood her aims and the nature of her work. The British government suspected her of being a Russian spy in India. Official Christianity financed plots to smear her character in order to discredit the nonsectarian nature of the spirituality she taught. Scientists and scholars laughed at many of her statements because they disagreed with the established beliefs of the times. For instance, her perennial teachers declared through her writings that the earth is roughly 4.3 billion years old, while the science of the day was certain that it could not be much older than 100 million years. Not until three-quarters of a century later did science catch up with the perennial teachings on this point.[23] As Marilyn Ferguson documented in *The Aquarian Conspiracy*, persecution of the ideas, practices, and insights that were first made public by HPB continues even one hundred years later, even though the perennial renaissance culture is finally making its presence felt everywhere.[24]

Apart from the unlikelihood that HPB could have single-handedly spearheaded the cultural revolutions of the twentieth century that are traceable back to her, HPB said all along that she was not only inspired by the perennial teachers and their disciples and representatives throughout the world, but was also helped by them in various ways. There are numerous documented instances of her receiving this kind of help.[25]

Further, according to those who knew her well—her family, friends from her youth, and her theosophical colleagues and students—the wisdom that came through HPB's works was not personally hers. In this way HPB and Krishnamurti are similar, for he also was not known to have anything like the abilities he displayed in his capacity as a teacher. Some may choose to see this as a mystery at the core of the lives of these two teachers. However, both of them made it very clear that the teachings they gave came from the teachers of the perennial philosophy. References to HPB being "an instrument" of the Masters have been given above. K's relationship to the perennial teachers are documented in Part II, but some details of that relationship may be advanced here. The first book K ever published is *At the Feet of the Master*. That little inspirational book begins with K's statement: "These are not my words; they are the words of the Master who taught me."[26] And ten days before he died, he said in what was clearly meant as a definitive statement on the source for his inner life, that "for seventy years that super energy—no—that immense energy, immense intelligence, has been using this body."[27]

Of Mysteries

The authors of books published to date about K cannot make any sense of what K called the process, and simply refer to it as a mystery. Two authors even use the word *mystery* in the titles of their books.[28] Evelyne Blau, in her exquisitely produced anthology, *Krishnamurti: 100 Years*, states:

> There may be elements in this book, as recounted by witnesses to extraordinary events, that may seem incomprehensible, confounding to our linear, rational thinking. But let us not linger too long with this part of the story—it is unknowable.[29]

While some aspects of K's inner life we may never understand fully, as Blau points out, those who have written about K's life may be more willing to accept a mystery here than is necessary. There was indeed, in one sense, a mystery in K's life, and he spoke to friends about this mystery on various occasions during his last two decades. This sense of the word *mystery* points to the sacredness that he referred to often in his talks and writings—to what cannot be known by the conditioned mind. This is much the same sense of the word as in the ancient Greek initiatory mysteries, in which candidates would find themselves confronted with the unknown, numinous aspect of existence. It is also close to Rudolf Otto's *mysterium tremendum et fascinans*, which is an important concept in twentieth-century theology.[30]

This expression conveys the sense of the word *mystery* when used to refer to an act of transformation. The individual confronting a deeper level of awareness feels out of depth, unable to rely on the usual human baggage of knowledge, experience, and conditioning. In such a state, nothing identified as "me" has any relevance whatsoever. Hence, the transformation implies a sense of awe akin to fear, since it involves the death of the "me." In the literature, people experiencing this often speak of their hair standing on end. Such is the *tremendum* aspect of this transformation. The *fascinans* aspect comes from the other sense of awe—that of seeing with unprecedented clarity and depth, and sensing communion with all that is.

However, this is not the sense of the word *mystery* most often used by those who have written about K's life. They surround K's process and the source of his work with mystery in the sense of "not appropriate to be examined further." Some followers of K have suggested that there is something intrinsically wrong in investigating the source of K's work, as such research might confuse people's understanding of K's insights and observations. Yet on a number of occasions K stated that certain aspects of his inner life *are* amenable to such explorations, and moreover, that it is eminently proper to make them.

On one occasion, in 1972, K told some members of the

Krishnamurti Foundation in Ojai that the source of his work could not be understood by the conscious mind, while at the same time he rejected the idea that it is a mystery:

> I feel we are delving into something which the conscious mind can never understand, which doesn't mean I am making a mystery of it. There is something. Much too vast to be put into words. There is a tremendous reservoir, as it were, which if the human mind can touch it, reveals something which no intellectual mythology—invention, supposition, dogma—can ever reveal.
>
> I am not making a mystery out of it—that would be a stupid childish trick. Creating a mystery out of nothing would be a most blackguardly thing to do because that would be exploiting people and ruthless—that's a dirty trick.
>
> Either one creates a mystery when there isn't one or there is a mystery which you have to approach with extraordinary delicacy and hesitancy, and, you know, tentativeness. And the conscious mind can't do this. It is there but you cannot come to it, you cannot invite it. It's not progressive achievement. There *is* something but the brain can't understand it.[31]

Yet, K was to have a radical change of mind about explorations into his inner life. Seven years later and in a different context, K indicated that the nature of the source of his insights and observations was something that *could* and *should* be looked into. What he says in the following passage is remarkable because he says that *others* could investigate his inner life, whereas he could not. Presumably this was at least partly because of the secrecy of initiatory oaths he had taken, as documented in Part Two.

Mary Lutyens, in the company of Mary Zimbalist, probed into the question of inquiry into the source of his inner life with K in 1979. (When K speaks of the head starting, he is referring to a very intense pain he felt in the head whenever the process, or a significant aspect of it, took place. When he speaks of the boy being vacant, he is referring to the absence, since childhood, of self-centered content in his mind. Both subjects will be discussed further in chapters 2 and 3, and in Part II.)

ML: Might someone else be able to find out? And would it be right to inquire?

K: *You* might be able to because you are writing about it. I cannot. If you and Maria [MZ] sat down and said, "Let us inquire," I'm pretty sure you could find out. Or do it alone. I see something: what I said is true: I can never find out. Water can never find out what water is. That is quite right. If you find out I'll corroborate it.

ML: You would know it if were right?

K: Can you feel it in the room? It is getting stronger and stronger. My head is starting. If you asked the question and said, "I don't know," you might find it. If I was writing it I would state all this. I would begin with the boy completely vacant.

ML: Do you mind it said that you want it explained?

K: I don't care. Say what you like. I'm sure if others put their minds to this they can do it. I am absolutely sure of this. Absolutely, absolutely. Also I am sure *I* can't find it.

ML: What if one could understand it but not be able to put it into words?

K: You could. You would find a way. The moment
     you discover something you have words for it.
     Like a poem. If you are open to inquire, put
     your brain in condition, someone could find
     out. But the moment you find it, it will be
     right. No mystery.
ML: Will the mystery mind being found?
K: No, the mystery will be gone.
MZ: But the mystery is something sacred.
K: The sacredness will remain.[32]

In the first quotation, K seemed to refer, in deliberately
nontechnical words, to something akin to Otto's *mysterium
tremendum et fascinans*. Here, in the second, K has made the subtle distinction, again in simple words, between the mystery and
the sacredness of the *mysterium tremendum et fascinans*. The
mystery that is the core of genuine religious experience remains,
while the mysteriousness that may surround it can be removed.
Because the latter can be removed, K felt it was proper to investigate the source of his inner life.

The origins of K's inner life touch intimately on the question of the existence and nature of the perennial teachers. For reasons discussed more thoroughly in chapter 3, it does not seem
possible to make sense of K's inner life unless these perennial
teachers were real human beings, though ones with extremely
sophisticated yogic abilities. If there were no perennial teachers in
charge of the process, then the process remains a mystery—
incomprehensible, unknowable. On the other hand, if what K said
from when he first experienced the process in 1922 until his death
in 1986 is accepted as true—that the process was conducted by the
perennial teachers—then the experiences connected with it can be
explained and need no longer remain a mystery.

Some of K's students consider the process a mystery that
should not be looked into. Others seem to fear that acknowledging K's rich esoteric life would contribute to the creation of a new

religion around K—something not at all in keeping with K's insights and observations, and thus inappropriate. But these views ignore the notion that "the truth shall make you free." If the truth is that K was consciously involved in the work of the perennial teachers, we must accept this fact and adjust our understanding accordingly.

Mystery Mongering

It seems there have always been some teachers of the perennial philosophy who have not been known publicly. That they are hidden from the ordinary world should not be puzzling. However, because they are hidden, people have mystified these teachers and thus brought on more confusion about who they were. After HPB made the world at large aware of the secret schools of perennial philosophy that have existed through the ages, zealotism joined hands with capitalist enterprise and a cottage industry of New Age occult schools was born. Some of the schools of thought that have some pedigree in HPB's work have been moved by a spirit of research and sensibility. Manly Palmer Hall's Philosophical Research Society and Edgar Mitchell's Institute of Noetic Sciences are two such schools. But a great many others, while broadcasting the perennial philosophy in one form or another, have also promoted their own concepts of who the perennial teachers are. It is these notions that are largely responsible for the rise of misunderstanding. It is thus not surprising that most sympathizers of K have shunned the notion of perennial teachers.

G. I. Gurdjieff also claimed to have been in contact with the teachers of the perennial philosophy. It would be interesting to examine whether evidence suggests that his teachers were the same as those who helped HPB with her work. If nothing else, this might explain why the early leaders of the Gurdjieff movement— P. D. Ouspensky, A. R. Orage, and Thomas and Olga de Hartmann—had come to Gurdjieff from the theosophical movement. In the context of Gurdjieff's work the perennial teaching emphasizes "self-remembering." Similarly, in the original teachings of the theosophical movement, self-understanding and transformation were the very core of the teaching.

HPB never promoted the worship of her teachers. Yet even as early as HPB's time, her teachers tended to be regarded as objects of worship, rather like Christian saints. This has contributed to the erroneous perception of theosophy as a new-fangled cult that has appropriated teachings from all over the world, particularly from Asia. But whatever misconceptions may exist about these teachers, the fact remains that HPB's teachers were intent on bringing about major transformations on the planet, and that psychological and spiritual mutation lay at the core of their teachings.[33]

HPB, K, and the Perennial Teachers

HPB and her colleagues always described the teachers of the perennial philosophy as men and women of flesh and blood who find no enticement whatsoever in the life of the world and seek a life of relative peace, away from ordinary civilization. They have been said to live often in communities with others like themselves, whose primary interest is the pursuit of insight and compassion and research into the nature of *what is*. Such pursuits cannot be carried out in the midst of civilization, where the majority of humanity do not have such interests. According to HPB, the lack of seriousness as well as the intrinsic violence of the majority are the main reasons for surrounding the perennial philosophy with secrecy. At the same time, however, the perennial teachers hold the promotion of human welfare at heart, and so they are also interested in coming in contact with likeminded people who are nevertheless living in the world.

HPB's description of the activities of the teachers of the perennial philosophy is in fact not unlike a description of those of K himself. Throughout his long life, he spent a great deal of time alone, often in communion with nature, intensely engaged in research into *what is*. Those who attended his talks or read his books were also people interested in creating a better society by bringing about transformation in their personal lives. Thus the followers and sympathizers of K form a group similar to the secret transformative perennial schools that have existed throughout history for the same ends. K's work seems to be, in fact, an appropriate continuation of perennial work that has gone on throughout the ages, of which HPB's work was an immediate precursor.

Authors such as Carl Jung, Alan Watts, Aldous Huxley, Joseph Campbell, and Ken Wilber tell us that the perennial philosophy has been a very real factor throughout history and therefore its teachers are just as real. As the evidence and reasons presented in what follows suggest, K's inner life could have taken place only if there is a perennial philosophy and there are teachers of that philosophy. In fact, the richness of his psychic and spiritual life can itself be regarded as evidence for the existence of this lineage and its teachers.

CHAPTER TWO

A New Perspective

A CENTURY AFTER BLAVATSKY'S PASSING, THE
existence of an energy field around every living thing, including
human beings, has become more widely accepted, thanks to
research in a variety of areas. The idea of forms of subtle energy
that flow through living organisms is also gaining currency. The
energy systems in the body known as kundalini and the chakras
can now be described in terms of subtle, ultra-subatomic energy-
matter. [1]

Kundalini and *chakra* are Sanskrit words and are used in
the South Asian schools of yoga and tantra. However, all major
civilizations have recognized, depicted, and made use of these subtle energy patterns, though they have understood and described
them in different ways. Such references are found, for instance, in
the cultures of Tibet, China, Japan, ancient Egypt, ancient Greece,
and precolonial North and South America. More recently, they
have been recognized in the culture of Renaissance Europe.[2] The
ubiquitousness of practices and writings on this subject at the
very least commends serious consideration of the existence of
these energies in the human organism.[3] This psycho-physiological perspective on humankind seems to hold answers to problems
in what the European philosophical tradition calls "the philosophy of mind," and so is of interest not only to philosophers but
also to researchers in fields like physiology and psychology.[4] After
all, the subtle energy patterns are said by trained clairvoyants to
be the material basis of psychological phenomena such as emotions and thoughts. (The expression "trained clairvoyants" was
used by CWL to refer to people who had been tutored in some

way by the perennial teachers, even when they had been born somewhat clairvoyant or had developed clairvoyance in some other way. He used this expression to distinguish such perennial candidates from other clairvoyants).[5]

The wisdom on this subject from many areas of the world is largely unavailable, in some cases because the literature is known incompletely, in others because it has not been made public or has been substantially destroyed. Tantra, on the other hand, is a living tradition whose practitioners now include people from Europe and America, thanks to the perennial renaissance. This means that at least significant portions of it are out in the open. Thus tantric terminology has become particularly useful. Nevertheless, one should be aware that this terminology brings with it the particular conceptual framework of tantra.

A Special Language

The available Indian and Tibetan sources that refer to these psycho-physiological energy patterns use language that would be meaningful only to a tantric scholar or practitioner. For instance, the *Sat-cakra-nirupana*, a tantric work that, according to its translator, is meant to *clarify* our understanding of kundalini, begins with the following statement:

> In the space outside the Meru, placed on the left and the right, are the two Siras, Sasi and Mihira. The Nadji Susumna, whose substance is the threefold Gunas, is in the middle. She is the form of Moon, Sun, and Fire; Her body, a string of blooming Dhatura flowers, extends from the middle of the Kanda to the Head, and the Vajra inside her extends, shining, from the Medhra to the Head.[6]

A little further on we are given a definition of kundalini:

Over [the Svayambhu Linga] shines the sleeping Kundalini, fine as the fibre of the lotus-stalk. She is the world-bewilderer, gently covering the mouth of Brahma-dvara by Her own. Like the spiral of the conch-shell, Her shining snake-like form goes three and a half times around Siva, and Her lustre is as that of a strong flash of young strong lightning. Her sweet murmur is like the indistinct hum of swarms of love-mad bees. She produces melodious poetry and Bandha and all other compositions in prose or verse in sequence or otherwise in Samskrta, Prakrta and other languages. It is She who maintains all the beings of the world by means of inspiration and expiration, and shines in the cavity of the root (Mula) Lotus like a chain of brilliant lights.[7]

However useful to practitioners or enlightening to scholars such powerful, poetical presentations may be, the style and the specialist language make them inaccessible to those outside the circle of tantra's serious students. The wisdom of tantra thus has remained unrecognized until the time of the perennial renaissance, which was brought about by the work of HPB and those inspired or influenced by her. One of the great contributions by the early disciples of HPB was a conceptual framework that made it possible to speak about kundalini and the chakras in a universally meaningful and accessible way.

Tantric literature would never have become as popular as it has without the theosophists' efforts to demythologize and make more widely accessible the meanings of these ancient texts. Even Indian and Tibetan scholars have increasingly made use of theosophy's more universal language. This suggests not only the logical and historical priority of the perennial philosophy over the many regional versions of the teachings found throughout the world; it also suggests that Blavatsky's theosophy is not a syncretistic system built up from regional teachings, but is *the source* of all those teachings, as HPB and her teachers stated.

Chinese Energy Wisdom

The ancient Chinese tradition also developed a system of research that was perhaps the earliest clear explanation of the subtle energies. The elaborate and careful descriptions of the Chinese stand in contrast to the poetical and mythical presentations found in tantric literature.[8] Such descriptions still form the core of Chinese medical diagnosis and therapy today.[9] In fact, there are numerous reports of relatively simple cures of chronic diseases, such as cancer and arthritis, brought about by Chinese physicians working with the subtle energies.[10]

The Chinese understanding of the subtle energies began to come into its own worldwide only in the last quarter of the twentieth century. Without question, the Chinese system contributes to our understanding of what a human being is. The fact that these energies can be manipulated successfully for health, as well as for martial arts purposes, tells us that they are not visions, mythical teachings, or superstitions, but are as real as other forms of equally invisible energy, such as electricity and nuclear energy.

Yet despite its relatively analytical and descriptive nature, the regionality of the Chinese approach to the healing arts keeps it from being universally acceptable to all. For one thing, different regional approaches describe the subtle energies differently; for instance, except for the relatively arcane schools of Taoist yoga, in the Chinese approach kundalini and its flow through the chakras are not described the way they are in tantra—and in Krishnamurti's experiences.[11] For another, to benefit fully from this healing art as it is known and practiced in China requires accepting a number of principles of Taoism and Chinese culture. There is nothing intrinsically wrong with this, but adopting a Chinese/Taoist perspective, like adopting any other regional perspective, may not appeal to everyone.

In the process of becoming known more widely, the Chinese approach has taken full advantage of the receptive New

Age milieu created by the perennial renaissance. Its scholars have even borrowed some of the terminology and conceptual structures of theosophical writings (signally, those of C. W. Leadbeater), as have the Indian and Tibetan systems.[12] For these reasons, the perennial perspective remains invaluable as the source of a universality not available in any regional tradition. Perennial expositions on subtle energies can and do incorporate the wisdom of the Chinese system as well as that of tantra and other energetic systems from around the world. It is this universality that has appealed to people everywhere and made the work of the early theosophists unique in world history.

A Victorian Lens

It is valuable to keep in mind that the terminology and descriptions used publicly for the perennial teachings by the early theosophists were cast in the language of the Victorian era. Later observers of these theosophists often forget, or fail to see, that they were true pioneers in uncovering and broadcasting these insights, and they could not but express them in terms of the language and concepts of their era.

But as K often said, the word is not the thing. The way something is expressed (whether in Victorian or new-paradigm or any other style) is not as important as its substance. Perhaps the best way to read the early theosophical literature is to consider ourselves anthropologists who have just unearthed something from a foreign culture—even when that culture happens to be the one we were born into. We need take from it only what we find of value in it for our own lives. This is, in fact, the phenomenological approach, used in contemporary philosophy and psychology, which sets out to "bracket off" (suspend) all presuppositions one might have in researching any issue.

A New Perspective

Anyone inquiring into the inner life of Krishnamurti

would do well to keep in mind the material nature of the subtler energies and that they are universal, that is, not culture-dependent. K's psychic experiences have often been discussed as if they belonged exclusively to the tantric tradition of India. Once K's experiences are understood not in terms of an Indian system of beliefs and practices but simply as *human* experiences that do not belong to any culture, a more accurate picture of what was happening to him is possible. In other words, K's experience of the process was not merely or exclusively a result of cultural influences.

The language used to describe many aspects of the process includes tantric terms, which is understandable since the tantric tradition was the best-preserved perennially inspired school at the time. And K, after all, was born in India. But no tantric text contains the science-inspired descriptions of the flow of subtle energy in the process that are found in perennial renaissance literature. That was not possible before the work of C. W. Leadbeater. What are now widely accepted as the "true" meaning of words such as *chakra* and *kundalini* were the original contribution of the perennial renaissance.

Another factor to keep in mind is that those who have written about K and his experiences have exhibited a prejudice against things theosophical—whether teachings, history, or references to the character of the movement's leaders—even though none of these authors has provided good arguments or well-researched facts to fully justify this attitude. Interestingly—and ironically—they have used theosophical explanations and terminology to discuss K's inner life while in the same breath denying or ignoring their theosophical source. Clearly, a more open, research-oriented attitude is needed when examining K's inner life. The present inquiry is an attempt to do just that.

CWL

Among the early theosophists, C. W. Leadbeater (CWL) was the pioneer who made a detailed clairvoyant study of the subtle energies. He provided the language and the conceptual and aesthetic images that have now become commonplace in discussions of these energies in perennial renaissance literature. Besides his significant influence on the understanding of the perennial teachings, Leadbeater also played a critical role in Krishnamurti's early development. Thus it is appropriate to look briefly at some implications of his work.

During his time—and for several decades after his death—there was heated debate over the accuracy, and even the reality, of CWL's clairvoyance. Thus it is interesting to see how his psychic ability has stood up to the more rigorous scrutiny of researchers almost a century later. CWL did clairvoyant research in numerous areas. Some—such as investigations into Krishnamurti's previous incarnations—are extremely difficult to assess.[13] And people's opinions are likely to be based on whatever prejudices they bring to the inquiry.

Other areas of CWL's clairvoyant explorations, however, are more amenable to investigation. Here CWL's remarkable abilities appear unquestionable. For instance, from 1895 until shortly before his death in 1934, CWL did extensive clairvoyant research into the structure of the physical elements.[14] Though he was the senior researcher, he did much of this work with AB—up until 1913 when she decided not to continue using her clairvoyance. They called their investigations "occult chemistry." To inquirers in subsequent decades these investigations seemed to have been mere fantasy. The most important assessments were made by the Theosophical Research Centre Science Group, several members of which belonged to the prestigious British Royal Society. As late as the 1950s, these scientists—who as theosophists were willing to look into the issue with an open mind—had come to inconclusive findings:

> In some few cases the occult structures seem better suited than the orthodox to explain the facts of organic chemistry, but in others there is difficulty in

reconciling the occult structures with the available data. . . . Our brief comparison of the occult and orthodox theories of atomic structure, clearly reveals one fact at least—that much work remains to be done before the rapprochement which we believe to be eventually inevitable is actually realised.[15]

However, in 1980 Dr. Stephen M. Phillips of Cambridge published the results of his research into CWL's psychic abilities in this field.[16] In summary he wrote:

In conclusion, the clairvoyant description of matter appears to have very close contact with chemistry, nuclear physics and the quark structure underlying the physical universe. . . . At present one can with a measure of confidence claim that quarks were observed by Annie Besant and C. W. Leadbeater, using yogic techniques, 69 years before scientists suggested that they existed.[17]

The reason why previous investigators had assessed CWL's clairvoyance either negatively or inconclusively is that CWL had been describing quarks and their behavior, which were discovered by physicists only decades later. This underscores the reality of CWL's clairvoyant abilities. He could not have gotten the information from scientific sources, because there were none in his lifetime; nor was the notion of quarks even speculated about in the literature. Moreover, CWL's observations were not a set of casual or imprecise remarks, but were the results of extensive and careful research conducted over a period of forty years. Out of his research he provided specific descriptions, with drawings, of the subatomic structure of all the physical elements.

Another topic that has been researched intensively since CWL's death is the aura, or psychic field, that surrounds the human body. Here again, much of what CWL had stated on the subject had been a matter of belief or disbelief for decades. However, a number of researchers have discovered remarkable similarities—even identity—between CWL's descriptions and their own findings. Drs. J. Moss and K. L. Johnson of the Neuro-Psychiatric Institute of California, who conducted research on the human aura, commented in 1974:

> We are amazed at similarities between our pho-
> tographs and the drawings and descriptions of
> human auras by psychics Annie Besant and C. W.
> Leadbeater.[18]

Although these findings point strongly to CWL's clairvoy-ant abilities in areas amenable to rigorous scientific investigation, they do not guarantee that he was equally accurate in other aspects of his clairvoyant work. They do suggest, however, that his work should be considered seriously.

CWL also conducted extensive clairvoyant investigations in connection with Krishnamurti. In fact, the present study is in part an inquiry into some of the most debated claims made by CWL regarding K.

Pioneer

Scholars and explorers of the subtle energies who lived prior to C.W. Leadbeater were limited to speaking of what they knew using the terminology and concepts of their particular tra-ditions. Descriptions of kundalini and the chakras, for instance, were given in poetical, mythological, arcane terms meaningful only to tantric practitioners. CWL demythologized the subject through his clairvoyant explorations conducted in a scientific spirit and through his subsequent expositions using language informed by science. He made this research available to an inter-national audience by describing what he saw in terms of the perennial philosophy—thus following in the footsteps of HPB—

but using declarative sentences and a purely descriptive language that was his unique creation.[19]

His use of the language as well as his conceptual framework may on occasion seem dated. He was after all a Victorian, and it is through the filter of the verbal and even conceptual mannerisms of that subculture that we receive his perennial insights. Nevertheless, it is possible for anyone to understand Leadbeater when he writes:

> In ordinary superficial conversation a man sometimes mentions his soul—implying that the body through which he speaks is the real man, and that this thing called the soul is a possession or appanage of that body—a sort of captive balloon floating over him, and in some vague sort of way attached to him. This is a loose, inaccurate and misleading statement; the exact opposite is the truth. Man is a soul and owns a body—several bodies in fact; for besides the visible vehicle by means of which he transacts his business with his lower world, he has others which are not visible to ordinary sight, by means of which he deals with the emotional and mental worlds.
>
> . . . Students of medicine are now familiar with [the body's] bewildering complexities, and have at least a general idea of the way in which its amazingly intricate machinery works. . . . Naturally, however, they have had to confine their attention to that part of the body which is dense enough to be visible to the eye, and most of them are probably unaware of the existence of that type of matter, still physical though invisible, to which in Theosophy we give the name of etheric. This invisible part of the physical body is of great importance to us, for it is the vehicle through which flow the streams of vitality which keep the body alive, and without it as a bridge to

convey undulations of thought and feeling from the astral to the visible denser physical matter, the ego could make no use of the cells of his brain. It is clearly visible to the clairvoyant as a mass of faintly-luminous violet-grey mist, interpenetrating the denser part of the body, and extending very slightly beyond it.

The chakras or force-centres are points of connection at which energy flows from one vehicle or body of a man to another. Anyone who possesses a slight degree of clairvoyance may easily see them in the etheric double, where they show themselves as saucer-like depressions or vortices in its surface. When quite undeveloped they appear as small circles about two inches in diameter, glowing dully in the ordinary man; but when awakened and vivified they are seen as blazing, coruscating whirlpools, much increased in size, and resembling miniature suns. We sometimes speak of them as roughly corresponding to certain physical organs; in reality they show themselves at the surface of the etheric double, which projects slightly beyond the outline of the dense body.[20]

Significantly, CWL originated a whole genre of literature on the subtle energy patterns in the human aura, the chakras, and kundalini. Because of the descriptive literary style in which he wrote about these formerly arcane subjects, he made it very easy for others to subsequently write or speak about them, though they rarely give him credit. Whatever one may think of the topic, his manner of presenting it represented a genuinely creative effort.

Moreover, from the time CWL publicized his clairvoyant research until the 1970s, no comparable works on the aura or the chakras were published. During these decades, the writings of

CWL (and to a lesser extent those of his colleagues and pupils, such as Geoffrey Hodson, Phoebe Bendit, and Dora van Gelder Kunz) were the only universally accessible and understandable sources for clairvoyant expositions of these subjects. CWL's influence was considerable. For one thing, his clairvoyant work inspired a number of artists, including Wassily Kandinsky in Europe and Agnes Pelton in America.[21]

CWL certainly made it clear with regard to his research that he did not consider his perceptions the final word. He often said that he was doing pioneer work, and therefore other researchers should take pains either to corroborate or correct his work. This has been done. Other clairvoyants have corroborated much of what he said, and have also corrected some of it on finer points.[22]

The pioneering work of CWL has made it possible for even scientific researchers to make investigations into the nature of kundalini, and for a more universal idiom to be employed when speaking of these formerly recondite subjects. For instance, in his introduction to what could be considered a definitive anthology on kundalini, John White explains:

> Kundalini is the personal aspect of the universal life force named *prana* by the yogic tradition. This primal cosmic energy is akin, if not identical, to *ch'i* (Chinese), *ki*, (Japanese), the Holy Spirit, and various other terms from cultures that identify a life force that is the source of all vital activity. Prana has not yet been identified by modern science, but ancient wisdom maintains that it is the means for raising human awareness to a higher form of perception, variously called illumination, enlightenment, cosmic consciousness, *samadhi*. Kundalini, often referred to as the "serpent power" because it is symbolized by a coiled snake, can be concentrated and channeled through the spine into the brain—a process likewise not yet identified by modern sci-

ence. The systematized process for accomplishing this upward flowing of energy is known as kundalini yoga.[23]

Such a clear exposition would never have been possible had it not been for the pioneering efforts of HPB and her colleagues, foremost of all CWL.

The impact of his work in the context of the present study needs to be especially acknowledged, since most authors who have written about chakras, auras, kundalini, or similar matters either ignore CWL altogether or criticize him in terms of their own preconceived notions.[24] This is true despite the fact that all of these authors draw on CWL's linguistic and conceptual framework, since he was the pioneer in this field. Authors writing about Krishnamurti have also questioned CWL's clairvoyance without providing evidence for their claims against him on this point.

CWL, the Process, and Kundalini

CWL's contributions are critical to a clear understanding of Krishnaji's process. Otherwise K's inner experiences are labeled "mysteries," "visions," or "delusions," or they have to be described in the specialist language of a particular sect. It was the rise of kundalini up Krishnaji's spine and its active, painful action in his head that held center stage in the psycho-physiological aspects of the process. Concerning the serpent fire, as kundalini is often called, CWL wrote:

> This force . . . exists on all planes of which we know anything; but it is the expression of it in etheric matter with which we have to do at present. It is not convertible into either the primary force already mentioned or the force of vitality which comes from the sun, and it does not seem to be affected in any way by any other forms of physical energy.

On attempting to investigate the conditions at the centre of the earth we find there a vast globe of such tremendous force that we cannot approach it. . . . The force of kundalini in our bodies comes from that laboratory of the Holy Ghost deep down in the earth. It belongs to that terrific glowing fire of the underworld. That fire is in striking contrast to the fire of vitality which comes from the sun, which will presently be explained. The latter belongs to air and light and the great open spaces; the fire which comes from below is much more material, like the fire of red-hot iron, of glowing metal. There is a rather terrible side to this tremendous force; it gives the impression of descending deeper and deeper into matter, of moving slowly but irresistibly onwards, with relentless certainty.

. . . We hear much of this strange fire and of the danger of prematurely arousing it; and much of what we hear is undoubtedly true. There is indeed most serious peril in awakening the higher aspects of this furious energy in a man before he has gained the strength to control it, before he has acquired the purity of life and thought which alone can make it safe for him to unleash potency so tremendous. But kundalini plays a much larger part in daily life than most of us have hitherto supposed; there is a far lower and gentler manifestation of it which is already awake within us all, which is not only innocuous but beneficent, which is doing its appointed work day and night while we are entirely unconscious of its presence and activity. We have of course previously noticed this force as it flows along the nerves, calling it simply nerve-fluid, and not recognizing it for what it really is. The endeavour to analyse it and to trace it back to its source shows us that it enters the human body at the root chakra.

Like all other forces, kundalini is itself invisible; but in the human body it clothes itself in a curious nest of hollow concentric spheres of astral and etheric matter, one within another, like the balls in a Chinese puzzle. There appear to be seven such concentric spheres resting within the root chakra, in and around the last real cell or hollow of the spine close to the coccyx; but only in the outermost of these spheres is the force active in the ordinary man. In the others it is "sleeping," as is said in some of the Oriental books; and it is only when the man attempts to arouse the energy latent in those inner layers that the dangerous phenomena of the fire begin to show themselves. The harmless fire of the outer skin of the ball flows up the spinal column, using (so far as investigations have gone up to the present) the three lines of Sushumna, Ida and Pingala simultaneously.[25]

Like other expounders of the perennial philosophy, CWL used terminology from various religions and philosophies in his expositions, and the careful reader may note how that terminology gains a different meaning when put back in the perennial context.

CWL's clairvoyant findings are not only relevant to K's process but are in accord with K's observations. CWL consistently described emotions and thoughts as composed of ultra-sub-atomic particles of energy-matter. Therefore, according to his perceptions, there is no clear demarcation between the observer and the observed. This implication of his work is in agreement with K's insights, as well as with twentieth-century physics.

K himself knew and confirmed the value of CWL's work. In the 1970s, after Mary Lutyens' first volume of memoirs on K was published, academics and other professionals met with K on various occasions. More than once in these meetings Leadbeater and Besant were criticized as having been misguided in many ways. K found himself defending CWL and AB, pointing out that "these were very serious people."[26]

Discovery

Leadbeater is a central figure in any study of K's life, for it was he who "discovered" the boy Krishna on Adyar Beach in the spring of 1909. Immediately upon seeing him, CWL confided to a few close colleagues that he had never seen an aura so free of selfishness, and that the boy would become a great speaker.

One of those colleagues, Ernest Wood, was astonished at CWL's words. He knew Krishna and his brothers very well, as he had befriended them in the process of attempting to tutor them, and he was certain Leadbeater was wrong. In Wood's estimation— and apart from the fact that the boy did not know English— Krishna was retarded and would probably die at a young age, as had some of his siblings. (As it was, all of his siblings were dead by the early 1950s, while K lived until 1986.) As Mary Lutyens wrote in her memoir of K:

> It could not have been Krishna's outward appearance that struck Leadbeater, for apart from his wonderful eyes, he was not at all prepossessing at that time. He was under-nourished, scrawny and dirty; his ribs showed through his skin and he had a persistent cough; his teeth were crooked and he wore his hair in the customary Brahmin fashion of South India, shaved in front to the crown and falling to below his knees in a pigtail at the back; moreover his vacant expression gave him an almost moronic look. People who had known him before he was "discovered" by Leadbeater said there was little difference between him and his [retarded] youngest brother, Sadanand. Moreover, according to Wood, he was so extremely

weak physically that his father declared more than
once that he was bound to die.[27]

Later, looking more closely at Krishna's aura and presumably as he studied clairvoyantly some fifty of the boy's previous
incarnations, CWL became convinced that not only would
Krishna develop into a much greater speaker than AB (who was a
legend in her own time as a speaker, even among nonsympathiz-
ers), but the Buddha Maitreya, whose incarnation as the succes-
sor of Gautama Buddha is expected by Buddhists within this time
period, would "overshadow" Krishna. The Lord Maitreya (as
CWL and other Theosophists called him), known as the Christ in
the West, would thus give out the keynote teaching for the new
era that Blavatsky had referred to in her writings.

Needless to say, CWL's declarations, which were supported
and restated by AB, created an immense uproar in the
Theosophical Society, and the organization was split many ways
as a result. These declarations caused an immense amount of
trouble for both Besant and Leadbeater, and the remainder of
their lives would have been far simpler and happier if they had
not made them. CWL stated on a number of occasions that he
personally would never have pushed the onslaught of notoriety
on the extremely shy and sensitive boy, but that he and AB made
these declarations under the direction of the perennial teachers;
they were doing the Masters' work. If CWL and AB had invent-
ed all this—as a number of authors have asserted, though without corroboration—it was a most unintelligent thing for them to
have done, since they got only grief in return, and their theosophical work suffered as well. Yet no one has ever accused either
of them of lack in acumen.

In fact, this issue is without question the most difficult in
theosophical history for later Theosophists to explain. CWL and
AB spent more energy on promoting "the Coming of the World
Teacher" than on anything else they undertook throughout their
very long and active lives. If they were mistaken, suspicion must
be cast on much of the rest of their work as well. In subsequent

decades, most Theosophists chose to "look the other way" on this issue, yet they almost universally disagreed with Besant and Leadbeater about it. In fact, many Theosophists went out of their way to disavow any connection with Leadbeater in particular. This put them in the anomalous position of largely accepting the meta-physical and clairvoyant teachings that had been given through CWL and AB—though often not acknowledging them by name—while at the same time rejecting the one teaching CWL and AB both considered most important.

A statement on this subject by Dora Kunz, who was presi-dent of the Theosophical Society in America in the 1970s and 80s, is particularly significant, in light of the fact that she not only knew CWL personally (she had been his disciple as a girl and young woman), but was herself a well-known trained clairvoyant. She worked for several decades with medical doctors to help them, through clairvoyant methods, arrive at otherwise difficult diagnoses.[28] In other words, her clairvoyance, though rigorously tested, has never been questioned. From her personal perspective, the most important application of CWL's clairvoyance was in relation to Krishnamurti:

[CWL] was without a doubt clairvoyant. The best known and impressive demonstration of his clair-voyance was his "discovery" of Krishnamurti. Leadbeater was walking on the beach by Adyar when he saw two brothers also walking there. They were very poor and badly fed, not much to look at, but he saw their auras and he recognized a tremen-dous potential in one of the boys, Krishnamurti. CWL never had much money, but he helped to sup-port the boys from his own income, and he interest-ed Mrs. Besant in them. She adopted the boys and sent them to England, and Krishnamurti turned out to be a unique person. Whatever CWL saw in that starving boy's aura, he picked him out, and Krishnamurti has made his own contribution to modern society.[27]

Kunz is careful here about stating the actual claims CWL made regarding K. After all, this subject is still controversial in theosophical circles. Yet this is a remarkable statement coming from someone who was thoroughly acquainted with all of CWL's work, whose own clairvoyance is unquestioned, and who was not connected with Krishnamurti's work once he broke away from the Theosophists early on. In other words, in making such a statement she had nothing to gain, no ax to grind, and perhaps much to lose, given the unpopularity of Krishnamurti in most Theosophical circles. Yet she considered CWL's revelations regarding Krishnamurti the most important of all his clairvoyant work.

Whatever one may think of his claims regarding the Telugu boy, CWL's impact on people's attitudes toward extrasensory perception and other paranormal abilities and what may be possible through them has been indubitably phenomenal. He was the first person to speak of the subtler realms in those terms, using a language that would be meaningful to a worldwide public. Anyone since his time who has spoken of energy patterns, psychic fields, centers of force, or vibrations (or "vibes," a term whose theosophical origins few people know), has been following in his footsteps.

CHAPTER THREE

Mutation

PUPUL JAYAKAR'S DESCRIPTION OF K'S PROCESS at the beginning of chapter 1 suggests that K was an accomplished yogi, someone who had spent many years in subtle and elaborate practices to the exclusion of much else. K, however, had been doing no such thing. From 1911 through 1921, when he lived in England, he spent his time studying under a tutor to enter Oxford (he never passed the exams) and learning about everyday things. Biographical accounts show that he was involved with theosophy, or anything that could be construed as spiritual practice, only in the most peripheral way. His remarks at the time about theosophy—other than his communications with Besant and Leadbeater—show, if anything, a lack of interest on his part.

Unlikely Yogi

Mary Lutyens, who knew K intimately from 1911 when he first went to England at the age of sixteen, wrote:

> The boy Krishna I had known had been quite vacant, childish, almost moronic, interested really in nothing except golf, and mechanical things such as cameras, clocks and motor-bicycles.[1]

Her reference to him as the boy Krishna, though he was a young man, underscores the point that he was clearly not an accomplished yogi, especially given his down-to-earth interests and disregard for yoga or any other spiritual practice.

Annie Besant was K's legal guardian between 1911 and 1921, though she was not with him during that time. She spent those years in India, partly because it would have been difficult to carry on her theosophical work in Europe during the war and partly because she was deeply involved in India's independence movement and in creating a number of cultural organizations in India. Besant never pushed others into sharing her beliefs. For her, theosophy was not so much a belief system as a path to transformation.[2] Krishnaji said shortly after she died:

> Dr. Besant was our mother, she looked after us, she cared for us. But one thing she did not do. She never said to me, "Do this," or "Don't do that." She left me alone. Well, in these words I have paid her the greatest tribute.[3]

AB also conveyed to K's tutors that they should not attempt to mold his mind in any way outside of the conventions of his studies. His great passions then were playing golf and volley ball, finding out as much as possible about cars (an avocation he never fully abandoned) and racing them, and learning how to dress well. Meditation was not on his list of daily activities. His life was that of a wealthy young man. He was surrounded by rich Victorians who were teaching him by example their manners and perspectives.

The available documents show that he returned to "the work" in 1921 more out of a sense of duty and out of gratitude to AB than anything else. He was apparently weary of much of what he had seen in theosophical circles for several years. Some of the remarks he made in 1921-22 (in letters, or recounted by others in anecdotes) suggest a sense of guilt for not having adequately fulfilled the expectations connected with his mission. It was generally a period of inner struggle: On one hand he was unhappy with the predominant understanding of theosophy in the Theosophical

Society. On the other hand, he knew the time was near for him to begin to fulfill the grandiose expectations held by those who were aware of Besant and Leadbeater's declarations made concerning the "Coming" of the World Teacher.

Beginnings

The first manifestations of the process began shortly after Krishnaji and his brother had arrived in Ojai from Australia in 1922. While still in Australia, a message for Krishnaji was brought through by CWL from one of the perennial teachers connected with theosophical work, the Master Koot Hoomi (or KH):

> Of you, too, we have the highest hopes. Steady and widen yourself, and strive more and more to bring the mind and brain into subservience to the true Self within. Be tolerant of divergences of view and of method, for each has usually a fragment of truth concealed somewhere within it, even though oftentimes it is distorted almost beyond recognition. Seek for that tiniest gleam of light amid the Stygian darkness of each ignorant mind, for by recognising and fostering it you may help a baby brother.[4]

This message had "a profound effect" on Krishnaji, according to Mary Lutyens. Shortly after, he settled in Ojai and began to meditate daily, something he had not done since shortly after arriving in England in 1911. This was so unexpected that he wrote to Lady Emily Lutyens (Mary's mother):

> All this is rather surprising you, isn't it? I am going to get back my old touch with the Masters & after all that's the only thing that matters in life & nothing else does. At first it was difficult to meditate or to concentrate & even though I have been doing it for

only a week, I am agreeably surprised.[5]

K started meditating for roughly half an hour daily only fourteen days prior to when the process commenced on August 17, 1922. Just a few days after beginning, he started practicing a form of meditation that might have triggered the process. This suggests that the process was not something he consciously initiated, or the result of anything he did. In fact, even as late as 1961, he wrote in his journal (later published as *Krishnamurti's Notebook*) about the process in terms that leave no room for the possibility that he did anything to induce it:

> The pressure and the strain of deep ache is there; it's as though, deep within, an operation was going on. It's not brought on through one's own volition, however subtle it might be. One has deliberately and for some time gone into it, deeply. One has tried to induce it; tried to bring about various outward conditions, being alone and so on. Then nothing happens. All this isn't something recent.[6]

From his own comments it is clear that there was little intentionally to do with the tremendous initiatory experiences K was soon to have—experiences that would in turn have a transforming effect on people worldwide. As K was to say often throughout his life, what comes from the depth always comes "uninvited, unexpectedly." In other words, throughout the process there was an element of what Christians might refer to as grace. K's contribution to the process seems to have consisted exclusively of two conditions: 1) The vacancy of his mind; this is the kind of emptiness spoken of in many spiritual traditions, such as yoga, where it is called *sunya*, and Zen Buddhism, where it is called *sunyata*. 2) His predisposition to be of service in the work of the perennial teachers; put simply, this was an inner *goodness*, a predisposition to "do the right thing" at deep levels and under all circumstances. However, these two qualities would not have been sufficient for the process to take place.

If one rules out the possibility that an outside agent initiated and conducted the process, the other possible explanations seem to be that he went through periods of severe hallucinations throughout his life, that kundalini was somehow awakened in him spontaneously, or that there was deception of some kind. Before exploring these possibilities, however, the process itself should be examined in some detail.

The Process

Throughout *Krishnamurti's Notebook*, which is a diary K kept from June 1961 through January 1962 (though it was not published until 1976, after Lutyens' first book on K's life), he says in many different ways that "the purification of the brain is necessary." He spoke of this in the context of the excruciating physical pain that generally came along with the psycho-physiological process he underwent. It seems as if K wrote this journal in order to document his own impressions while the process was going on. Yet it also contains some of the clearest and deepest expositions of his insights and observations. An example would be the following:

> All night it was there whenever I woke up. The head was bad going to the plane [to fly to Los Angeles]. The purification of the brain is necessary. The brain is the centre of all the senses; the more the senses are alert and sensitive, the sharper the brain is; it's the centre of remembrance, the past; it's the storehouse of experience and knowledge, tradition. So it's limited, conditioned. Its activities are planned, thought out, reasoned, but it functions in limitation, in space-time. So it cannot formulate or understand that which is the total, the whole, the complete. The complete, the whole, is the mind; it is empty, totally

empty and because of this emptiness, the brain exists in space-time. Only when the brain has cleansed itself of its conditioning, greed, envy, ambition, then only it can comprehend that which is complete. Love is this completeness.[7]

This passage was written on June 19, 1961. K had been experiencing the process recurrently since at least April of that year, and continued to do so throughout the writing of the journal. On May 12 he had written about it to Mrs. Jayakar's sister Nandini. At the time, he was in England giving talks and holding meetings. He wrote to Nandini:

The wheels of Ooty are working, unknown to any, and other things are taking place. It is so extraordinary, and words seem so futile. Days are too short and one lives in a day, a thousand years.[8]

His phrase "the wheels of Ooty" refers to the period in 1948 when the two sisters, shortly after they had first met him, were with him in the Indian hill station of Ootacamund and were witnesses to manifestations of the process. *Wheel*, of course, is the English word for the Sanskrit *chakra*. Clearly, K was saying that during the process his chakras were vivified. This is widely recognized in the literature as what happens when the serpent fire of kundalini rises up the spine. Even a treatise meant for the general public, such as the *Sivananda Companion to Yoga*, includes a brief discussion of the movement of kundalini from the lowest, or *muladhara*, chakra at the base of the spine to the highest, or *sahasrara*, chakra at the crown of the head:

As Kundalini passes through each of the various chakras, different states of consciousness are experienced. When it reaches the Sahasrara, the yogi attains samadhi. Though still operating on the material plane, he has reached a level of existence beyond time, space and causation.[9]

K continued to make references to the "wheels of Ooty" in subsequent letters. On June 1, for instance, he wrote that

> The wheels of Ooty are working furiously and painfully.[10]

The day after he left England (to fly to Los Angeles, as mentioned in the *Notebook* passage quoted above), his friend Doris Pratt, who at the time was apparently not fully aware of the esoteric nature of these experiences, wrote about his visit in a letter:

> [T]here were some very strange and difficult times when all life and energy seemed to be drained from his body and when he became "weak and ill" to an alarming degree. These occasions only lasted a few moments in their essence, but necessitated rest afterwards. On quite a few occasions he cried out aloud at night and on one or two occasions Anneke [Korndorffer] heard him and was very troubled. On other occasions he would mention at breakfast that he had been calling out and that he hoped he had not disturbed us. Similarly on several occasions at meal times he suddenly dropped his knife and fork and appeared to be kind of transfixed for a moment or two, and then to go limp and faint so that one thought he might drop to the floor.
>
> I questioned him about it because I wanted to know whether there was anything at all the onlooker could do. He replied there was nothing we could do except keep quiet, relaxed and not worry,

but also not touch him at all. I pressed him a bit, and he said while he himself knew exactly what was happening, he was unable to explain it to us. He said it was linked with the happenings [related to the process] which were alluded to in the unexpurgated book by Lady Emily [Lutyens].

During the eight weeks I was living in the same house I felt on many occasions that I was an onlooker at a most profound and tremendous mystery. . . . There was the man who during his own morning meditation period, spread a mantle of intense quietude over the house which even a rhinoceros like myself could feel. Then there were those mysterious attacks and some equally mysterious healings.[11]

"Mysterious healings," incidentally, refers to K's ability to heal others, which—like his clairvoyance, singing of mantras, and performance of certain rituals—is generally played down in books about his life. Perhaps their authors preferred to avoid acknowledging the esoteric implications of these abilities and practices; or perhaps they wished to avoid possible associations with the Messiah, given that K, like Jesus, had the ability to heal by imposition of hands and there had been a messianic mystique surrounding K all his life.[12]

When K referred to the head being "bad," as in the passage quoted above from the *Notebook*, he was speaking of a painful physical aspect of the process in which kundalini burned through the synapses and various centers in his brain. Passages such as these make a clear connection between what K was undergoing and the psychological and even physiological mutation that is the heart of his insights and observations, and is meant to apply to any human being. Clearly, transformation is not an easy matter for anyone. The psychological dimension of K's understanding of mutation has a family resemblance to Rudolf Otto's *mysterium tremendum et fascinans,* which was discussed in chapter 1. This kind of transformation takes place at deep levels and affects all aspects of one's life. Shifts in behavior or experiences that effect changes only in limited areas of human experience are not of this type and are not transformation in K's integral sense of that word.

Mutation

From the beginning K spoke of the need for radical transformation or mutation: without such mutation humanity would not have a spiritually meaningful future, and perhaps would have no future at all. However, it was only during the last years of his life that he elucidated more carefully the notion that this mutation was not only psycho-spiritual—which is the way audiences had understood it—but also biological, meaning a mutation of the brain cells.

In a dialogue in the early 1980s, published as *The Future of Humanity,* K and physicist David Bohm explored the question of whether humanity can change its pervasive self-destructive patterns of behavior. Early on in their dialogue they noted that knowledge and thought are not adequate to make us move away from those patterns and on to more creative and harmonious relationships with each other and the environment. In the preface to the book, Bohm outlined the content of the discussion, and remarked:

> But if knowledge and thought are not adequate, what is it that is actually required? This led in turn to the question of whether mind is limited by the brain of mankind, with all the knowledge that it has accumulated over the ages. This knowledge, which now conditions us deeply, has produced what is, in effect, an irrational and self-destructive program in which the brain seems to be helplessly caught up.

If mind is limited by such a state of the brain, then the future of humanity must be very grim indeed. Krishnamurti does not, however, regard these limitations as inevitable. Rather, he emphasizes that mind is essentially free of the distorting bias that is inherent in the conditioning of the brain, and that through insight arising in proper undirected attention without a center, it can change the cells of the brain and remove the destructive conditioning. If this is so, then it is crucially important that there be this kind of attention, and that we give to this question the same intensity of energy that we generally give to other activities of life that are really of vital interest to us.[13]

The notion that it is possible to bring about a mutation in the brain cells within a human lifetime would have been unacceptable in conventional academic circles earlier. Until very recently, brain cells were thought to be the only human cells that do not undergo significant short-term transformations. In Deepak Chopra's words, "It was long thought that we are born with a set number of brain cells that never divide to form new ones, yet recently it has been found that the DNA in neurons is active, which may lead to new conclusions."[14]

Further, only in the late twentieth century have scientists begun to note that evolution in nature does not take place gradually through very small changes and adaptations, as was thought previously. Rather, evolution is now understood to occur in sudden spurts of mutation that take place, for reasons not yet clearly known, after long periods of relative equilibrium that often last millions of years. As biologist James Lovelock wrote. "[T]he evolution of the environment is characterized by periods of stasis punctuated by abrupt and sudden change."[15]

Interestingly, Blavatsky and her teachers also said that mutations take place abruptly, and further, that mutations occur at the endings and beginnings of major cycles. That is, they not only taught what is now accepted in biology, but also provided an explanation of it, which science has not yet done. During HPB's time, however, conventional science did not give particular significance to cycles, and scientists were convinced that evolution was a gradual process. So in spite of the perennial renaissance's influence in the more creative fringes of science, this teaching was largely ignored in academic circles.[16]

The recent developments in the biological sciences seem to confirm K's insistence that psycho-biological human mutation takes place immediately, not gradually as a result of certain activities or practices. As John White wrote in *The Meeting of Science and Spirit*:

> [N]ew research indicates that even in old age, the neural cells of the cerebral cortex respond to an enriched environment by forging new connections to other cells. (The cerebral cortex is the "thinking" or "intellectual" part of the brain.) In other words, the brain can grow nerve cells at almost any age in response to novelty and challenge. A study of rats showed that neurons increased in dimension and activity, glial cells (which support neurons) multiplied, and the dendrites of neurons (branches of neurons which receive messages from other cells) lengthened. The dendritic increase allows for more, and presumably better, communication with other cells.
>
> . . . There is nothing firmly conclusive in this intriguing research, but it reminded me of something I wrote in the introduction to *The Highest State of Consciousness* (1972). There I suggested that enlightenment involves a repatterning of the brain's neural networks. Integration or unification is a primary aspect of the mindstate called

enlightenment. Since mind and brain are obviously closely related, it seems clear that whereas before enlightenment the brain's nervous system had unconnected or "compartmentalized" areas (the neurological analog of a "fragmented" understanding), in enlightenment there is a breakthrough resulting in an integration of the nerve pathways through which we think and feel. Our multiple "brains" become one brain. The neocortex (the "thinking-intellectual" part), the limbic system and thalamus (the "feeling-emotional" part), and the medulla oblongata (the "instinct-unconscious" part, at least according to Carl Jung) attain a previously nonexistent but always possible mode of intercellular communication. A threshold is passed, probably explainable in terms of both cellular electrochemical change and growth of new nerve-ending connections. However it may be accomplished in neurophysiological terms, the result is intimately associated with a new state of consciousness, a new mode of perception and feeling associated with the discovery of nonrational (but not irrational) forms of logic— forms which are multilevel/integrated/simultaneous rather than linear/sequential/either-or.[17]

These recent developments are in fact central to Deepak Chopra's landmark work in the medical field, particularly as it applies to aging versus the possibility of physiological regeneration. Dr. Chopra summarizes much of this research in his best-selling book *Ageless Body, Timeless Mind*. Relevant to our discussion, he makes connections between physiological changes and the possibility of transformations in the brain cells:

We are the only creatures on earth who can change our biology by what we think and feel.

. . . It would be impossible to isolate a single thought or feeling, a single belief or assumption, that doesn't have some effect on aging, either directly or indirectly. Our cells are constantly eavesdropping on our thoughts and being changed by them. A bout of depression can wreak havoc with the immune system; falling in love can boost it. Despair and hopelessness raise the risk of heart attacks and cancer, thereby shortening life. Joy and fulfillment keep us healthy and extend life. This means that the line between biology and psychology can't really be drawn with any certainty. A remembered stress, which is only a wisp of thought, releases the same flood of destructive hormones as the stress itself.

Because the mind influences every cell in the body, human aging is fluid and changeable; it can speed up, slow down, stop for a time, and even reverse itself. Hundreds of research findings from the last three decades have verified that aging is much more dependent on the individual than was ever dreamed of in the past.

. . . The biochemistry of the body is a product of awareness. Beliefs, thoughts, and emotions create the chemical reactions that uphold life in every cell. An aging cell is the end product of awareness that has forgotten how to remain new.

. . . Impulses of intelligence create your body in new forms every second. What you are is the sum total of these impulses, and by changing their patterns, you will change.[18]

Perennial Mutation

Mutation of the brain cells was a pivotal concept in the perennial teachings presented by HPB, her teachers, and her colleagues. They said that the twentieth century would mark the beginning of several major world cycles;[19] it would be a very critical period for humanity, and human mutations of evolutionary proportions involving mutation of the brain cells would become possible.

Given its intimate connection with the core of early theosophical teaching, the creation of a new human type and a new age of mankind was an issue discussed with great passion among the early theosophists. In *A Study in Consciousness,* her seminal work published at the turn of the century, Annie Besant spoke of brain cell mutation in terms of the innate potential in all human beings for moving on to new horizons in consciousness:

> [The] enlarging of waking-consciousness is accompanied with development in the atoms of the brain, as well as with the development of certain organs in the brain, and of the connections between cells. . . . So long as these physical developments remain unaccomplished, Self-consciousness may be evolved . . . but . . . its workings do not express themselves through the brain and thus become part of the waking-consciousness.[20]

Basic to the perennial teaching given by the theosophists was the notion, implied in AB's words, that for a faculty to become reality it must be part of waking consciousness in the physical brain—not merely an interesting intellectual theory or even an accomplishment on the "inner planes." For that to happen, however, the individual must engage in a transformative lifestyle conducive to such physical and psychological mutations. If and when they took place, such mutations would usher in a new human type, a new humanity, a new age. This is the point that would be insisted on later by K, as the earlier quotation from Bohm states.

In other words, even though evolutionary mutations take place at critical times determined by world cycles, they do not happen willy-nilly; they require engagement on the part of a few pioneering members of the species who undergo transformations. This is the way biological evolution is now said to take place: only a few members of a species undergo evolutionary mutations, whenever mutations happen. So also with the creation of a new human type: mutation in the brain cells of a few individuals would be enough. Theosophists believed the proper way to bring about such mutations in the brain was through the spiritual path outlined in the perennial philosophy (as they understood it) and in the esoteric teachings of the major religions and other traditions.

The preceding are some of the points of agreement between the theosophical teachings, as they were understood through the first third of the twentieth century, and K's expositions. A major difference, at least on the surface, is K's insight that before any such mutation can take place—and therefore before a new humanity can be created—there must be a psychological dying to the known. This means, in part, abandoning one's identifications with a particular culture, system of ideas, religion, and with the expectations built up over a lifetime. This is an awesome prospect for many of us. It is also an aspect of the *mysterium tremendum et fascinans*.

Ironically, this difference may be only a misunderstanding that arose out of early theosophists' attempts to communicate the ancient wisdom to a wider audience. In their zeal to make the formerly secret teachings available to the public at large, they presented the perennial teachings in the form of conceptual systems and methods of practice. The popularity of Leadbeater's writings (and later of others, such as Alice Bailey) shows the success of this decision. In retrospect, however, it had a detrimental effect. Most people came to understand the perennial philosophy as a conceptual system and a series of predetermined, repeatable practices. Transformation and dying to the known were relegated to mere conceptual categories, where they clearly do not belong. After all, conceptualizing about dying to the known is as valuable to mutation as a menu is to a hungry person.

Dying to the Known

Dying to the known has been a key element of the perennial philosophy for millennia. In fact, candidates sometimes even were shut inside coffins for days on end to have them gain a deep and unfaltering sense of it. Dying to the known was also at the heart of the teaching given by HPB and her teachers.[21] Unfortunately, whenever the perennial philosophy has been taken up and blended with particular cultures or systems, this crucial teaching of transformation has been sidelined from its central place of importance. The same happened with theosophy in the early years of the perennial renaissance. For instance, there was a great deal of talk about "entering the Path"; but this was understood as following a precisely outlined set of rules. This sort of practice has great appeal to the mind, with its penchant for organizing everything in logical categories. But for this very reason, it belongs to the realm of the conditioned mind, which by nature is not transformative.[22] Mutation, or transformation, on the other hand, implies non-identification with categories and systems. The mere acceptance of intellectual constructions about spiritual evolution cannot bring about a new age for humankind; instead, it leaves everything as it has been, though giving the impression of change.

When K insisted on actual transformation, and when he flatly denied any value in the purely conceptual edifices of Theosophy, most Theosophists were perplexed. For the most part they did not understand—much less know what to do with—what he was saying. Most people find the level of engagement implied in K's observations about transformation too arduous. As K made very clear, however serious we may be about religious, philosophical, or social improvement, most of us actually prefer to persist on a course of action that, besides being frivolous from the perennial standpoint, is dangerous to our personal and global welfare. This subject will be discussed more thoroughly, particularly in chapter 8.

Closed Loops

Annie Besant's statement quoted above may now prove to be not only in full agreement with the prominence K gave to mutation in his explorations, but also at the leading edge of scientific understanding a century later. As Bohm explains, echoing John White's musings of the early 1970s:

> It is worth remarking that modern research into the brain and nervous system actually gives considerable support to Krishnamurti's statement that insight may change the brain cells. Thus, for example, it is now well known that there are important substances in the body, the hormones and the neurotransmitters, that fundamentally affect the entire functioning of the brain and nervous system. These substances respond, from moment to moment, to what a person knows, to what he thinks, and to what all this means to him. It is by now fairly well established that in this way the brain cells and their functioning are profoundly affected by knowledge and thought, especially when these give rise to strong feelings and passions. It is thus quite plausible that insight, which must arise in a state of great mental energy and passion, could change the brain cells in an even more profound way.[23]

In cybernetics a closed, or recursive, loop is a series of instructions that repeat themselves endlessly. For instance, a computer programmed to write *prejudice* in a closed loop would continue writing the word until the computer is shut off or a "break" is keyed in. It seems as if up to this point in evolution the human brain cells have connected with one another in a way analogous to closed loop patterns. Correspondingly, human thought has functioned in terms of "closed loops" in numerous areas of existence. For instance, if one is an African American or a Jew living in Israel or a Christian in Ireland or a person with a serious illness, one expects certain experiences to follow inevitably. The nature of closed loops implies that our lives will remain full of fear, confusion, and violence as long as we are unwilling to die completely to these recursive patterns in the brain. K's explorations suggest that it is those recursive patterns in the brain that keep us from being sensitive to ourselves, to one another, and to *that which is*. That is, conceptual systems imply the use of recursive patterns and therefore can *never* lead to transformation. Both K and the perennial teaching tell us that so long as the ways we feel, think, and behave are characterized by recursive or closed loops, there cannot be a new humanity or a new age.

K's psycho-spiritual experiences may hold important keys for bringing about such a new age for mankind. During the process, K's dendrites, axons, and nerve endings may have been literally "on edge," ever open to some new possibility rather than following well-worn paths—paths determined largely by our evolution as a species and by patterns of behavior that were successful previously. The physical stress and nervous fatigue such a constant state of alertness implies may explain much of K's behavior witnessed by others ("slipping off," fainting, becoming weak, and so forth), as well as the constantly recurring pain. As K wrote in his journal at a time when he was experiencing the excruciating pain in the brain connected with the process:

> Destruction is essential. Not of buildings and things but of all the psychological devices and defences, gods, beliefs, dependence on priests, experiences, knowledge and so on. Without destroying all these there cannot be creation. It's only in freedom that creation comes into being. Another cannot destroy these defences for you; you have to negate through your own self-knowing awareness.
>
> Revolution, social, economic, can only change outer states and things, in increasing or nar-

rowing circles, but it will always be within the limited field of thought. For total revolution the brain
must forsake all its inward, secret mechanisms of
authority, envy, fear and so on.

The strength and the beauty of a tender
leaf is its vulnerability to destruction. Like a blade of
grass that comes up through the pavement, it has
the power that can withstand casual death.[24]

These words suggest an intimate relationship between the
esoteric process of kundalini burning through K's brain cells to
activate new synapses (and possibly to trigger the creation of new
brain cells and other cerebral developments), the content of K's
insights and observations, and the necessity for a physiological as
well as psychological mutation in each of us, thereby creating a
new humanity. In fact, all three may be but different ways of
looking at precisely the same thing.

The Nature of the Process

This brief account of the nature of the process (which is
considered more thoroughly in Parts II and III) is consistent with
the perennial teaching in both its ancient and more modern expositions, with what CWL and K said about the process, and with K's
insights and observations. However, those who have written
about K in the past have given other, very different explanations
for the process. Therefore, before proceeding it is valuable to look
carefully at these various alternative explanations, which can be
grouped under the following: hallucinations, spontaneous awakening of kundalini, deception, hypnosis, and self-delusion.

Hallucinations

As the Notebook makes evident, there was an incontro-
vertibly intimate relationship between the esoteric process K
underwent, and his insights and observations. Given this close

connection, if the process were a hallucination, his insights and observations would have to be of the same quality. However, K's expositions, which were on complex areas of psychology, philosophy, and spiritual life, were formidably clear and penetrating till the end of his life. Such clarity and depth seem incompatible with hallucinations. This critical point makes it extremely difficult to consider his inner experiences as hallucinations or visions.

In her foreword to the *Notebook*, Mary Lutyens explained her own understanding of the process, which further clarifies that it was not a series of hallucinatory episodes:

> A word is needed to explain one of the terms used in it—"the process." In 1922 . . . Krishnamurti underwent a spiritual experience that changed his life and which was followed by years of acute and almost continuous pain in his head and spine. The manuscript shows that "the process," as he called this mysterious pain, was still going on nearly forty years later, though in a much milder form.
>
> "The process" was a physical phenomenon, not to be confused with the state of consciousness that Krishnamurti variously refers to in the notebooks as the "benediction," the "otherness," "immensity." At no time did he take any painkilling drugs for "the process." He has never taken alcohol or any kind of drug. He has never smoked, and for the last thirty years or so he has not so much as drunk tea or coffee. Although a life-long vegetarian, he has always been at great pains to ensure a plentiful and well-balanced diet. Asceticism is, to his way of thinking, as destructive of a religious life as over-indulgence. Indeed he looks after "the body" (he has always differentiated between the body and the ego) as a cavalry officer would have looked after his horse. He has never suffered from epilepsy or

any of the other physical conditions that are said to give rise to visions and other spiritual phenomena; nor does he practise any "system" of meditation. All this is stated so that no reader should imagine that Krishnamurti's states of consciousness are, or ever have been, induced by drugs or fasting.[25]

Incidentally, distinguishing one's needs from those of the body and the analogy of a cavalry officer's relationship to his horse come straight out of *At the Feet of the Master*. Unsupported claims have been made that CWL wrote this little inspirational book. However, K wrote it when he was fourteen. K, as well as witnesses at the time, said that the Master KH had instructed him to prepare for his first perennial initiation—a fact that K corroborated in the 1930s.[26] The little book is apparently K's recollections of what the Master had taught him. One of these teachings was:

> The body is your animal—the horse upon which you ride. Therefore you must treat it well, and take good care of it; you must not overwork it, you must feed it properly on pure food and drink only, and keep it strictly clean always, even from the minutest speck of dirt. For without a perfectly clean and healthy body you cannot do the arduous work of preparation, you cannot bear its ceaseless strain. But it must always be you who control that body, not it that controls you.[27]

Contrary to beliefs held by many theosophists and Krishnamurti students alike, K took this teaching from his Master (which can be found in perennial Hinduism) seriously to the end of his life.

From what K said in the *Notebook* and elsewhere, there was an inescapable connection between the process he was undergoing and the necessity for all of us to "cleanse the brain." He said all along in his talks and writings that the brain must be cleared of the debris of conditioned patterns of response. In his own pioneering case, that apparently implied a psycho-physiological mutation that was extremely painful, possibly because of the depths to which it was carried out and the enormous energy that evidently was flowing through his system.

Anyone claiming that K was hallucinating whenever the process was going on would be forced to make a remarkable statement: When K functioned as a teacher, he divulged landmark insights in fields such as philosophy and psychology, but otherwise his life was largely a grand series of hallucinations that continued for almost eighty years. Further, the hallucinations theorist would have to show that everyone who met the Masters in the early days of theosophical history was also hallucinating; for those same Masters were apparently the ones who initiated K and conducted the process. Moreover, it is hard to believe those Masters were hallucinations given the impact of the perennial renaissance, which they are credited with bringing about.

In other words, there is a seamless continuity between the process, K's insights and observations, and the perennial lineage and its modern expositions through the perennial renaissance. To dismiss the process as a hallucination is to deny the validity of what K said and his own accounting of its source. In sum, the hallucinations theory seems to fall short of anything close to an adequate explanation for the process.

Spontaneous Awakening

Probably the most spectacular well-known case of spontaneous development of kundalini is that of Gopi Krishna.[28] Without the direct guidance of a guru, he practiced daily meditation for hours at a time over years, following instructions in a number of tantric books on how to arouse kundalini. Apparently, he was extremely lucky not to have had any of the negative experiences that can occur when practicing tantra without the help of a knowledgeable and reliable guide. In effect, he ignored the warning label, "Do not try this at home," that comes implicitly with these practices.

The clairvoyant and theosophist Geoffrey Hodson, who presumably developed his clairvoyance through approaches suggested by his perennial teachers, wrote dozens of books on his super-sensible experiments. He spoke of children he knew who had become clairvoyant by innocently using breathing patterns that seemed right out of tantric texts; this comes closer to a truly spontaneous awakening of kundalini.[29] (As noted briefly in chapter 1, the vivification of the chakras as kundalini rises up the spine may produce clairvoyance, as well as other psychic results.) In this category are also cases where clairvoyance developed due to a powerful jolt to one of the psychic centers. C.W. Leadbeater mentions such a case: a Canadian woman who had a bad fall and, when she came to, found she had become clairvoyant permanently.[30]

Visualization is one of the techniques used for awakening kundalini, and K had been doing what could be interpreted by some as visualizations of the Lord Maitreya for a few days before the process began on August 17, 1922. The following is the full description of that practice. Incidentally, this account suggests that K was clairvoyant, given the way he speaks of the different levels of awareness:

Since August 3rd, I meditated regularly for about thirty minutes every morning. I could, to my astonishment, concentrate with considerable ease, and within a few days I began to see clearly where I had failed and where I was failing. Immediately I set about, consciously, to annihilate the wrong accumulations of the past years. With the same deliberation I set about to find out ways and means to achieve my aim. First I realized that I had to harmonize all my other bodies with the Buddhic plane [the level of awareness immediately beyond the conceptual mind] and to bring about this happy combination I had to find out what my ego wanted on the Buddhic plane. To harmonize the various bodies I had to keep them vibrating at the same rate as the Buddhic, and to do this I had to find out what was the vital interest of the Buddhic.

> With ease which rather astonished me I found the main interest on that high plane was to serve the Lord Maitreya and the Masters. With that idea clear in my physical mind I had to direct and control the other bodies to act and to think the same as on the noble and spiritual plane. During that period of less than three weeks [actually, closer to ten days], I concentrated to keep in mind the image of the Lord Maitreya throughout the entire day, and I found no difficulty in doing this. I found that I was getting calmer and more serene. My whole outlook on life was changed.[31]

On the surface, K's attempt to put himself in harmony with the Lord Maitreya might seem sufficient to account for what happened. Some might interpret aspects of what K was doing as visualization, even if that was not consciously his intention; and since visualization is one technique for awakening kundalini, some might say this triggered the process. However, if this is the full explanation, it would be the most amazing known case of the power of visualization, given the tremendous consequences that resulted from it. Not only the process but everything that K taught would have to be explained as its result. Usually, visualization can lead to results such as clairvoyance, some psychic abilities, or even a limited degree of psychological transformation. K's process, however, implied mutation at great depth that impacted not only him but the many others influenced by his insights and observations. If all that was the result of five or six half-hour visualizations, that would indeed be amazing. Furthermore, since K subsequently abandoned all appeals to the image of the Lord Maitreya or other teachers, visualizations are an even less likely explanation of the process than hallucinations; for the visualizations of a few days would then have to explain a lifetime of reawakenings of kundalini.

K's state of being may have led him to begin what may be interpreted as visualizations, and the perennial teachers may have recognized this as an opportunity to introduce the transformations that were to take place in him. That is, K's predisposition to be of service to the perennial teachers may have created ideal conditions for what was to transpire. Such a predisposition may be similar to what the *Yoga Sutras* refer to as *Ishwara pranidana*, total surrender to the divine. In yoga as well as other religious traditions, surrender to *that which is* is often sufficient for experiencing theosophical, or divine, states of awareness. However, the perennial teachers as K's spiritual mentors, and K's predisposition to be of service—whether it was akin to *Ishwara pranidhana* or not—were present years before the process began. So the spontaneous awakening of kundalini through visualizations of the Lord Maitreya cannot account for all aspects of the process.

If spontaneous awakening of kundalini is considered a sufficient, or even partial, explanation of the process, the hallucination theory would also be implied. For every time K experienced the process in the presence of other people, he referred constantly and insistently to the several "others" who he said were in charge of the proceedings, and described himself as merely a vehicle for a colossal intelligence that he clearly identified as not his own. If these "others" were products of his imagination, one must consider again the hallucinations theory. As noted above, this theory is untenable, or at least very weak, since it implies that K's teachings came out of hallucinations as well. Since the notion that the process was exclusively the result of spontaneous awakening of kundalini depends on the presence of hallucinations, this theory is also invalidated.

If we take K's own words as evidence, they deny the possibility that the process was exclusively the result of an internal experience such as kundalini awakening. For one thing, K referred all his life—from the beginning of the process until just a few days before his death—to an outside agency as responsible for the process. This leads us back to Pupul Jayakar's statement, quoted at the beginning of chapter 1, that a guru is necessary to protect the yogi from physical or psychological injury when kundalini is awakened. But there was no such expert physically present at any point during K's experiences of the process. The only "experts" mentioned are the perennial teachers who started the perennial renaissance. Since these teachers were said to have yogic abilities, their physical presence would not have been required.

An analogy comes to mind. It is now possible to put a robot on the surface of Mars and give it commands from Houston, Texas, even though there is no apparent physical connection between Houston and Mars. If someone several centuries ago had heard of such an event, it would have been considered witchcraft, or it would not have been believed. Perennial schools have been around for millennia, and some perennial teachers are said to have developed the ability to use a kind of remote control between human beings. Ancient books on yoga and tantra contain "formulas" for developing such abilities. In other words, there is nothing supernatural about their employment, just as there is nothing supernatural about remote control between one gadget and another.

The real difficulty in accepting such a possibility is not necessarily theoretical. The problem comes because developing such abilities requires a radical transformation of one's lifestyle. These ancient sciences are intrinsically psychological, and the perennial philosophy has always been highly practical in requiring the psychological engagement of its "scientists"—the perennial philosophers and their students. Deep down, the unwillingness to submit to the "lab conditions" of the ancient science—which demands emptiness from conditioning—is the real problem for many contemporary people. On the other hand, modern science requires leaving the human psyche out of scientific experiments as completely as possible. Perhaps understanding these differences would help people realize that there is nothing "spooky" or "supernatural" about the perennial teachers being involved in the process—or in the creation of the contemporary perennial renaissance.

It does not seem likely that spontaneous awakening of kundalini could have produced K's process. Nor was there any expert physically present—no single guru, as Jayakar describes in the passage quoted near the opening of chapter 1. On the other hand, if, as K said all along, there were several perennial teachers involved in what he at one point called an "operation," that would be an important explanation for the source of the process. Spontaneous awakening of kundalini is at best a necessary but not a sufficient explanation of the process.

Deception

The process might also be explained as a deception. This explanation might appeal to those who are ignorant of the relevant facts, or who deny the existence of subtle energies and their masterful manipulation by perennial teachers. Such people would be inclined to ignore evidence discussed here already, such as the impressive research of CWL and other clairvoyants into areas related to the subtle energies; the clairvoyant medical diagnostic work of Dora van Gelder Kunz; the effectiveness of acupuncture, which operates on a subtle energy model; and the fact that many people can develop clairvoyance and related abilities.

Still, the possibility of deception must be considered. Deception could be, broadly speaking, of two types: one unconscious, the other more deliberate. The former might more appropriately be called "delusion" and would mean that K deceived himself regarding his inner life. Perhaps the experiences connected with the process were projections prompted by inner psychological urges. Or he might have been so impressionable as a teenager that others could hypnotize him into believing he was seeing the Masters and was the vehicle for the Lord Maitreya. A few authors have speculated along these lines, such as Stuart Holroyd, as noted in chapter 1. But no one has researched this possibility carefully and evaluated the implications this view entails. That is attempted in the section on self-delusion.

The other form of deception would mean that K deliberately lied about his inner life. The only author who has put forth this view is Radha Rajagopal Sloss.[32] Since she is the daughter of the Rajagopals, who lived under K's protection for about thirty years, her book might have been informative and of value to anyone interested in K's life and work. However, Sloss relies on her mother's memories from some forty years earlier as her exclusive source, even though she admits that her mother was emotionally imbalanced at the time some of the relevant events in her book took place. The book's disparaging and narrow view of K has prompted a number of responses to point out some, though not all, of its numerous inaccuracies.[33]

Since Sloss's book is so poorly founded, one can say that as yet no one has presented a credible case for K willfully deceiving anyone regarding his inner life. The evidence to the contrary is overwhelming, spanning acquaintances and friendships over almost eighty years. Nevertheless, the question of delusion in some form is a valid one. Discussing it carefully is also difficult and involved.

Hypnosis

There are two possible forms of delusion: being deluded by someone else, as in hypnosis, and deluding oneself.

Some authors have proposed that CWL hypnotized, or attempted to hypnotize, K as a young man. At first blush this seems a possible explanation. But if K were as impressionable as this theory requires, it means he was mesmerized for life by notions planted in his psyche during the few months that CWL had access to Krishna. And that access was limited and almost always in the presence of others. That is, he presumably would have taken the suggestions about the Masters and his own role as the vehicle of the Lord Maitreya so much to heart that they fueled the process for him for the rest of his life. Given the physiological and psychological complexities connected to the process, the profound impact of K's insights and observations on several generations of intelligent people, and other factors considered in this discussion, hypnosis seems a very weak explanation.

There are several other difficulties with this hypothesis. The main one also arises when considering hallucinations and spontaneous development of kundalini: it implies a complete split in K's personality throughout most of his very long life. It means K the teacher was totally unaware of K the initiate. This flies in the face of K's own researches, which call for a high level of awareness and mindfulness from moment to moment. A split in K's personality would imply that even he was not maintaining that level of attentiveness. If K the initiate was merely hypnotized, the close connections K the teacher made between the process and his insights are invalidated. It would mean that K the teacher could not see critical psychological processes taking place in his own psyche.

For these and related reasons, anyone aware of the depth and clarity of K's insights and observations would find it very difficult to accept the theory of hypnosis. This is particularly the case in light of comments K made, especially in the *Notebook*, about the intimate relationship between the process and his investigations.

The hypnosis hypothesis also breaks down in the context of the facts of K's life. He was accommodating all along to those who were close to him and invariably would let others do as they pleased, even when it impinged directly on administrative aspects of his work. In fact, this trait is what led a number of authors to point out how suggestible he was. Mary Lutyens, for instance, states:

> When he was first "discovered" by Leadbeater it must have struck the latter that the boy's empty mind was ideally fertile soil for the planting of his own Theosophical ideas.[34]

This statement implies that Lutyens *knew* CWL's thoughts and intentions; she seems to claim clairvoyance for herself!

However, far from hypnotizable, K was most uncompliant and indomitable when it came to anything having to do with deeper matters. He not only broke with the Theosophists; he transcended all notions that theosophy was a conceptual system. His was a break at very great depths. As discussed in Part III, he broke new ground in insisting on the necessity for transformation. If his malleable demeanor in everyday matters gave a mistaken impression, it should be obvious that in what mattered, *no one* left an impression on him. And the process was an integral part of what mattered to him.

Lutyens followed the comment above by saying:

> All those years of study and Theosophical conditioning left hardly a mark on K's mind.[35]

Though Lutyens' remarks reveal an anti-Theosophical, anti-Leadbeater prejudice in her work, they also argue against the notion of hypnotism as an explanation of K's inner life, which after all also implies that CWL was a hypnotizer. But from the beginning K made it very clear that he had not been "conditioned" by the Theosophists.

Even in Lutyens' description of Krishnaji's period of growth and formation among the Theosophists from 1911 to 1921, it is clear that no one was trying to condition him in any way. CWL did give him instructions about his spiritual life and was directly involved in his relationship with the perennial teachers for a few months between 1909 and 1911. But it is difficult to construe CWL's function as Krishnaji's tutor and mentor in these matters as some form of hypnosis.

Interestingly, HPB had also been dubbed a hypnotizer by some critics of the theosophical movement, who claimed she mesmerized those close to her to make them do whatever she wanted. It is useful to see what she said about hypnosis, since the same understanding was shared by theosophists generally, including CWL.

All know that there is a tacit, often openly-expressed, belief among a few of the Fellows of the T.S. that a certain prominent Theosophist among the leaders of the Society *psychologizes* all those who happen to come within the area of that individual's influence. Dozens, nay, hundreds, were, and still are, "psychologized." The hypnotic effect seems so strong as to virtually transform all such "unfortunates" into irresponsible nincompoops, mere cyphers and tools of that theosophical Circe. This idiotic belief was originally started by some "wise men" of the West. Unwilling to admit that the said person had either any knowledge or *powers*, bent on discrediting their victim, and yet unable to explain certain abnormal occurrences, they hit upon this happy and logical loophole to get out of their difficulties.

The theory found a grateful and fruitful soil. Henceforth, whenever any Fellows connected theosophically with the said "psychologizer" happen to disagree in their views upon questions, metaphysical or even purely administrative, with some other member—"on despotism bent"—forthwith the latter comes out with the favourite solution: "Oh, they are psychologized!" The *magic* WORD springs out on the arena of discussion like a Jack-in-the-box, and forthwith the attitude of the "rebels" is explained and plausibly accounted for.

Of course, the alleged "psychology" has really no existence outside the imagination of those who are too vain to allow any opposition to *their* all-wise and autocratic decrees on any other ground than phenomenal—nay, *magical*—interference with their will. A short analysis of the Karmic effects that would be produced by the exercise of such powers may prove interesting to theosophists.

Even on the terrestrial, purely physical plane, moral irresponsibility ensures punishment. Parents are answerable for their children, tutors and guardians for their pupils and wards, and even the Supreme Courts have admitted extenuating circumstances for criminals who are proved to have been led to crime by a will or influences stronger than their own. How much more forcibly this law of simple retributive justice must act on the psychic plane; and what, therefore, may be the responsibility incurred by using such psychological powers, in the face of Karma and its punitive laws, may be easily inferred.

. . . From the occult standpoint, the charge is simply one of black magic, of *envoûtement*. Alone a *Dugpa* [black magician], with "Avitchi" ["hell" in Tibetan cosmology] yawning at the further end of his life cycle, could risk such a thing. Have those so prompt to hurl the charge at the head of persons in their way, ever understood the whole terrible meaning implied in the accusation? We doubt it. No occultist, no intelligent student of the mysterious laws of the "night side of Nature," no one who knows anything of Karma, would ever suggest such an explanation. What adept or even a moderately-informed chela [disciple] would ever risk an endless future by interfering with, and therefore *taking upon himself, the Karmic debit of all those whom he would so psychologize as to make of them merely the tools of his own sweet will!*[36]

"Psychologizing," or hypnotism, is apparently still a popular explanation more than a century later, for it is found in current books on K's life. However, hypnotism was a very serious matter to theosophists. Though mesmerism in some form is considered acceptable for such things as healing or alleviating pain, control of another person is absolutely warned against and is profoundly incompatible with the perennial path. As CWL explained:

> The domination of the will by that of another produces effects that few people realise. The will of the victim becomes weaker, and is more liable to be acted upon by others.[37]

Anyone suggesting hypnotism as an explanation for K's inner life would have to explain its profound inconsistency with the perennial teaching and practice. That has never been done by anyone making claims along these lines.

Self-Delusion

A final possible explanation of K's inner life is that it all came from the unconscious. That is, some inner urge might have led K to create a fantasy world of Masters, clairvoyant experiences, and belief in himself as vehicle for the Lord Maitreya. His cultural background could have supported this, for in India there is a belief in the periodical manifestation of avatars. The inner demands could have gained momentum from K's intimate contact with theosophists, who were expecting the coming of the World Teacher in the twentieth century. These possibilities might have been enhanced by K's innate tendency to please others.

Whatever their source, inner urges have been identified by various ancient approaches to meditation and psychology as phenomena that need to be seen, acknowledged, understood, and transcended. In twentieth-century Western psychology (which had its origins in the theosophical milieu, in which such teachings were a staple), such urges have been said to come from unconscious or subconscious levels of awareness.

This explanation may be attractive from the standpoint of formal psychology. But once K's own insights and observations are taken into account, this theory also begins to break down.

Some of K's own observations on psychology, and particularly on the unconscious, are found in a series of dialogues K had with physicist David Bohm and David Shainberg, head of psychiatry training at Columbia University. The dialogues are available in a series of videotapes, and also in much edited form in the book *The Wholeness of Life.*

The reader should keep in mind that K had no formal education and was not a reader of books of psychology or philosophy. (His reading was largely confined to newspapers, and "thrillers," such as Agatha Christie's.) Yet he was the first person to point out seriously the nonexistence of the unconscious. This was, in fact, one of the reasons that led Shainberg to pursue K's acquaintance. As the following passage is taken out of context, some of what is said may not be completely clear to anyone not familiar with K's work. For instance, the passage begins with a discussion of a thinker without thought, and of the observer being the observed. These are subjects that K went into at great depth elsewhere,[38] including in this series of dialogues. The topic of the ending of time, referred to briefly toward the end of the passage, is another subject K explored at great depth elsewhere.[39]

> Krishnamurti: Is there a thinker without thought?
> Bohm: No.
> K: Exactly. There you are. If there is no experiencer, is there an experience? So you have asked me to look at my images, which is a very serious and very penetrating demand. You say, look at them without the observer, because the observer is the image-maker, and if there is no observer, if there is no thinker, there is no thought—right? So there is no image. You have shown me something enormously significant.
>
> Shainberg: As you said, the question changes completely.

K: Completely. I have no image.

S: It feels completely different. It's as if there is a silence.

K: So I am saying, my consciousness is the consciousness of the world, because, in essence, it is filled with the things of thought—sorrow, fear, pleasure, despair, anxiety, attachment, hope—it is a turmoil of confusion; a sense of deep agony is involved in it all. And in that state, I cannot have any relationship with any human being.

S: Right.

K: So you say to me: To have the greatest and most responsible relationship is to have no image. You have pointed out to me that to be free of images, the maker of the image must be absent. The maker of the image is the past, is the observer who says "I like this," "I don't like this," who says "my wife, my husband, my house"—the me who is in essence the image. I have understood this. Now the next question is: Are the images hidden so that I can't grapple with them, can't get hold of them? All you experts have told me that there are dozens of underground images—and I say, "By Jove, they must know, they know much more than I do, so I must accept what they say." But how am I to unearth them, expose them? You see, you have put me, the ordinary man, into a terrible position.

S: You don't have to unearth them once it is clear to you that the observer is the observed.

K: Therefore you are saying there is no unconscious.

S: Right.

K: You, the expert! You, who talk endlessly about the unconscious with your patients.

S: I don't.

K: You say there is no unconscious.

S: Right.

K: I agree with you. I say it is so. The moment you see that the observer is the observed, that the observer is the maker of images, it is finished.

S: Finished. Right.

K: Right through.

S: If you really see that.

K: That's it. So the consciousness which I know, in which I have lived, has undergone a tremendous transformation. Has it? Has it for you? And if I may ask Dr. Bohm also—both of you, all of us—realizing that the observer is the observed, and that therefore the image-maker is no longer in existence, and so the content of consciousness, which makes up consciousness, is not as we know it—what then?

S: I don't know how you say it. . .

K: I am asking this question because it involves meditation. I am asking this question because all religious people, the really serious ones who have gone into this question, see that as long as we live our daily lives within the area of this consciousness—with all its images, and the image-maker—whatever we do will still be in that area. Right? One year I may become a Zen-Buddhist, and another year I may follow some guru, and so on and so on, but it is always within that area.

S: Right.

K: So what happens when there is no movement

of thought, which is the image-making—what then takes place? You understand my question? When time, which is the movement of thought, ends, what is there? Because you have led me up to this point. I understand it very well. I have tried Zen meditation, I have tried Hindu meditation, I have tried all kinds of other miserable practices, and then I hear you, and I say, "By Jove, this is something extraordinary these people are saying. They say that the moment there is no image-maker, the content of consciousness undergoes a radical transformation, and thought comes to an end, except in its right place." Thought comes to an end, time has a stop. What then? Is that death?

S: It is the death of the self.

K: No, no.

S: It is self-destruction.

K: No, no, sir. It is much more than that.

S: It is the end of something.

K: No, no. Just listen to it. When thought stops, when there is no image-maker, there is a complete transformation in consciousness because there is no anxiety, there is no fear, there is no pursuit of pleasure, there are none of the things that create turmoil and division. Then what comes into being, what happens? Not as an experience, because that is out. What takes place? I have to find out, for you may be leading me up the wrong path![40]

The content of this discussion, and the fact that K did not get his insights from books or from speculations about what others have said, should make it apparent that K was keenly aware of the workings of the mind. While it does not prove that he was not driven by inner urges, this does imply a more difficult defense of the self-delusion theory.

The Masters

During K's original experiences of the process in 1922, and at every subsequent manifestation reported by him or by others, there was no guru physically present; yet K and the others present in 1922 reported that the perennial teachers were there. All the witnesses said that whatever was happening to Krishnaji was carried out by the Masters and overseen by the Lord Maitreya—who K and others said was also present on several occasions. The Lord Maitreya is supposed to be one of the principal figures associated with the perennial philosophy and to have manifested in the past as Krishna, as the Christ, and as Quetzalcoatl, among other great teachers. He is the one ultimately responsible for all perennial teachings throughout the world during the present cycle.

K's brother Nityananda (Nitya), one of the witnesses to the first manifestations of the process, identified the experience of 1922 as part of an initiation ceremony carried on by the perennial teachers. In his account, he recalls a similar previous situation when the two brothers had been in Taormina, Italy, where K had gone through his second initiation. In Ojai, at the beginning of the process, K had been chanting the mantra sung every night in Adyar by members of the Esoteric School of Theosophy (who were expected to follow the path of deconditioning). Nitya recalled:

> Long ago in Taormina, as Krishna had looked with meditative eyes upon a beautiful painting of our Lord Gautama in mendicant garb, we had felt for a blissful moment the divine presence of the Great One, who had deigned to send a thought. And again this night, as Krishna, under the young pepper tree, finished his song of adoration, I thought of the

Tathagata [Gautama Buddha] under the Bo tree, and again I felt pervading the peaceful valley a wave of that splendour, as if again He had sent a blessing upon Krishna.

We sat with eyes fixed upon the tree, wondering if all was well, for now there was perfect silence, and as we looked I saw suddenly for a moment a great Star shining above the tree, and I knew that Krishna's body was being prepared for the Great One. I leaned across and told Mr. Warrington of the Star.

The place seemed to be filled with a Great Presence and a great longing came upon me to go on my knees and adore, for I knew that the Great Lord of all our hearts had come Himself; and though we saw Him not, yet all felt the splendour of His presence. Then the eyes of Rosalind [Williams] were opened and she saw. Her face changed as I have seen no face change, for she was blessed enough to see with physical eyes the glories of that night. Her face was transfigured, as she said to us, "Do you see Him, do you see Him?" for she saw the divine Bodhisattva [the Lord Maitreya], and millions wait for incarnations to catch such a glimpse of our Lord, but she had eyes of innocence and had served our Lord faithfully. And we who could not see saw the Splendours of the night mirrored in her face pale with rapture in the starlight.

Never shall I forget the look on her face, for presently I, who could not see but who gloried in the presence of our Lord, felt that He turned toward us and spoke some words to Rosalind; her face shone with divine ecstasy as she answered, "I will, I will," and she spoke the words as if they were a promise given with splendid joy. Never shall I forget her face when I looked at her; even I was almost blessed with vision. Her face showed the rapture of her heart, for the innermost part of her being was ablaze with His presence but her eyes saw. And silently I prayed that He might accept me as His servant and all our hearts were full of that prayer. In the distance we heard divine music softly played, all of us heard, though hidden from us, were the Gandharvas [angels of music].

The radiance and the glory of the many Beings present lasted nearly half an hour and Rosalind, trembling and almost sobbing with joy, saw it all; "Look, do you see?" she would often repeat, or "Do you hear the music?" Then presently we heard Krishna's footsteps and saw his white figure coming up in the darkness, and all was over. And Rosalind cried out, "Oh, he is coming; go get him, go get him" and fell back in her chair almost in a swoon. When she recovered, alas, she remembered nothing, nothing, all was gone from her memory except the sound of music still in her ears.[41]

Nitya's description may understandably be assessed as over-zealous, emotional lyricism. However, it corroborates what K himself said until the end of his life—though in more subdued and serene language—about the presence of the Masters and the Lord Maitreya.

Simplicity

K's process cannot credibly be explained as a hallucination, a spontaneous manifestation of kundalini, or some form of deception, nor was any guru ever physically present. Yet the process was closely related to—it was at the source of—K's subtle and life-transforming expositions. Moreover, there seems to have been an intimate connection between K's process and the mutation required for creation of a new humanity. The only credible explanation for the process seems to be that it was initiated, guided, and protected by the perennial teachers personally, using their yogic abilities. This is what Krishnamurti himself said all along about these experiences, as subsequent chapters show.

From all the evidence available, it seems that K's only—and critical—contributions to the process were his vacuity of conditioning and his predisposition to serve the perennial teachers. That is, at no point did he have the kinds of expectations, ambitions, fears, and demands that most of us seem to have. This may be what CWL meant when he said he had never seen anyone with such a selfless aura. It is precisely such emptiness that the most sophisticated systems of meditation aim at obtaining, and it often comes—if it comes at all—only after decades of intense practice. As Mary Lutyens explained:

> It's interesting that when Krishnamurti first asked me to write his biography, he said to me, if he was writing the biography he would start with the vacant mind. And then he went on to enlarge on how he'd always had, he said, a vacant mind. And he seemed to think that the vacant mind was so much a part of him, a part of his teaching.[42]

Perhaps this psychological emptiness combined with a predisposition to serve were preconditions for fulfilling his mission. Yet again, as discussed in this chapter, they would not be sufficient, since something like grace also seems to have been a factor. However, if there is any truth to the claims Leadbeater and Besant made about K, these qualities of his must have been vital.

PART TWO

THE PASSION

CHAPTER FOUR

Initiation

KRISHNAJI'S FIRST EXPERIENCE OF THE PROCESS in 1922, seen in retrospect, has all the signs of an initiation. This initiation appears to have been conducted for Krishnaji by several of the Masters. Prominent among them was the Lord Maitreya, who is perceived in the perennial philosophy as a "Planetary Spirit" or avatar not connected exclusively with any particular religion. Though called Maitreya in the Buddhist tradition, he is known by different names, such as Kalki Avatar in Hinduism, Sosiosh in Zoroastrianism, and Christ in Christianity.[1]

A connection between K and the perennial teachers is bound to seem bizarre and even unbelievable to some, particularly to admirers of K who find it incompatible with what they understand to be his message. After all, K railed for some seventy years against following others in psychological-spiritual matters. However, strange as it may seem to someone unacquainted with the perennial philosophy, K's own statements as well as all the evidence available reveal his intimate relationship with those perennial teachers. So to discredit this relationship is to disagree with K himself.

The word *initiation* is used in a number of contexts even in mainstream society. It is associated with rituals of induction into an organization and also with rites of passage from one stage of life into another. In New Age schools, the word shows up in connection with vague notions of human development. Therefore, it would be appropriate to clarify the meaning of the term in the present context and as it applies to K's life.

Dying to the Known

In perennial schools, initiation is an event that takes place in the context of a symbolic or mythic reenactment of a psychological death the candidate experiences. The candidate dies to the old associations, identifications, and expectations of daily life—implying that a greater field is opened up by the process of dying to the known. One purpose of initiation, then, is to help the candidate awaken to a richer, wiser, more compassionate life than was possible as long as he or she continued the old ways. The initiation is partly confirmation of a tendency—or even an actuality—already present in the candidate. Further, it strengthens the link between the candidate and anyone else in the world who "has been to the mountain top" and seen from a more universal perspective, and now lives freer of the conditioning of any culture, system, or expectations.

A reason why initiations and ceremonies in general have been of great importance throughout human history is that they employ nonverbal, mythical modes of communicating with the psyches of the participants. This symbolic "language" conveys subliminal messages to the candidate that the conscious mind is not likely to accept. The conscious mind is conditioned according to a particular culture or pattern of behavior—and is what most of us identify with.

The Twentieth-Century Revolution

HPB and her teachers made significant comments to the effect that the creation of a new human type would begin in the twentieth century. They said that humanity was psychologically ready for major shifts in consciousness, and larger numbers of people could now be exposed to formerly secret teachings and practices. They also commented that their own efforts were largely to make public what used to be hidden away in the perennial teaching. The public exposure and demythologizing of ancient approaches and practices could mean but one thing: The perennial teachers were scuttling the old symbols and related paraphernalia and getting ready to give out their ancient message in a radically new form.

The developments in the twentieth century in such diverse fields as art, psychology, and mythology provide much credibility for these statements. The rise of nonobjective art in the twentieth century, for instance, was both a result and an internal component of the work of the perennial renaissance. In painting, the new art brought wider awareness of the power of color, composition, and shape even when denuded of any objective element recognizable by ordinary consciousness. The science of psychology, which was born largely in the perennial renaissance milieu, directed attention to internal processes of removing self-delusion that were reserved for initiates into the perennial teaching in former days. The birth of the scholarly subject of mythology, useful as a tool for demythologizing, was similarly inspired by the early perennial renaissance according to James Webb.[2] Important pioneers in this field, like Joseph Campbell and Carl Jung, have clearly indicated the perennial source of much of their work. Webb has also documented amply how the bohemian elements in twentieth-century theater and cinematography have always been inspired by perennial sources.[3] Their colossal success has popularized the dramatic arts, whose origins can be traced back to cathartic initiatory experiences that liberated elements of the psyche that would otherwise remain dormant and unexpressed.

A corollary to these developments is that initiation would also be demythologized. It could now be stripped of those elements that the new consciousness might perceive as unnecessary frills, or even as obstacles to deeper transformation. Initiation could take on a different and presumably deeper meaning.

Tribal Rituals

Initiation has a more universal meaning in circles influenced by the perennial philosophy than it has had in particular cultures in the past, or even in many modern New Age subcultures. In an initiation ritual belonging to a particular culture or system of beliefs, the candidate is encouraged to feel a sense of kinship with other members of the group who have also gone through the ceremony. This is an approximation of the sense of oneness with everyone and everything that is part and parcel of a perennial initiation. However, it is only a limited sense of oneness, since in tribal initiations anyone outside the circle of the tribe is not included in that spirit of kinship.

Tribal initiations seem to gain much of their subliminal power from the fact that the candidate acts out certain steps and takes certain oaths in the presence of many witnesses. An example would be marriage ceremonies as they are practiced throughout the world. It is as if a collective consciousness were witnessing the act and giving it sanction, while at the same time delimiting parameters of behavior by enjoining the candidate to follow certain conventions. Even when initiation ceremonies contain an element of the numinous, which does not belong to any culture and thus represents something beyond the tribe, the important factor is generally believed to be the fact that the numinous has expressed itself in this *particular* form. In other words, the emphasis is not on the numinous. If it were, a total break with the values and practices of the tribe would occur at some deep, significant level, since the numinous is universal, not particular.

There is often an element of taboo with tribal rites, whereby participants do things and share in attitudes that are normally prohibited by the laws of the tribe but considered special and positive in the context of the ceremony. However, far from a true break away from the tribe, these are integral to becoming more a part of it. The participants share a feeling not unlike that of accomplices in a crime, thus strengthening group bonding. In tribal initiations the emphasis tends to be on the importance of the tribe vis-à-vis the world outside the tribe. Even in perennial renaissance circles where initiation is an integral part of the teaching, elitism in connection with stages of initiation is common. This is despite the fact that elitism is completely foreign to initiation as it was practiced in perennial circles for millennia.

In fact, a careful reading of K's biographical materials

shows that this issue is one of the main reasons why he broke away from the Theosophists. He came to perceive that the vast majority of Theosophists felt themselves part of an elite. They did not seem to have the level of commitment required to go through an initiation in the perennial sense—that is, dying completely to the known, which includes notions of oneself as superior or inferior.

As noted in chapter 3, whenever one defines oneself as an "X"—whatever quality or identity "X" may stand for—one is behaving in terms of closed loops in the brain's synaptic patterns. Then initiation—transformation—is not possible. This is reminiscent of what Martin Heidegger meant by *Dasein* as the "inauthentic" self, which can only "find" itself in the act of defining itself as being an "X."[4] Among early Theosophists and New Agers, it became common to speak of "elder brethren" and "younger brethren," referring to people who were presumably more or less "evolved." One reason K separated himself from the Theosophists now seems to have been because he found himself surrounded by people who were at heart unwilling to die to the known, yet spoke endlessly—mostly in terms of notions they had taken from books—of initiation and "the Path" said to lead to it. His breaking away may also point to a radically new approach to initiation and transformation on the part of the perennial teachers. This new approach would imply *authenticity*, to use Heidegger's term. Perhaps humanity could now engage in transformation in ways not possible before. That would indeed indicate the beginning of a new era.

A New Era

On behalf of these early Theosophists and New Agers it may be said that the perennial teaching as presented by K was unique in a number of critical ways; therefore, the bewilderment he created is understandable—and perhaps even to be expected. He presented the ancient teaching in an entirely new manner that might have been better understood by people already exposed to twentieth-century developments in art, mythology, philosophy, psychology, and to the new paradigms in science, religion, and other fields. But these developments would not take place until much later in K's lifetime, even though his message implied them from the beginning.

Other factors made it difficult for anyone to follow K to the fullest. For instance, even though the perennial teaching has all along been about dying to the known, in the past a door leading to the known had always been left ever so slightly ajar. Perennial teachers had apparently determined that those candidates who were capable of breaking through their conditioning entirely would eventually move further on in dying to the known. Those unable to go that far would hopefully at least take their cultural values and religious practices more seriously. K, however, broke cleanly with any associations with a particular culture or manner of thought and behavior. This had never been done before by any known perennial teacher. It points to K's special position in the history of the perennial lineage. It may also mark the significance of the twentieth century in the presentation of perennial teachings before the world, as HPB and her teachers had claimed.

If K's insights and observations truly denoted a new beginning for perennial work, it is not surprising that early Theosophists and New Agers could not follow him very far. Nor should their efforts as they confronted a radically new approach be belittled. In fact, if anything, their puzzlement came because they *understood* what the problem was: K was breaking with the perennial past. This cannot be said of many of K's subsequent sympathizers, who generally have shown no interest in or knowledge of the perennial philosophy and its critical place in K's life and teachings.

Perhaps K was the spearhead of an effort on the part of the perennial teachers to make the perennial practice of initiation more common, rather than something only a handful of people take part in. If so, then we could also say that K carried further the movement, begun by HPB, to put behind us the secrecy and occultism formerly surrounding the perennial philosophy, mak-

ing it more accessible to everyone. This would be achieved largely by eliminating the mythical and conceptual elements essential
to initiation in the past, presenting it instead as strictly the
process of psychological and spiritual transformation.

America

If the above assessment is true, then K's presence in the
twentieth century is an important landmark in the history of the
perennial philosophy. In any case, that is how K himself perceived
his position. It also means that K's work is intimately related to
what the perennial renaissance is really about: individual human
transformation in connection with deeper, global transformation.
This has been the purpose of perennial initiation for millennia.

Although the door of initiation or transformation has
always been open in perennial circles everywhere, very few people have been willing to undergo the psychological and spiritual
rigors of passing through it. One reason for this is that, before the
founding of America, there had never been a pluralistic society in
which critical perennial values were widely acknowledged by a
majority of the population.[5]

As HPB suggested in passages quoted in chapter 1, perennial elements have always been present in all societies, religions,
and philosophies. What makes America different is that several of
the pillars on which its society rests were crafted in perennial
shops. The notions of equality, fraternity, and freedom had been
integral to the perennial philosophy for millennia. They became
widely known in French—as *egalité*, *liberté*, and *fraternité*—
because of the greater notoriety of the bloody and dictatorial
French Revolution, but they were first publicly declared by the
American Revolution. In Europe, the Rosicrucians, Masons, and
others in secret societies had been teaching these principles for
centuries previously. (Present-day organizations bearing those
names tend to be shallow vestiges of the societies that preceded
them, as scholars such as Frances Yates have shown abundantly.)[6]
Members of these societies had worked for centuries toward the

creation of a society in which the individual, rather than a political structure or a belief system, would be considered "sacred." Such a social environment would be appropriate for transformation on a large scale. This may be why the creation of a good society was paramount in K's insights and observations.[7] Blavatsky and Besant were also deeply involved throughout their lives in movements for social reform in sympathy with perennial values.[8]

Before the founding of America, all societies were based on hierarchical models. Even in Asian countries, where the perennial philosophy developed its more significant publicly known strongholds in recent centuries, the hierarchical model, with all its ruthlessness and lack of respect for the individual, has been the blueprint for social behavior. Given this model's long history and pervasiveness, people have been deeply conditioned to accept it. That may be why even in America, where elitist attitudes and practices are often prosecutable in court, throughout the twentieth century numerous people still adhered to tribal assumptions, and even identified themselves as Americans in terms of their prejudices rather than their belief in freedom and equality before the law.

American corporations and their use and abuse of power are identified as "America" in the minds of many, both in the United States and around the world, and are largely responsible for the "Yankee go home!" syndrome everywhere. Rather than representing the American value of respect for the individual, these corporations are excellent representatives of the *ancien régime* of hierarchical values. Corporations by nature tend to run on principles of dictatorship based on greed, not on respect for either the individual or life in general. It is largely the rise to power of corporate leviathans that turned the United States toward materialism in the twentieth century.

The Battle for Shambhala

This dark inroad into America's founding values has led some to speculate whether the mythical Battle for Shambhala (a Buddhist version of the biblical Armageddon—the "final" battle between good and evil) might not have begun in the twentieth century. Edwin Bernbaum has written a landmark study on this subject, *The Way to Shambhala*. He cites a passage from the ancient *Vishnu Purana* to corroborate his belief that we are in the midst of the Battle for Shambhala. The passage describes the time for that epic battle—and the return of the world teacher—thus:

> Then property alone will confer rank; wealth will be the only source of devotion; passion will be the sole bond of union between the sexes; falsehood will be the only means of success in litigation; and women will be objects merely of sensual gratification. Earth will be venerated but for its mineral treasures. . . . [9]

Intriguingly, HPB quoted the same passage when she was speaking of our time as the beginning of a new era. In that context, she saw a direct, intimate connection between corporate earnings and the grand prophesies, and also identified medical drugs as an important element in humanity's nemesis.[10] Her prescience here ought to give one pause, given that in her day neither corporations nor drugs had the dominant place in society they occupy in our times. She also identified the present time with manifestation of the Kalki Avatar. As noted by Bernbaum and others, the Battle for Shambhala is associated in the minds of some Tibetan Buddhists with the manifestation of the Lord Maitreya.

Even two centuries after America was founded, the universalist, perennial values have still not taken hold on the population and are not truly part and parcel of daily life. In this, the project of America is not different from any other perennial effort in history. Perennial values have always been difficult for most people to incorporate into their daily lives. Thus today we find that the same hierarchical models are still in effect in every part of the world—including the United States. On the other hand, it seems that if no America, however imperfect, had been created in the

eighteenth century, very likely there would have been no theosophical movement (with its emphasis on universal brotherhood)
in the nineteenth, and no Krishnamurti (with his uncompromis-
ing exposés of the dangers of *any* kind of identification or authority) in the twentieth. People used to be, and still are, killed or put
away in the Bastilles of the world for making statements that
strike one as tame in the light of Krishnamurti's revolutionary
expositions. Notably, K's expositions took place in a milieu created by HPB's work, and exclusively in countries that had been
touched somehow by the spirit of the American Revolution.
Despite his wide travels, K never spoke in a totalitarian country,
and even refused to travel to his beloved India if a "state of emer-
gency" (when individual rights are temporarily suspended) was
declared by the government.

If K's presentation of the perennial teaching for the world,
then, was a landmark event in the history of humanity, and an
integral part—a culmination as well as a new beginning—of
perennial efforts through many centuries, the intimations for the
future found in the writings of HPB and her colleagues gain credibility. For instance, they spoke of a new era beginning in the
twentieth century and said the centerpiece of that effort would be
in America, particularly California. In fact, the meaning of the
expression "new age, " which gained wide currency because of its
significance for Theosophists, is the creation of a new human
type. This would presumably be a human being whose brain
synapses would not function in terms of closed tribal loops.
Initiation would gain a wider meaning in the new age—the creation of a new humanity.

The Mythical Key

HPB said numerous times, in *The Secret Doctrine* and elsewhere, that the esoteric or perennial teaching was given out in
what she called "the mystery language," which employs seven
"keys" or modes of perception and communication. One of these
is the psychological key, and K's way of teaching is the best exam-

ple of it to date, although other exponents of the perennial philosophy, such as Nagarjuna in the past and G. I. Gurdjieff in recent times, have also used it. Another key is the mythical, which is employed in various forms of art, including rituals such as initiation ceremonies.[11]

All of the perennial teachers and many of their associates and agents (such as HPB and some of her colleagues and followers) are said to be initiates in the perennial sense. That is, they have died to the known in some significant way at great psychological-spiritual depths. They have thus awakened to more alert states of awareness, and to the experience of humanity as one entity and life in general as one whole in which all of us are cocreators.

According to HPB and to work such as that of Huxley, Campbell, and Jung, every major civilization has had esoteric schools where candidates prepared for initiations and, if they were successful in the preparation, underwent the life-transforming experiences of initiation into a new life. With the presence of the perennial teachers in all major civilizations of the world, and presumably involved in major developments in those cultures, it is no surprise to find vestiges of their doings and sayings in the more mundane activities and traditions of many cultures.

For instance, religious rituals such as Bar Mitzvah in Judaism, and baptism and confirmation in Christianity, and other experiences in particular religious traditions are approximations of the perennial act of transformation, which may or may not be expressed as an initiation ceremony, as noted in chapter 3. The same is true of military ceremonies, and even of "unofficial" practices in that subculture, such as hazing. The military and martial arts have always had a deeper dimension for their serious practitioners than simply cultivation of machismo, or preparation for killing and being killed. They focus in various ways of facing pain—and even death—with equanimity, and so have a dimension that can be termed religious, given the developed moral code associated with these arts.

Yet despite the similarities, the conventional and perennial approaches to initiation differ in important ways. The human brain apparently accommodates a transcendent happening in the context of its identification with a particular religion or (sub)culture. It translates the experience—which is always dynamic and open-ended—into a repeatable pattern in terms of closed or recursive loops. The opportunity for true transformation is lost because of participation in particular systems, methods, or organizations and the psychological identification that accompanies it. As K wrote in the *Notebook*:

> Control in any form is harmful to total understanding. A disciplined existence is a life of conformity; in conformity there is no freedom from fear. Habit destroys freedom; habit of thought, habit of drinking and so on makes for a superficial and dull life. Organized religion with its beliefs, dogmas and rituals denies the open entry into the vastness of mind. It is this entry that cleanses the brain of space-time. Being cleansed, the brain can then deal with time-space.[12]

Schools Perennial and Contemporary

The concept of the university is another example of a mundane activity that has roots in the work of the perennial teachers. The university was first conceived by Pythagoras, who is widely acknowledged as the "father of Western civilization" and—just as important for our discussion—the "father" of esoteric teachings in the West. It was he who coined the words *esoteric* and *exoteric*. He also founded the first known university in the world, the Pythagorean School, on which Plato later partly modeled his Academy.[13]

A vestige of the university's esoteric pedigree is the celebration, held upon completion of course work, called "commencement," which is but a synonym for the more esoteric word *initiation*. Both words suggest that the moment of initiation—or graduation—is in one sense a culmination, but in a more real and deep sense a beginning of the practice of the skills and knowledge one has acquired. Though a more or less mundane celebration, the graduation ceremony still carries hints of its esoteric origins. For instance, the baccalaureate degree traces its name to "laureates" (initiates) of the Bacchic mysteries. The ceremony thus makes use of the mythical key—however ignorant of this the participants may be.

Despite the vestiges of perennialism still visible in contemporary universities, the differences between these and perennial schools are profound. They differ in their goals, their means, and their interests. Examining these differences is important for appreciating the value of perennial schools in general and initiation-transformation in particular.

All perennial schools have one primary goal: the transformation of humankind through the transformation of individual candidates. Their main goal, then, is "trans-ethical"; that is, not merely "ethical" in the sense of pursuing a particular set of beliefs or expectations. Interestingly, a veritable plethora of philosophers, and in some cases "new schools" of thinking, have shown since the nineteenth century how and why ethics as a rational pursuit is defunct. Pragmatism, existentialism, logical positivism, deconstructionism, and neo-pragmatism are a few contemporary schools that have shown abundantly, even while using the analytical, conceptual mind to make their cases, that such a mind cannot provide metaphysical foundations for ethics. On this point they are in perfect agreement with the best of Asian philosophy, exemplified by Nagarjuna in Buddhism, Lao-tse in Taoism, and Shankaracharya in Vedantic Hinduism.[14]

Ludwig Wittgenstein (1889-1951), for instance, showed that all the things that truly matter to human beings (ethics, aesthetics, love, communion with the divine) are real and important but are also part of what he called "the mystical"—that which one

cannot talk about sensibly.[15] If there is to be some form of morality and truth—if nihilism is to be avoided—what is required is
what Nietzsche called a "revaluation of values."[16]

Precisely such a revaluation—or more properly, "trans-
valuation"—of all values lies at the heart of the main goals of
perennial schools. Perennial schools have always seen the analytical mind as useful for understanding and resolving problems of a
mechanical nature but absurdly inappropriate for dealing with
issues that "truly matter," to paraphrase Wittgenstein. That is,
before there can be wisdom, insight, and compassion, there must
be the death of all conditioning. A profound psychological transformation is required. This transformation—usually called "initiation"—is a prerequisite for further participation in the activities
of the school, for, as K observed, true intelligence is present only
in the company of both insight and compassion.[17]

By contrast, the contemporary university depends almost
exclusively on self-centeredness. Contemporary higher education
uses the analytical mind as the foundation of research. Its main
goal is to *train* young people to be integral parts of the corporate
structure. Financial support for universities comes mostly from
corporate sources, and in turn, corporations tend to see universities as hatcheries for "new blood" to conduct their pursuit of
power.

A university based on perennial values could *never* contribute to such corrosion of the human spirit. Unfortunately, it is
difficult to create such an institution. The efforts of perennially
inspired schools—such as Montessori, Waldorf, and Krishnamurti
schools—have concentrated on pre-university education. There
are a handful of "eclectic" universities that have a perennially-
inspired approach to their curriculum. These include the
California Institute of Integral Studies in San Francisco, the
Nyingma Institute of Buddhist Studies in Berkeley, and John F.
Kennedy University in Orinda—perhaps not coincidentally, all in
California. But these schools fight an uphill battle largely because
they tend to lack substantial funding from large corporations. If

an institution of higher learning with perennial foundations were created, initiation-transformation might become more prominent and widespread even in mainstream society, and the wisdom of the ancient practice of initiation would become manifest to meet the current urgent need for transformation.

Jung and the Bardo Thödol

An excellent example of an initiation is provided in the *Bardo Thödol,* or *Tibetan Book of the Dead.* In his "Psychological Commentary" on that work, Carl Jung ascribed precisely the same meaning to initiation in ancient perennial circles as we have discussed here. Blavatsky had said that in Tibetan and other Mahayana Buddhist circles one could find living traditions that are fairly good approximations of perennial teachings. This and other statements by HPB's colleagues prompted a number of people who had been touched by her work, such as Jung, to look into them.[18]

W. Y. Evans-Wentz was also among the many influenced by HPB, and for many decades—until the 1970s, after the Tibetan diaspora—his work was universally regarded as the best available on Tibetan Buddhism. Even after the works of others (like Lama Anagarika Govinda and Chogyam Trungpa Rinpoche) made their mark, Evans-Wentz's books continue to have great influence, perhaps because of their perennial roots. He employed HPB's literary style, defended the universality of the perennial teaching, and declared the genuineness of HPB's knowledge of Tibetan Buddhism's esoteric doctrines.[19]

His best-known production is his translation and commentary on the *Bardo Thödol.* This text is a series of instructions or injunctions to be read to a recently deceased person, somewhat like the ritual of extreme unction in Christian churches. The intention is to help that person experience a psychological death—the kind of death that ultimately matters, according to the perennial philosophy—at the same time as he or she experiences the death of the physical body.

The reader may note the similarity between Jung's comment on the primacy of the soul in the quotation that follows and CWL's statement quoted in chapter 2, in which he said that a human being is not a physical body that *has* a soul, but rather is a spiritual being that may or may not express itself through a physical body. When Jung speaks of what is "given," he is clearly referring to the same dynamics noted by CWL. The reader may also note Jung's reference to sacrifice in the sense found in perennial sources, where there are even expositions of the "Law of Sacrifice." Gurdjieff, who was one of these perennial sources in the twentieth century, also explored the importance of sacrifice in an esoteric sense.[20] Jung wrote:

> It is highly sensible of the *Bardo Thödol* to make clear to the dead man the primacy of the soul, for that is the one thing which life does not make clear to us. We are so hemmed in by things which jostle and oppress that we never get a chance, in the midst of all these "given" things, to wonder by whom they are "given." It is from this world of "given" things that the dead man liberates himself; and the purpose of the instruction is to help him towards this liberation. We, if we put ourselves in his place, shall derive no lesser reward from it, since we learn from the very first paragraphs that the "giver" of all "given" things dwells within us.
>
> . . . A great reversal of standpoint, calling for much sacrifice, is needed before we can see the world as "given" by the very nature of the soul. It is so much more straight-forward, more dramatic, impressive, and therefore more convincing, to see that all the things happen to me than to observe how I make them happen. Indeed, the animal nature of man makes him resist seeing himself as the maker of his circumstances. That is why attempts of this

kind were always the object of secret initiations, cul-
minating as a rule in a figurative death which sym-
bolized the total character of this reversal. And, in
point of fact, the instruction given in the *Bardo
Thödol* serves to recall to the dead man the experiences of his initiation and the teachings of his *guru*,
for the instruction is, at bottom, nothing less than an
initiation of the dead into the *Bardo* life, just as the
initiation of the living was a preparation for the
Beyond.

Such was the case, at least, with all the
mystery cults in ancient civilizations from the time
of the Egyptian and Eleusinian mysteries. In the initiation of the living, however, this "Beyond" is not a
world beyond death, but a reversal of the mind's
intentions and outlook, a psychological "Beyond" or,
in Christian terms, a "redemption" from the tram-
mels of the world and of sin. Redemption is a separation and deliverance from an earlier condition of
darkness and unconsciousness, and leads to a condition of illumination and releasedness, to victory and
transcendence over everything "given." . . . The
Bardo Thödol is, as Dr. Evans-Wentz also feels, an
initiation process whose purpose it is to restore to
the soul the divinity it lost at birth.[21]

The "great reversal of standpoint" referred to by both
CWL and Jung as an implicit aspect of initiation is the subject of
Marvin C. Shaw's book *The Paradox of Intention*, which has
become a kind of classic in religious studies. Shaw's approach to
the topic of the reversal—or "paradox"—of one's standpoint is
closer to Krishnamurti's than to Jung's, in that his is a more existential perspective. Though Shaw does not speak of initiation as
such, his "reversal of intention" is precisely the same kind of
reversal that both CWL and Jung identified as an integral compo-

nent of initiation. Shaw opens the explanation of the nature of his book with a quotation from Suso:

If any man cannot grasp the matter, let him be idle and the matter will grasp him.
— HEINRICH SUSO, *The Exemplar*

This book is a study of a single, simple idea, that of reaching a goal by giving up the attempt to reach it. The difficulty which some readers may have in understanding this is not caused by any complexity or abstractness in the concept, but by the fact that it seems contrary to common sense and everyday practice. Normally, we assume that goals are reached through the expenditure of mental and physical effort, and the so-called paradox of intention strikes us as perhaps intriguing, as some sort of mental puzzle, but finally as illogical and unavailing. Now if this or any other difficulty arises, and the point of what you are reading escapes you, you have an opportunity to put into practice this paradoxical method we are attempting to understand. Simply take the advice of the medieval Christian mystic Suso quoted above, let go of the effort to grasp the meaning, read on, and the meaning which evades you may well arise on its own.

. . .[W]hen our action is at its best and we have achieved real proficiency and expertness in something, it has the character of being flowing or self-moving. When we are doing our best, in a sense, we act without acting. . . . When we are adroit and skillful, we find that we have let go of the intensity of effort. Relating this to religious conversion introduces a new and intriguing element to which we must return.

At this point, however, there is a possibility of misunderstanding. The danger is that getting the goal by giving up the attempt to get it may be taken as itself a technique, and a book devoted to a study of this idea then will appear as yet another self-help book. If the principle is rightly understood, it is a criticism and rejection of the idea that life is fulfilled through technique. Therefore, it is an "anti-self-help book," a book which maintains our problem is precisely that we approach ourselves as projects to be completed. The hunger and need manifest in the present rush hour of the manuals of happiness comes from an excess of concern about how life is managed and happiness contrived, and not merely from the fact that we haven't yet found the recipe suited to our temperament. . . . A manual of happiness is just what we do not need and, in fact, cannot have, for the claim we will be exploring is that the very idea of getting the goal through efforts renders those efforts counter-productive.[22]

Shaw's book—which is highly recommended to anyone serious about understanding this issue and the nature of religious experience—expresses in very clear terms the need in all of us for what K called "dying to the known." All the available evidence suggests that dying to the known is a multidimensional and never-ending process. This may partly explain why there are many different types of initiation—some about dying to relatively superficial aspects of the "given" in our lives, others concerning deeper and more comprehensive ways to die to the known. Generally speaking, the term *initiation* has the latter meaning in a perennial context. The mythical reenactment that takes place during an initiation ceremony is presumably symbolic of a process that should have been going on for the candidate at some level already. Part of the purpose of the reenactment is to jog subliminal aspects of the candidate's awareness into accessing a deeper understanding of what it means to die to the known. In this sense, the initiation's effects are said to continue long after the ceremony ends.

CHAPTER FIVE

Process and Authority

NUMEROUS ELEMENTS OF K'S PROCESS SUGGEST
that it began as an initiation conducted by the Masters, and thereafter consisted of either the aftereffects of that initiation or its
deeper levels, which were to last the rest of his life. Both
Krishnamurti and Leadbeater stated independently at the time
that K's process was an initiation, and every statement K made
subsequently on the subject affirmed the same.

Certain elements of K's process were common to perennial initiations in general. These were: the awakening of kundalini,
a nonlinear awareness of several dimensions simultaneously,
physiological changes (in his case a visible and painful lump on
the nape of the neck), and a significantly deepened sense of oneness with humanity and with all that is. However, there are
aspects of K's initiation, recorded in documents from the period,
that had not previously been associated with initiations. These
point to the uniqueness of K's initiation, and further, to the significance of his presence in the twentieth century. Some of these
aspects are considered in what follows.

The lengths of time perennial initiations require are also
significant. An initiation along with the inner preparations connected with it are said to take three, seven, fourteen, seventeen,
twenty-one, or forty days. Perennial initiations also invariably
take place at significant times in the world cycle, and at times that
are astrologically appropriate. K's very first initiation, (which
took place in India previous to the initiation that marked the
beginning of the process in 1922), is an example of this. It
occurred on January 11, 1910, an astrologically propitious time

according to the prominent astrologer and theosophist G. E. Sutcliffe. Sutcliffe had said in 1909 that if the Christ were to come back, there would be no better time astrologically for his rebirth than that date.[1]

Some elements of K's experience during the process are strikingly similar to descriptions Leadbeater provided of the steps of one of his own initiations. The information on what took place in K's psycho-physiology and how it was apparently conducted by the Masters is scant and incomplete. CWL, on the other hand, carefully documented aspects of his own initiation that presumably could be made public, so looking carefully at CWL's experiences can yield insights into K's process.

CWL's Initiation

CWL's account points out the significance of the amount of time an initiation requires. It also shows that an initiation is a living process and therefore need not happen as exactly as the analytical mind might expect. In his autobiographical fragment, *How Theosophy Came to Me*, CWL described how he became clairvoyant in the summer of 1885 under the tutorship of the Master KH:

> He asked me whether I had ever attempted a certain kind of meditation connected with the development of the mysterious power called *kundalini*. I had of course heard of that power, but knew very little about it, and at any rate supposed it to be absolutely out of reach for Western people. However, He recommended me to make a few efforts along certain lines, which He pledged me not to divulge to anyone else except with His direct authorization, and told me that He would Himself watch over those efforts to see that no danger should ensue.

Naturally I took the hint, and worked away steadily, and I think I may say intensely, at that particular kind of meditation day after day. I must admit that it was very hard work and sometimes distinctly painful, but of course I persevered, and in due course began to achieve the results that I had been led to expect. Certain channels had to be opened and certain partitions broken down; I was told that forty days was a fair estimate of the average time required if the effort was really energetic and persevering. I worked at it for forty-two days, and seemed to myself to be on the brink of the final victory, when the Master Himself intervened and performed the final act of breaking through which completed the process, and enabled me thereafter to use astral sight while still retaining full consciousness in the physical body—which is equivalent to saying that the astral consciousness and memory became continuous whether the physical body was awake or asleep. I was given to understand that my own effort would have enabled me to break through in twenty-four hours longer, but that the Master interfered because He wished to employ me at once in a certain piece of work.[2]

Based on the literature on initiation, a good rule of thumb is that the longer an initiatory experience lasts, the deeper is its significance. As CWL wrote in his classic on the subject, *The Masters and the Path*:

The time occupied by the ceremony of initiation varies according to several considerations, one of which is the amount of knowledge that the candidate brings with him. Some traditions put the period as three days and nights, but it is often finished in much less time. One at which I was present took two nights and a day of seclusion, but others have been condensed into one night, by leaving much that used to be included to be finished later by the higher pupils of the Masters. Some of the old Initiations lasted so long because the candidates had to be instructed in astral work. There are also buddhic experiences which must be realized, for a certain amount of development of the buddhic vehicle is required for Initiation, as some of the teachings which must be given at that level could not otherwise be understood.

. . .The actual ceremony of Initiation takes less than six hours, but a certain amount of time is given to the candidates both before and afterwards. The Masters always congratulate the candidates after the Initiation, and each says a few kindly words. They take the opportunity of such a gathering to transmit certain orders to Their pupils; and generally it is an occasion of great rejoicing, at any rate among all the younger members. It is a victory for all when another neophyte is admitted, when one more is safe forever.[3]

In Krishnaji's case, the initiation, including a period of intensive preparation, took forty-nine days. The inner work connected with it continued the rest of his life, becoming intensified at certain significant times. The longer length of time indicates that this initiation was unusual and unique. But there was nothing unusual about the amount of work required after the initiation itself. Leadbeater explained regarding his own case:

It must not for a moment be supposed, however, that the attainment of this particular power was the end of the occult training. On the contrary, it proved to be only the beginning of a year of the hardest work that I have ever known. It will be understood that I lived there in the octagonal room [in Adyar] by the river-side alone for many long hours every day, and practically secure from any interruption except at the meal-times which I have mentioned. Several Masters were so gracious as to visit me during that period and to offer me various hints; but it was the Master Djwal Kul who gave most of the necessary instruction.

... The pupil has to be tested in all sorts of ways and under all conceivable conditions; indeed, towards the end of the tuition sportive nature-spirits are especially called in and ordered in every way possible to endeavour to confuse or mislead the seer. Unquestionably it is hard work, and the strain which it imposes is, I suppose, about as great as a human being can safely endure; but the result achieved is assuredly far more than worth while, for it leads directly up to the union of the lower and the higher self and produces an utter certainty of knowledge based upon experience which no future happenings can ever shake.[4]

K's Initiation

Although the purpose of K's "process" initiation was apparently totally different from CWL's, certain elements were similar: the tremendous pain; the kundalini awakening under the supervision of the same perennial teachers, who also offered congratulations; and in the end, the same unshakable certainty about the spiritual life.

A significant difference between the two is that CWL, though working under the instruction of the teachers, was in charge of the proceedings until the final step, which was taken care of by Master KH. Krishnaji, on the other hand, was almost completely a willing spectator to his process, which was done to him and through him by the perennial teachers. Rather than engaging in a particular meditation or exercise, he found himself witnessing mystical perceptions in states other than ordinary consciousness even while remaining in the waking state. Described by witnesses, who of course could only see what his body—his "physical elemental," as he explained it—was doing, his behavior appeared rambling, as if he were experiencing the disjointed perceptions often associated with delirium. He described the way the process began:

On the 17th of August, I felt acute pain at the nape of my neck and I had to cut down my meditation to fifteen minutes. The pain instead of getting better as I had hoped, grew worse. The climax was reached on the 19th [the third day]. I could not think, nor was I able to do anything, and I was forced by friends here to retire to bed. Then I became almost unconscious, though I was well aware of what was happening around me. I came to myself at about noon each day. On that first day while I was in that state and more conscious of the things around me, I had the first most extraordinary experience.

There was a man mending the road; that man was myself; the pickaxe he held was myself; the very stone which he was breaking was a part of me; the tender blade of grass was my very being and the tree beside the man was myself. I almost could feel and think like the roadmender, and I could feel the wind passing through the tree and the little ant on the blade of grass I could feel. The birds, the dust and the very noise were a part of me. Just then there was a car passing by at some distance; I was the driver, the engine and the tyres; as the car went further away from me, I was going away from myself. I was in everything, or rather everything was in me, inanimate and animate, the mountain, the worm and all breathing things. All day long I remained in this happy condition. I could not eat anything, and again at about six I began to lose my physical body, and naturally the physical elemental did what it liked; I was semi-conscious.

The morning of the next day [the 20th] was almost the same as the previous day. I ate nothing throughout the day, and I could not tolerate too many people in the room. I could feel them in rather a curious way and their vibrations got on my nerves. That evening at about the same hour of six I felt worse than ever. I wanted nobody near me nor anybody to touch me. I was feeling extremely tired and weak. I think I was weeping from sheer exhaustion and lack of physical control. My head was pretty bad and the top part felt as though many needles were being driven in. While I was in this state, I felt that the bed on which I was lying, the same as on the previous day, was dirty and filthy beyond imagination and I could not lie on it.

Suddenly I found myself sitting on the floor and Nitya and Rosalind asking me to get into bed. I asked them not to touch me and cried out that the bed was not clean. I went on like this for some time till eventually I wandered out onto the verandah and sat a few moments exhausted and became slightly calmer. I began to come to myself and finally Mr. Warrington [general secretary, that is, head of the Theosophical Society in the United States] asked me to go under the pepper tree which is near the house. There I sat cross-legged in the meditation posture. When I sat thus for some time, I felt myself going out of my body. I saw myself sitting down and with the delicate, tender leaves of the tree over me. I was facing the East.

In front of me was my body and over the head I saw the Star bright and clear. Then I could feel the vibration of the Lord Buddha; I beheld Lord Maitreya and Master K.H. I was so happy, calm and at peace. I could still see my body and I was hovering and within myself was the calmnes of the bottom of a deep unfathomable lake. Like the lake, I felt that my physical body with its mind and emotions could be ruffled on the surface, but nothing, nay nothing could disturb the calmness of my soul.

The presence of the mighty Being was with me for some time and then They were gone. I was supremely happy for I had seen. Nothing could ever be the same. I have drunk at the clear pure waters at the source of the fountain of life and my soul was appeased. Never more could I be thirsty, never more could I be in utter darkness. I have seen the Light. I have touched compassion which heals all sorrow and suffering; it is not for myself, but for the world. I have stood on the mountain top and gazed at the mighty Beings. Never can I be in utter darkness; I have seen the glorious and healing Light. The fountain of Truth has been revealed to me and darkness has been dispersed. Love in all its glory has intoxicated my heart; my heart can never be closed. I have drunk at the fountain of joy and eternal Beauty. I am God-intoxicated![5]

The three perennial teachers K named as central to this initiatory experience were the Buddha (Gautama), the Lord (or Buddha) Maitreya, and the Master KH. According to the perennial teachings, one member of the perennial brotherhood is responsible for all the major religious or philosophical teachings within a cycle, which lasts thousands of years. The Buddha is said to have been the previous holder of this office, and his incarnation as Gautama Buddha is said to have been his last. The Lord Maitreya is said to be the present teacher and to be responsible for originating all religious or philosophical matters for the next many thousands of years. The Master KH is said to be the next in line.

The star that Krishnaji mentioned is the "Star of Initiation," which is supposed to appear at perennial initiations. (K's brother Nitya also mentioned the star in his description of K's initiation quoted in chapter 3.) None of the published accounts of K's initiation have explained the star's significance, and in some accounts it has been misinterpreted. In fact, this five-pointed star became the symbol of the Order of the Star, the organization founded in 1910 to prepare for the "Coming of the World Teacher." Its members wore silver star pins to express their intention to undergo initiation in order to prepare for the Coming.

The presence of the star underscores the fact that this was an initiation, and references to it are found throughout the early theosophical literature. For instance, Leadbeater described the final moments of K's first initiation, in 1910:

> Over [the Lord Maitreya's] head flashed forth the Blazing Star which conveys the assent of the King [of the brotherhood], and all bowed low before it. . . . Under the influence of that tremendous magnetism, the tiny Silver Star of Consciousness which represents the Monad in the candidate swelled out in glowing brilliancy until it filled his causal body, and for a wonderful moment the Monad and the ego were one, even as they will be permanently when Adeptship is attained. The Lord placed His hands upon the head of the candidate and, calling him by his true name, said: "In the Name of the One Initiator, whose Star shines above us, I receive you

into the Brotherhood of Eternal Life.". . . So the wonderful ceremony ended and the Masters gathered round the new Brother and gave him hearty congratulations as the Blazing Star disappeared.[6]

Forty-Nine Steps

The final act of congratulations was also part of K's "process" initiation years later in Ojai. On the night of October 5, 1922, exactly forty-nine days after the process began on August 17, the first phase of this grand initiation was concluded. Nitya reported:

> Later, when both Rosalind and I were in the room Krishna began talking to people we could not see. The work had been assured of success and apparently they were congratulating him, and the room was full of visitors all desiring to rejoice with Krishna; but there were too many for his comfort. We heard him say "There is nothing to congratulate me about, you'd have done the same yourself."[7]

Forty-nine days was apparently the length of time for the deepest and most secret initiation that we know of before the present cycle: the initiation of Gautama Buddha. He is said to have sat under the Bo (or Bodhi, "Wisdom") Tree for forty-nine days before he attained enlightenment. The *Jataka* relates how Gautama gave up pursuing enlightenment through fierce austerities, broke his fast with rice and milk offered by a young girl, and then

> sitting down with his face to the east, he made the whole of the thick, sweet mild-rice into forty-nine pellets of the size of the fruit of the single-seeded palmyra-tree, and ate it. And he took no further

nourishment until the end of the seven weeks, or forty-nine days, which he spent on the throne of wisdom after he had become a Buddha.[8]

In Krishnaji's case, however, forty-nine days is how long it took to complete only the first phase of a process that would take the rest of his life to unfold.

The number forty-nine comes up often in HPB's writings, for she taught that seven is a key number for understanding many mythical and esoteric teachings, and forty-nine is the sevening of seven.[9] W. Y. Evans-Wentz provided a brief explanation of the reverence for the numbers seven and forty-nine in connection with the initiation-like procedures of the *Bardo Thödol*:

> Turning now to our text itself, we find that structurally it is founded upon the symbolical number Forty-nine, the square of the sacred number Seven; for, according to occult teachings common to Northern Buddhism and to that Higher Hinduism which the Hindu-born Bodhisattva Who became the Buddha Gautama, the Reformer of the Lower Hinduism and the Codifier of the Secret Lore, never repudiated, there are seven worlds or seven degrees of *Maya* [illusory phenomena of nature; the Shakti of Brahman in Hinduism, Ain Soph in Judaism] within the *Sangsara* [phenomenal universe]. . . . As in the embryonic state in the human species the foetus passes through every form of organic structure from the amoeba to man, the highest mammal, so in the after-death state, the embryonic state of the psychic world, the Knower or principle of consciousness, anterior to its re-emergence in gross matter, analogously experiences purely psychic conditions. In other words, in both these interdependent embryonic processes—the one physical, the other psychi-

cal—the evolutionary and the involutionary attainments, corresponding to the forty-nine stations of existence, are passed through.

Similarly, the forty-nine days of the *Bardo* may also be symbolical of the Forty and Nine Powers of the Mystery of the Seven Vowels. In Hindu mythology, whence much of the *Bardo* symbolism originated, these Vowels were the Mystery of the Seven Fires and their forty-nine subdivisional fires or aspects. They are also represented by the *Svastika* signs upon the crowns of the seven heads of the Serpent of Eternity of the Northern Buddhist Mysteries, originating in ancient India. In Hermetic writings they are the seven zones of after-death, or *Bardo*, experiences, each symbolizing the eruption in the Intermediate State of a particular seven-fold element of the complex principle of consciousness, thus giving the consciousness-principle forty-nine aspects, or fires, or fields of manifestation.

The number seven has long been a sacred number. . . . Its use in the *Revelation* of John illustrates this, as does the conception of the seventh day being regarded as holy. In Nature, the number seven governs the periodicity and phenomena of life, as, for example, in the series of chemical elements, in the physics of sound and colour, and it is upon the number forty-nine, or seven times seven, that the *Bardo Thödol* is thus scientifically based.[10]

The fact that the first phase of Krishnaji's initiation took forty-nine days is underscored here, because even though the beginning and ending dates of the process have been published, the significance of this length of time has not been pointed out before.[11] This means that neither K nor Nitya nor CWL nor AB made any public reference to this fact; nor have those who have written about K's life taken notice of it. However, from the documentation discussed here, this length of time marks the first phase of the process as an initiation. It also echoes the Buddha's initiation, which was unique from a perennial perspective, as it presaged the most important avataric teaching of the previous cycle.

Was K's "process" initiation informed by similar avataric connotations? That is precisely what CWL and AB said. That is also what K himself said throughout his life. His insights and observations, while at the leading edge in fields like philosophy and psychology, were also like nothing anyone had taught before. These considerations make the fact that his initial experience lasted forty-nine days another reason to consider his as a grand initiation, with epochal implications.

Primacy of Mutation

Writings on K's life have provided much evidence showing that the process continued, though in gradually less painful forms, until the end of his life. This evidence also shows that he never ceased to be profoundly and consciously involved in his sacred mission for the Masters and the Lord Maitreya. K rarely stated this unequivocally in his public addresses. If he had done so, he would have had to answer endless questions about Masters and avatars, rather than focus on the work he was here to do. His work was not about promoting authority, including the authority often exercised by people with some psychic ability. Though K apparently had such abilities, he ceaselessly stressed that his work was exclusively to help bring about mutation. If he had catered to people's demands for authorities and sensational performances, he would have been barraged with triviality from the press and others who were not serious but were simply curious about "the Masters and the Messiah." As it is, he did undergo this kind of "tabloid celebrity" to some extent for thirty or forty years—approximately through the 1950s.

Sidney Field, in his short and revealing memoir,

Krishnamurti: The Reluctant Messiah, recounted an anecdote that simultaneously reveals K's direct knowledge of psychic faculties (an important aspect of his inner life) and one reason why he shunned them. It took place during the last Camp held in Ojai (subsequently, K held weekend talks at the Oak Grove, also in Ojai), which took place in 1928.

> During this last Camp gathering, I volunteered to bring Krishnaji's lunch, prepared on the Camp grounds, to Arya Vihara. It was always a problem to keep the soup from spilling during the five-mile trip by automobile. One day, as I handed him his tray, I asked him in jest, "Wouldn't this be much simpler if you could just levitate yourself over the Camp and descend by the dining room?"
>
> To my surprise, he said, quite seriously, "I have the key to all that, but I'm not interested."
>
> I said it would be wonderful and most practical to have some of those powers. He responded with his usual affirmation that the only thing worth having was Liberation. To reinforce his point, he told me a little story about a great yogi he had known in India, who had developed all kinds of *siddhis* (powers acquired through meditation) and could do amazing things, which he had witnessed himself, such as levitating, rendering himself invisible, and growing plants from seeds in a few minutes. Before he left the yogi's home, the great magician said to him, "I would happily trade all my *siddhis* for a glimpse of Nirvana."[12]

K reasserted having such psychic abilities as late as 1962. Pupul Jayakar related that in a private discussion with her and with other Indian friends

> [K] told us that, as a child [before meeting CWL and
> AB], he had many extrasensory powers—the capac-
> ity to read thought, or what was written in an
> unopened letter. He could make objects materialize,
> see visions, and foretell the future. He had the power
> of healing. But he had put all these powers aside nat-
> urally. He had never felt any interest in them.[13]

Apparently, the only way to protect his mission from an
onslaught of frivolity and mere curiosity was to distance it as
completely as possible from association with esoteric matters. For
several decades after K's break with the Theosophists in 1929, he
apparently said nothing about his esoteric life to most people who
knew him. During this time, even those who were close to him or
wrote about him were not personally grounded in the perennial
philosophy and therefore were not in a position to comprehend.

K's stance is understandable. Many people were drawn to
the sensationalism of "being with the Messiah." For some, touch-
ing him, being photographed with him, or moving to Ojai where
he lived were deemed spiritually glamorous. It was also intellectually fashionable to "explain" K in terms of Indian philosophy,
or whatever other psychological or philosophical "itch" a person
may have been afflicted with. These people were apparently more
interested in such things than in working to bring about a mutation in their own lives—a process that is self-effacing, concept-
free, genuinely compassionate, and relatively thankless, arduous,
and lacking in excitement. It implies confronting face-to-face the
mysterium tremendum et fascinans.

Confusion about K's Mission

Throughout his life, K made many specific references to
facts in his life intimately related to the perennial teachers. All the
evidence supports unequivocally that he never denied their existence, never denied being in intimate contact with them, and

never denied that he was the vehicle for the Lord Maitreya. Nevertheless, from the time of the dissolution of the Order of the Star, on August 3, 1929, many believed that his breakaway step meant that he had rejected his mission or his place as the vehicle for the World Teacher.

For instance, in 1934, five years after breaking his official ties with the Theosophists and dissolving the Order of the Star, K received a letter from Lady Emily Lutyens. She was on all accounts the person closest to him at the time, and remained so until her death in 1964. Yet in her letter she stated that K had denied his role as the World Teacher. In his response K said "I have *never* denied it" [his emphasis], and "I have only said that it does not matter who or what I am but that they should examine what I say which does not mean that I have denied being the W.T. [World Teacher]."[14]

When she had that exchange of letters with K, Lady Emily Lutyens had been an international Theosophical lecturer for two decades and was in close contact with the major leaders of the movement. K called her "mum," which suggests the closeness of their relationship. So, she was deeply aware of K's work and of everything else connected with him. She was also witness to the process on many occasions. If even she could maintain such a level of confusion about K, it is not surprising that people who merely heard his talks or read his books would be confused as well. Her misconceptions may have stemmed from her lifelong commitment to a system of beliefs and practices (in her case, Theosophy). That is, like so many others, she was committed to the primacy of the analytical mind. At the same time she recognized something profound that came from K, and had deep affection for him.

Such confusion would be even more likely among the many persons who surrounded K in the last decades of his life, for these later friends would have had no basis for knowing of his rich inner life or its connection with the most formidable effort known to date on the part of the perennial teachers. Unlike his Theosophical friends, they did not know about perennial teachers and assumed that K denied the existence of *any* such teachers. The same confusion has spread to the many writers about K, who seem unable to see K's own observations about the significance of his esoteric life without the lens of prejudice.

Adding to this confusion was K's own attitude about his inner life. To him, his esoteric life was of utmost seriousness and even sacredness. Thus he would not, and could not, speak about it and allow it to become grist for the analytical mind's mill. As a result, even in the company of friends who disparaged theosophy out of ignorance, he would not attempt to correct anyone. Deeply sympathetic as he was toward the human condition, he would sometimes join in the light-hearted banter himself, rather than demean the sacred by allowing it to be transmogrified.

Of Masters, Authorities—and Confusion

It is common for people to insist on turning to someone in authority to tell them what to do in their spiritual and psychological lives. They seem unable to grasp the simple fact that no one outside ourselves can be held responsible for what happens to us. Despite the spotless clarity with which K set forth the danger and uselessness of surrendering to authority in psychological and spiritual matters, people continued to harass him with questions about their perceived need for such a leader. Often, they wanted to set him up as such. Or they wanted him to validate whichever spiritual authority they chose to follow.

For the first few decades of his work, it was mostly Theosophists and people influenced by them, such as early New Age adherents, who came to hear K yet refused to listen to what he was actually saying. They demanded that he be their guru, or they expected him at least to acknowledge the need for a teacher in spiritual and psychological matters. In the 1960s and 70s, his audience was filled with young people who had found their spiritual leaders among the gurus coming to America from Asia. (Few of them realized that the advent of Asian gurus was the result of the perennial renaissance opening up throughout the world to a wider audience.) Their questions were much the same as the ones the Theosophists had been asking since the 1920s. From the 1970s until K's death in 1986, a more intellectually sophisticated crowd—who believed in the therapist as the guide of our inner lives—inquired about (and lobbied for) the need for psychological and spiritual teachers. All through this time, Indians, for whom the guru-disciple relationship is a part of their culture, were making similar demands. All of these people—from the spiritual to the idealistic to the intellectual—were equally confused, in spite of the simplicity with which K spoke on these issues.

What K said can be put in an uncomplicated manner:

- He said that turning to authorities in psychological and spiritual matters is both useless and dangerous.[15]
- He said there *is* a place for psychological and spiritual teachers, but their function is exclusively to point in the right direction. A true teacher has no authority, just as a pointing finger has no authority, however useful it might be under the right circumstances.[16]
- He said there *are* exponents of the perennial philosophy, called Masters by Theosophists. He avoided talking much about them, but their constant presence in his life is evident in archival materials and in books about his life.[17]
- He spoke all along as if he was aware of these Masters on a daily basis, and as if he knew himself to be the vehicle for the teaching of the Lord Maitreya.

Despite K's clarity, however, the people who surrounded him from the late 1940s until his death displayed the same confusion and resistance concerning what he said about his inner life as they did regarding what he said about psychological-spiritual authority. They seem to have wanted to believe that K could not possibly have had anything to do with the esoteric. Based on this belief, they apparently ignored, suppressed, or gave outlandish interpretations to what was actually taking place, for the facts are now available in various memoirs and personal reports by those who knew him. They similarly ignored all references in K's work to the important place of teachers in people's lives. This attitude and the attitude of those who thirst for a spiritual authority both arise out of a person's conditioning. People refuse to see what is actually taking place or listen to what is actually said because the facts do not fit in with their preconceived notions.

Beginning in the 1960s, K began to acknowledge his mission as the vehicle for the Lord Maitreya in discussions with his closest associates, though still rarely in public. For instance, David Bohm, who is better known for his epoch-making theory of the implicate order of the universe than for his close friendship with K during the last two decades of their lives, explained after K's death:

> To the best of my knowledge, Krishnamurti looked at himself as an expression of what we might call the sacred, or the universe, the cosmos—that ground which is the source of creative intelligence, which is not manifest and beyond time, that is the ground of everything that is. And he thought that was expressing itself in some unique way through him at this particular stage of human history.[18]

Mary Lutyens' book *The Years of Awakening*, published in 1975, created an uproar and a great deal of puzzlement in Krishnamurti circles. This was the first time K's rich esoteric life, particularly his lifelong relationship with the Masters and the Lord Maitreya, had been made public since the 1920s. Yet despite this, numerous students of K's work, including authors who have written about his life, continue to believe that the Masters and the Lord Maitreya were not a part of K's life.

K, on the other hand, was quite clear. As reported later by Lutyens, shortly after Lutyens' book came out, Mary Zimbalist "asked him why, if the Masters existed, they had spoken then [in the heyday of the theosophical movement] but not now." This would have been an excellent opportunity for K to have said something like "there are no such Masters." Instead, his response not only affirmed their existence but also stated his relationship to the Lord Maitreya. The reason why the Masters were no longer manifesting as they had during the first five decades of theosophical work, according to K, is that

There is no need, now that the Lord is here.[19]

This and other similar statements K made are unequivocal, not leaving much room for interpretations suggesting that he denied either his connection with the Masters or his mission as a vehicle for the Lord Maitreya.

It is understandable that those directly involved in the events of the late 1920s and early 30s, when K was actively shaking himself free of connections with the Theosophical Society, would have spread rumors—or believed them—regarding what he said or did not say. After all, communications then were not what they became in later decades, and only a few people had direct access to K on a daily basis. Further, such high expectations had built up around his person, that his actions beginning with the dissolution of the Order of the Star would understandably have resulted in criticism and gossip. What is puzzling, especially to anyone aware of the presence of the perennial teachers through the perennial renaissance, is that this view of K should be continued by commentators on K's life, in contrast to the facts of what he said—and what he lived—all along, until the end of his life.[20]

CHAPTER SIX

The Experiment

IF WE ACCEPT THE WORDS OF K HIMSELF AND OF others who witnessed the early manifestations of the process, there should be no doubt about the presence of the Masters during these events.

A Dangerous Operation

Based on Nityananda's detailed notes of what took place, Pupul Jayakar reports that by the night of September 10, 1922, about the midpoint of the grand initiation,

> Nitya and Warrington soon realized that Krishna was undergoing very dangerous transferences of consciousness or awakening of *kundalini,* and felt the atmosphere "charged with" electricity; they felt as if they were guardians of a temple where sacred ceremonies were being performed. At times those who were with Krishna felt the presence of a Being who was conducting the operations, although they could neither see nor identify it. But Krishna's body, between spasms of pain, would converse with the unseen presence, who appeared to be a friend and a Teacher.
>
> . . . By September 18 a new phase began. The pain was more intense. Krishna was asking the unseen presence questions. His restlessness had

increased; his eyes were open but unseeing; he would shiver and moan; sometimes he would shout out in pain, "Please, oh, please give me a minute."[1]

In spite of Jayakar's statement in this passage that the Being who was present could not be identified, on many occasions the being or beings in question were identified as the perennial teacher or teachers, as other passages quoted earlier indicate. In the earlier years, the presence of the perennial teachers and the Lord Maitreya was acknowledged rather openly, though still within a small, inner circle of associates. For instance, Krishna described part of his initiation in 1910 thus:

> When I left my body the first night, I went at once to the Master's [KH] house and found Him there with the Master Morya and the Master Djwal Kul. The Master talked to me very kindly for a long time, and told me all about the initiation, and what I should have to do. Then we all went together to the house of the Lord Maitreya, where I had been once before, and there we found many of the Masters— the Venetian Master, the Master Jesus, the Master the Count, the Master Serapis, the Master Hilarion and the two Masters Morya and K.H.[2]

K also spoke of a "presence" several decades later, when he recorded his experiences of the process in 1961. For instance, in his entry for June 27, he referred to April of that year, when the process had started up again while he was in Il Leccio, Italy:

> That presence which was at *il L.* was there, waiting patiently, benignly, with great tenderness. It was like the lightning on a dark night but it was there, penetrating, blissful.[3]

In all of the descriptions of what took place during the process, Krishnaji never appears in any way as the initiator of the proceedings. Rather, there is always a "Being who was conducting the operations."[4] Moreover, as noted in chapter 3, the process does not seem to have been a series of hallucinatory episodes, nor the result of spontaneous development of kundalini. The precision required in guiding the kundalini energies in K's case suggests that the process was not some happenstance. The only sensible option left—and the one K himself said was true—is that certain perennial teachers were in charge of the proceedings of the process. According to every single item of evidence—all the accounts by everyone concerned, either in published or archival materials—this was K's understanding of what could be called the process's technical aspects.

If Pupul Jayakar was right—if reports of the early manifestations of the process consisted of "a classical description of the arousing of the *kundalini*"[5]—then they were also a description of the perennial teachers performing an extremely delicate and difficult psycho-biological procedure. From once the process began until the end of his life, K was always a hair's breadth away from dying, as numerous references in works on his life suggest.[6]

Even though the evidence is clear that there was an awakening of kundalini and that the perennial teachers were the ones making it happen, there is much about the process that remains unknown. Specific details of what was done to K are not available because, in Nitya's words, "He was told not to say anything of what was being done to him and he gave his promise."[7] Secrecy is common in perennial initiations, as the passages from Blavatsky's *Key to Theosophy* quoted in chapter 1 explained rather thoroughly. Nevertheless, what follows is an attempt to understand the nature of this procedure in the light of remarks made by K and CWL at the time and in the light of certain perennial teachings. Jayakar also relates a number of conversations with K in which he spoke of matters relating to the process.

The Physical Elemental Speaks

Jayakar relates the amazement with which she and her sister first responded to K's process. They first witnessed it in 1947, shortly after they had been introduced to him. The process seemed foreign to his spotlessly clear, no-nonsense insights and observations. They were particularly puzzled by what must have seemed like a split in K's personality whenever he was "away" from the body and only the "physical elemental" spoke, since they were not familiar with the perennial understanding regarding different bodies or levels of existence in all human beings.[8] Briefly, *elemental* is a term used in Theosophical books to name the fact that each "vehicle," or level of awareness, has "a mind of its own." In the references quoted in connection with the process, it is the physical elemental—the consciousness of the physical body—that is speaking. This elemental is said to have a connection to the sympathetic nervous system.[9]

Jayakar's description is also interesting because it suggests that the process was ongoing through the 1930s and 40s, even though there are no records of it from that period. If there had been evidence from that time, perhaps it was destroyed. K's "physical elemental" was apparently not altogether aware of the two sisters and seemed to expect that Rosalind Rajagopal was his watcher, as she had been in the 1920s. That expectation strongly suggests that the process did go on through the 1930s and 40s, and that Rosalind was his watcher during that period.

Late at night we woke to the sound of Krishnaji's voice calling from the veranda where he slept. His voice sounded frail, and we were bewildered and thought he was ill. After a great deal of hesitation, we went to the doorway that led to the veranda and asked him whether he was unwell. Krishnaji was calling for somebody, his voice was fragile and child-like. He kept on saying, "Krishna has gone away, when will he be back?" His eyes were open, but there was no recognition. Then he seemed to grow aware of us and asked, "Are you Rosalind?" And then, "Oh, yes, yes, he knows about you, it is all right, please sit here, wait here." Then again after a little while, "Don't leave the body alone and don't be afraid." The voice started calling for "Krishna" again. His hand would cover his mouth and he would say, "He has said not to call him." Then in the voice of a child, "When will he be back? Will he come back soon?" This went on for a while; he would be quiet, then shout for "Krishna," then chide himself.

After about an hour his voice became joyful. "He is back, do you see them? They are here, spotless." His hands expressed a fullness. And then the voice changed, it was again the familiar voice of Krishnaji. He sat up, apologizing for having kept us awake. He saw us to our room and left. The strangeness of it all bewildered us; we were dazed and did not sleep all night. Next morning at breakfast he looked fresh and young. We questioned him as to what had happened. He laughed and said he did not know. Could we describe what had happened? We did so. He said we would talk about it some time, which by then we had come to understand meant that he did not wish to discuss the matter further.[10]

Significantly, K was completely outside the sphere of theosophical influence when this incident happened. This shows that the process was most likely not the result of a theosophical belief system, as some have suggested with regard to K's experiences in the 1920s. After all, the nature of these experiences did not change qualitatively over a period of six decades. Rather, they were part of an ongoing process of mutation, as K clearly stated in the *Notebook* in the early 1960s. Anyone suggesting that the experiences of the 1920s differed from the later ones would need to show *how* they were different.

K did use theosophical language throughout his life to describe or attempt to understand the "technical" aspects of the process. It was the best available terminology to date to convey in words what was happening to him. However, K never used this terminology in a purely theoretical way, as is often done in New Age and Theosophical circles. For him, the language was merely a tool.

This is a critical distinction. It clarifies that he was not engaged in promoting a metaphysical system. K's approach was never conceptual or metaphysical. Without intending to associate him with particular schools of thought, one can say *metaphorically* that his approach was akin to those of existentialism and phenomenology. That is, rather than accept a certain background of knowledge or speculation as "given," K would explore all issues without presuppositions. For instance, in connection with the process, he found himself engaging with certain individuals. To convey something about this to others, he would sometimes use the theosophical terminology most suited for the purpose—*Masters.* That is, he would have the experience *first* and only later try to speak of it. This phenomenological use of language is profoundly different from someone reading books about the Masters, developing a belief system, and assuming it stands for "the truth."

A New Age Explosion

Krishnaji was very likely not inclined to discuss the process in detail in the 1940s, particularly with people—like Pupul Jayakar and her sister—who were unacquainted with the perennial teachers, the perennial philosophy, and K's understanding of his place as vehicle for the Lord Maitreya. To make them understand the apparent split in personality that occurred during the process, for instance, he would have had to explain the physical elemental, astral travel, and other Theosophical notions. However, the sisters were not theosophists and in her published work at least, Jayakar shows no interest in theosophy. Moreover, K tended to be reticent about such matters, since they distracted from his real work.

In the 1960s, however, K began to discuss the process to some extent. This shift may have been connected with important changes in his life at that time. He started to have closer relationships with more new people. Lady Emily Lutyens, who had been an important link with his early experiences of the process, died in 1964. His final break with the Rajagopals was imminent. The Krishnamurti Foundations were formed. The first account of his life began to be written.

Also, the perennial renaissance would begin to come into its own in the 1970s: the New Age phenomenon exploded into mainstream culture in that decade. There was increased interest in the work of Joseph Campbell, Carl Jung, and Ken Wilber, and in mythology and transpersonal psychology in general. Connections between leading-edge science and ancient perennial teachings began to be explored.[11] Humanistic psychology and a cornucopia of other psychology schools with clear perennial intentions, and even perennial pedigrees, began to flourish. Thus, when K's books came out in the late 1950s and early 1960s, among the endorsers were figures such as Rollo May.[12]

Apparently the time had come to let the perennial jinni out of the bottle. K's tentative disclosures in the 1960s were premonitory and may have come from a well-informed understanding of the major social changes about to happen. After all, the perennial authors of these developments were also behind his work (as we have seen in Part I), which was clearly the centerpiece of the perennial renaissance.

K's rich inner life was first made public in Mary Lutyens' memoirs, the first volume of which was published in 1975. An earlier attempt had been made in the 1950s by Lady Emily Lutyens, who had included what she knew of the process in *Candles in the Sun*.[13] At the eleventh hour, however, K implored her to remove all those passages from her book.[14] Clearly the time was considered not yet ripe for such disclosures.

K's psychic-spiritual states and his references to the perennial teachers and the Lord Maitreya continued through the later decades of his life as they had been in the 1920s. However, the terminology he used to refer to the Masters gradually changed over time. One can surmise at least two important reasons for this. For one, K's language underwent constant transformation through the years, always moving toward forms of expression less likely to be misused by minds conditioned to particular religions, ethnicities, or systems.[15] For another, K may have wanted to express himself in ways that would not be identified with Theosophy as a conceptual model, particularly for the sake of his Indian friends, who according to Jayakar's comments throughout her memoirs, often had deep-seated prejudices against anything theosophical.

Esoteric Fountainhead

In the winter of 1969, K talked informally about the early days with Jayakar, her nephew Asit Chandmal, and her sister, Nandini. Instances such as this conversation are of particular interest, since Jayakar not only displays in her book great animosity for things theosophical, she also states (though without supporting evidence) that K's experiences of the perennial teachers and the Lord Maitreya were merely visions. Yet in reporting this conversation she says:

> Krishnaji was exploring the mystery that surrounded the discovery of the boy, Krishnamurti. He was probing delicately, turning the ear to intimations and insights that might arise in discussion. His statements on the Theosophical Society were clear and precise. He made no comment as to whether they were true or illusion. Sensing the "otherness" in Krishnaji, we listened, asking few questions and letting him speak.

Krishnaji said that the Masters had told C.
W. Leadbeater to find a boy who was a Brahmin,
who came from a good family, and who had a "face
as described." It was the duty of the Theosophical
Society to protect the body of the child, and to provide an atmosphere of complete security for two
years. If the body was prepared and ready, Lord
Maitreya would give the boy the mind. When
Leadbeater saw Krishnamurti on Adyar beach [in
1909], he perceived that there was no selfishness in
the boy's aura.

. . . Krishnaji then advanced several theories to explain how the boy remained untouched.
Was it that, through birth and rebirth, the child had
evolved to perfection? Or had the Lord Maitreya
protected the body till it was mature? Had the boy
been born without a formal character or personality,
allowing him to remain vague, untouched by his
earlier years with his father, the school, the doctrines of the Theosophical Society, the luxury of the
life he lived in England?

. . . The boy, who was totally innocent and
unaffected, still had to be protected so that evil could
not touch him, could not enter him.

. . . Mrs. Besant had insisted that two initiates accompany Krishnaji all the time. She said,
"Since you are always alone within, you must never
be physically alone." There was a reservoir of the
good in the boy that should not be contaminated.[16]

The heart of K's investigations was to dispel illusions of
any sort, not promote them. If all the esoteric elements brought
out in this conversation were merely illusions and visions, why
would K have wasted his own time and that of his friends by

bringing up the subject? And why would he have brought it up in an atmosphere that suggested the seriousness and sacredness of the subject for K? The context suggests that K considered examination of the esoteric aspects of his life (such as the present inquiry) critical for understanding who and what he was. Further, as other discussions on this topic make clear, K regarded his work as originating in those esoteric sources, not in himself as a person. This is documented in part III.

Certainly this conversation is valuable in that it reveals K's own understanding of his inner life. Especially in light of his lack of tolerance for mystifications regarding his person, if he thought these things were illusory, he would have said so in no uncertain terms, as he did about anything he saw as illusory in his researches. For these reasons, Jayakar's prefacing remarks that "He made no comment as to whether they were true or illusion" only reflect her personal opinion. K's actual understanding of these esoteric matters becomes clear when in the same conversation he said he was still protected by the Lord Maitreya and the perennial teachers. Jayakar wrote:

> He said he needed protection even in 1969, for his character was still unformed . . . "The body still needs to be protected from evil." He paused again, and said, "I still feel protected."[17]

A vision cannot protect anyone. This comment affirms the incompatibility between K's own experience and Jayakar's interpretation of it as just a vision.

> He then spoke of the early years, when the boy Krishnamurti's body had to be completely protected and given security for two years; but the mind was not to be touched, for "the Lord would give him the rest." There were long silences between his sen-

tences. K said the body had to go through a lot of pain (as in Ojai and Ootacamund) because there were still imperfections in the brain.[18]

K proceeded to speak of his initiations. This in itself affirms that they had taken place and, secondarily, that K considered the perennial teachers and the Lord Maitreya real, not visions; for it is meaningless to speak of initiations—at least in K's context—without initiators, and they are the ones he said conducted the initiations. It is also obviously meaningless for him to speak of still being protected in 1969 unless he knew there were protectors, and the only protectors he referred to at that time were the perennial teachers and the Lord Maitreya. As he said to Jayakar in 1982 during a discussion with other Indian friends:

> I think there is a force which the Theosophists had touched but tried to make into something concrete. But, there was something they had touched and then tried to translate into their symbols and vocabulary, and so lost it. This feeling has been going on all through my life. . . . When I talk about it, something tremendous is going on. I can't ask it anything.
>
> [Jayakar asked:] Is it something outside of you? Does it protect you?
>
> [K responded:] Yes, yes—of that there is no question—[19]

Some authors have been confused by other statements K made, such as the following, made in 1979:

> The Maitreya is too concrete, is not subtle enough. . . . I have said it isn't the Maitreya, the Bodhisatva.

That protection is too concrete, too worked-out. But I've always felt the protection.[20]

Statements such as this give the impression that K meant some being or process other than Lord Maitreya when he spoke of the protection he felt throughout his life. However, in light of his statement that the Masters were no longer manifesting because now "the Lord is here" (noted in chapter 5), this interpretation needs to be looked at more searchingly. For the only "Lord" he could have been referring to is the Lord Maitreya. The only other "Lord" K ever spoke of was Gautama Buddha; but unlike Maitreya, Gautama Buddha was never spoken of as manifesting in direct connection with K's work, though K did refer to him as an inspiring influence. The issue of what *Maitreya* might mean is dealt with in more detail in Part III. Here it is enough to point out that it was the *word* "Maitreya" that K objected to as "too concrete."

Though K was speaking to people who had no theosophical background and were sympathetic neither to what he was saying nor to its implications, nevertheless he clearly felt it was important to tell them some of the facts of his inner life. Perhaps, in a way, it was easier for him to speak to them, as they might be more likely to hear what he said without "Theosophical" preconceptions. This could be an example of the importance of not holding onto any one view of things but remaining open to perspectives that on the surface seem incompatible. For as Nietzsche emphasized, every perspective, despite its limitations, makes a potentially important contribution to a complete understanding.

Such a comprehensive perspective is at the heart of why K objected to making the meaning of the word *Maitreya* "too concrete." The analytical mind with its penchant for precision and logical rigor would demand one and only one intended meaning for each word, statement, or verbalized concept. Such concreteness makes deeper understanding impossible. It excludes other valid, appropriate words, statements, and concepts because they appear incompatible and inappropriate from its more limited, shallow perspective. This may be a reason why devotees of the analytical mind have always had difficulty understanding K.

Another reason why K may have opened up on the subject of his inner life in the 1960s, after practically hermetic silence since the 1920s, may be because he knew information about it would come out sooner or later. Archival material abundantly documenting K's esoteric life extends across almost eight decades. K may have hoped he could set the record straight—at least on what did not have to remain secret—before all this became available. Furthermore, by the 1960s his work had become well established quite independently of Theosophical or esoteric associations, so his message was relatively safe from corruption from those quarters. While he was still among the Theosophists, K had objected to the way the topics of the Masters and initiation tended to be trivialized and made too "concrete," creating the illusion that the words referred to the speaker's "correct" image of what they were supposed to refer to. This too is documented and discussed in Part III.

Morphic Resonance

There is no reason to believe that K himself was a Master, in spite of his unusual sensitivity and other rare qualities. It seems more likely that he was an ordinary human being who was chosen as the object of a sophisticated perennial-science experiment intended to establish greater communication between ordinary consciousness and a consciousness that is far more comprehensive. As Mary Lutyens said in her concluding remarks in *Years of Fulfilment*:

> I am inclined to believe that K *is* being used and has been used since 1922 by something from outside. I do not mean that he is a medium. A medium is separate from what he or she "brings through," where-

as K and whatever it is that manifests through him
are for the most part one. His consciousness is as
permeated with this other thing as a sponge with
water. There are times, though, when the water
seems to drain away, leaving him very much as he
used to be when I first remember him—vague, gentle, fallible, shy, simple-minded, compliant, affec-
tionate, delighting to laugh at the silliest jokes, yet
unique in his complete absence of vanity and self-
assertiveness.[21]

K himself said the same thing to Lutyens regarding his
work:

If I deliberately sat down to write it, I doubt if I
could produce it. . . . There is a sense of vacancy and
then something comes. . . . If it were only K—he is
uneducated, gentle—so where does it come from?
This person [K] hasn't thought out the teachings. . . .
It is like—what is the Biblical term?—revelation. It
happens all the time when I am talking [giving
talks].[22]

An important implication of this experiment is that it ultimately relates to humanity in general, not exclusively to K as an
individual. If the mutation could be brought about in K's nervous
system, then it would become a possibility for all of humanity.
According to the biological theory of morphic resonance, what
any human being can do becomes available to the rest of humanity as a genuine possibility.[23] Incidentally, this scientific theory
formed in the late twentieth century has been an integral part of
the perennial teachings for millennia, though under other names.
For instance, theosophists spoke of "group souls."[24] One reason
why the perennial teachers do not often manifest themselves

directly and publicly except in connection with major cycles may be that it is more important to them that all human beings develop the capacity to live in greater communion with *that which is.* This would call for the kind of mutation that a few—perhaps only one human being—must undergo for it to become available to all members of the species.

Perhaps when K said "the Lord is here," he did not mean that some super-entity was manifesting through him alone; perhaps he meant that a more comprehensive state of awareness was now more accessible to all people. That state may have manifested through one individual—K—and from what K said toward the end of his life, that may not happen again for hundreds of years.[25] However, that state may now be more readily available for all of humanity. Blavatsky's teachers said that we are at the beginnings of several major cycles, a time when such spiritual-psychological mutations are more likely. If this is so, then any one of us who cares to engage in such a mutation may do so, taking advantage of the epochal moment. A Christian might call this "partaking of the body of Christ." In the new perennial "dispensation," however, all such myths and images are left behind, as they get in the way of the manifestation of deeper levels of awareness that are universal—never sectarian.

K's "Passion"

The process of cocreating that mutation in himself for humanity, however, was an excruciatingly painful one for K throughout his life. Jesus is said to have suffered a "passion," a period of deeply felt suffering, that lasted a few hours and culminated in his crucifixion. K's "passion" consisted of a series of intensely painful experiences that initially recurred several hours a day for many months. Afterwards, they came back in milder form at intervals throughout his life. Nitya reported the final stage of the first manifestation of the process (the culmination of K's initiation):

That night was a ghastly night of suffering and when I look upon it, it seems to me that it was the most agonising night that Krishna ever went through. He suffered terribly the following nights, and they seemed much worse, but I think this was due to the piteously enfeebled condition brought on by this night. Before the suffering actually started, we heard him talking to the Master in charge. He was told not to say anything of what was being done to him and he gave his promise; then he was told that the visitor would return later at 8.15. Krishna said "He is coming at 8.15, then let us start quickly." Then just before it was started, he had been standing up and we heard him fall with an awful crash and then we heard Krishna apologising "I'm so sorry I fell, I know I must not fall." All through the evening he was more conscious of his physical body than he had ever been before.

They told him that he must make no movement, for generally he was writhing and twisting with the pain. But now he promised "Them" he would not move and over and over again he said "I won't move, I promise I won't move." So he clasped his fingers tightly and with his knotted hands under him, he lay on his back, while the awful pain continued. He found it very difficult to breathe that night and he gasped for breath continuously and choked repeatedly and when the pain grew beyond endurance and he could no longer get his breath he just fainted. Three times he fainted that night, and the first time he did it, we did not know what had happened; we had heard him choking and gasping and sobbing with the pain and suddenly after a long-drawn gasp there was dead silence. When we called to him there was no answer and when we went into the room and felt our way towards him—for the room was inky black and we did not know where he lay—we found him lying on his back so still and his fingers so tightly locked that he seemed [a] tower out of stone.

We brought him to quickly and three times this happened. Every time he came to, he would apologise to Them for the waste of time and tell Them that he had tried his best to control himself, but that it had been beyond control. Sometimes They gave him a slight breathing space and the pain would cease and between the throes of suffering he would start making some joke with the one in charge and he would laugh as if the whole thing was a joke. And so it went on for an hour and a quarter.

. . . That night when we went to bed, just before we fell asleep Krishna began talking to someone I could not see. I heard Krishna's end of the conversation. Apparently a man had been sent by the Master D.K. [Djwal Khul] to keep watch over the body through the night; Krishna began to tell him how sorry he was to cause him all that trouble. This was one of the most noticeable things all through. Krishna's politeness and consideration was extraordinary, whether he was fully conscious or whether it was only the physical elemental speaking. The man came to watch every night after this for six or seven nights. Krishna was to say "I've seen Him now. Nothing matters."[26]

A number of accounts of K's process were recorded by different people in different parts of the world in the 1920s. This account, like all the others, portrays the perennial teachers as real individuals who were working on K's psycho-physiology to bring about important mutations in his body and psyche. Interestingly, the Master DK had also helped CWL in his psychic-spiritual development; apparently this perennial teacher was a specialist in the movement of kundalini. His association with K's process is one more item of evidence that the same perennial teachers who worked on K had started the theosophical movement. After all, K met the Master DK *because* the latter had been deeply involved in the creation and early development of the movement.

That the perennial teachers would work on a candidate in such a way is not unique to K's case. As CWL pointed out in reference to one of the major stages in the path of transformation:

> This danger-point in the life of the Initiate is indicated in the Gospel story by the temptation in the wilderness which followed the Baptism of Christ by John. The forty days in the wilderness symbolize the period during which the expansion of the mental body given in the second Initiation is being worked down into the physical brain, though for the ordinary candidate not forty days but forty years might well be required for its accomplishment. In the life of Jesus it was the period when His brain was being adapted to the incoming Christ.[27]

The manifestations of K's process continued for years after its forty-nine-day-long commencement. Two years later, for instance, Nitya wrote to Annie Besant from Ojai:

> Krishna's process has now taken a definite step forward. The other night, it began as usual, none of us expecting anything fresh or new. All of a sudden, we all felt an immense rush of power in the house, greater than I have ever felt since we have been here; Krishna saw the Lord and the Master; I think also the star shone out that night, for all of us felt an

intense sense of awe and almost fear that I felt
before when the star came out. Krishna afterwards
told us that the current started as usual at the base
of his spine and reached the base of his neck, then
one went on the left side, the other on the right side
of his head and they eventually met at the centre of
the forehead; when they met a flame played out of
his forehead. That is the bare outline of what happened; none of us know what it means but the power
was so immense that night that it seems to mark a
definite stage. I presume it should mean the opening
of the third eye.[28]

Mary Lutyens reported that, during a stay at Pergine, Italy
in the late summer of 1924,

Lady Emily reminded him of what St Paul had said:
"My little children for whom I travail in pain till
Christ is born in you," to which he retorted, "You
bet I have the pains right enough!"

He might well say this because his
"process" had started again on August 21 and was
more agonising than ever although this had not
seemed possible at Ojai. Nitya wrote to Mar de
Manziarly on September 14 that the process had
been a greater strain for the past three weeks than
he could ever remember.

Instructions were given through K [by the
Master] on September 4 that his room must be
closed by 3 p.m. and that no one must touch him
after that hour and that everything and everyone
must be exceptionally clean; nor must he eat before
his ordeal. At 6 p.m. he would have his bath and put
on Indian dress and go into his "torture chamber" as

Lady Emily called it. Only Nitya was allowed to go in with him. Lady Emily, Helen [Knothe] and [D.] Rajagopal, having had an early supper, usually spent the hour while the process was going on sitting on the stairs outside his door. After his ordeal they would sit with him in his room while he had his supper.

On the evening of the 24th, Lady Emily recorded that K had a presentiment that it was going to be "an exciting night", and sure enough the Lord Maitreya came and remained with K for a long time and left a message for the whole party. This message was read aloud to them by Nitya the next morning:

> Learn to serve Me, for along that path
> alone will you find me
> Forget yourself, for then only am I to be
> found
> Do not look for the Great Ones when
> they may be very near you
> You are like the blind man who seeks
> sunshine
> You are like the hungry man who is
> offered food and will not eat
> The happiness you seek is not far off; it
> lies in every common stone
> I am there if you will only see. I am the
> Helper if you will let Me help.[29]

Krishnaji received numerous messages of this kind from the Masters or from the Lord Maitreya, sometimes meant for others and relayed through him. They were usually expressed in a style totally different from his own manner of speaking, or that of anyone associated with him publicly at the time. Though specific reference to the Masters would cease in later years, it does not make sense to think that someone other than they would have taken charge of the delicate and dangerous proceedings of the process, and with them, of K's work. For as was discussed earlier, the relationship between K's process and his insights and observations is intimate and incontrovertible. In any case, according to K's statements and those of numerous witnesses, the process did go on throughout his life, which is to say that the perennial teachers and the Lord Maitreya were with him to the very end.

A Unique Experiment

The notion that K's process was an experiment conducted by the Masters that was unique in world history appears in a number of references. K's brother Nitya mentioned it in a letter to CWL, in which he reported a message from the Master KH brought through by Krishnaji. Nitya asked CWL questions that K himself was also asking.

> Krishna's body repeated this message [from the Master] on the night of 26th [November 1923], immediately after the process was over for the evening.
>
> "The work that is being done now is of gravest importance and exceedingly delicate. It is the first time that this experiment is being carried out in the world. Everything in the household must give way to this work, and no one's convenience must be considered, not even Krishna's. Strangers must not come there too often; the strain is too great. You and Krishna can work this out.
>
> "Maintain peace and [an] even life."
>
> I have a feeling that the reference to the "experiment" is not only to the fact that this kind of thing is generally done in a monastery, but also per-

haps that They are trying something new in the preparation of the body.

Do you know at all if something similar to what is going on now, was part of the preparation of the body of Master Jesus when the Lord came last time?[30]

Nitya's comments and last question suggest that he did not study the message from the Master carefully, since it says clearly that this was *the first time* this experiment had ever been conducted. Given that it was the first time, K's process would not be completely explainable as the rising of kundalini and the vivification of the chakras, as discussed earlier; for the extensive literature of Tantra and similar bodies of knowledge is based on esoteric experiences that have occurred before. Further, the mechanics of the process were shrouded in secrecy all along. Thus getting some insight into K's process seems, at least at first blush, nearly impossible. However, a few stray comments by Krishnaji himself and by CWL, considered in the light of Blavatsky's writings, may shed some light on it.

CWL'S Puzzlement

Interestingly, in spite of CWL's very developed clairvoyance, he did not understand what was being done to K. In fact, he expressed deep concern about what was happening, indicating that he had no knowledge of anything like it ever having happened before. He wrote in a letter to AB on May 12, 1923:

It is evident that in all higher matters the methods of progress differ for each individual. I do not understand why such terrible physical suffering should come to our Krishna. Surely the Brahmin body is exceptionally pure, and should need less in the way of preparation than the average European vehicle. In

160

my own case I have no recollection of anything in
the least commensurate with this when I was passing through the same stage, though there was certainly a great deal of excessive discomfort in the
development of the Kundalini. It may be, as you
suggest, that this is part of the preparation of that
body for its Great Occupant, yet nothing has been
said as to any hastening of the Coming. But it might
well be that years must elapse after the completion
of this preparation, in order that the body might
fully recover from it before having to undergo the
strain of the actual occupancy. The case is so unique
that I suppose the truth is that we can only wait and
watch.[31]

K made several comments after the 1960s to the effect that
his brain was still not a perfect vehicle and thus the process needed to continue into his later life—a perception remarkably close
to CWL's comment. CWL's remarks also suggest what would be
stated more clearly by the Master later the same year (1923) in
the message Nitya reported in his letter, namely, that this was an
experiment unique in the history of humanity.

An aspect of the process that must have concerned CWL
even more was mentioned in Nitya's account of what began
immediately after the first phase of the process, in 1922, ended.
Nitya referred to an excruciatingly painful opening being made in
Krishnaji's head, and his constant request to the Masters to close
it rather than continue to open it. Jayakar summarized Nitya's
account, quoting him intermittently:

The location of the pain was constantly shifting. . . .
On October 6 [the day after the initiation itself cul-
minated], the agony had shifted to the scalp.
Something seemed to have been opened in his head,
which was causing him indescribable torture. At one

moment he shouted, "Please, close it up, please close it up." He screamed with pain, but they kept opening it gradually. When he could no longer endure the pain, Krishna screamed and then fainted. At the end of forty minutes he lay without the slightest flicker of movement. Slowly, consciousness returned.

. . . That night again the presence came to watch over him while he slept.

. . . The next night, according to Nitya, "They appeared to be operating on his scalp again." He was agonized and cried out in pain—even fainting eight times—when it became too severe. "He begged them to open it slowly and gradually so that he could get used to it by degrees." He was choking and had difficulty in breathing.

. . . Soon, a change was apparent. By now he could leave his body with extraordinary ease and rapidity, and the return no longer brought on shivering. He was to say later that night that *they had left open the center in his head* [italics added]. The man whom they could not see came again to keep watch.[32]

This opening left in his head may be a clue to the uniqueness of this experiment and simultaneously may explain CWL's great anxiety concerning what was happening to K.

Initiation and Closure

If indeed the Masters had left open the center in Krishnaji's head, and if this was integral to the process, then this was an unprecedented experiment indeed. A little-known fundamental rule regarding opening the psychic centers is that they must be sealed again once the specific procedure, which is said to be intrinsic to some perennial initiations, is completed. It is said that during the initiation itself, the candidate suddenly experiences levels of awareness and dimensions of being that are beyond ordinary consciousness. This is possible because of the opening, or vivification, of certain chakras, along with related changes in the brain. But the intensity of the experience and the strain it causes on the nervous system require that the chakras be closed again and the kundalini brought back down to the root chakra at the base of the spine. According to the literature, if this is not done, the candidate may go insane, or suffer the maiming or destruction of some physical organ, or in some cases may die. However, after the closure, the candidate may subsequently arouse kundalini again little by little, each time opening up the psychic centers somewhat more and becoming acclimatized to the new dimensions of awareness, until eventually it is safe to operate at those levels without fear of something going wrong.

Given the extreme secrecy of perennial initiations, very little is available in print about this. However there *is* some information accessible, in a roundabout way. CWL, who had become a bishop in 1914, gave clairvoyant descriptions of some Christian rituals in *The Science of the Sacraments*, which includes drawings and paintings to represent what he said he could see. He explained that for every material event there is a corresponding flow of energy made up of ultra-subatomic particles. He called them "ultimate physical atoms," and described them as roundish, heart-shaped vortexes made up of clearly-defined lines of energy. Scientist Stephen Phillips identified these later with what we now call quarks.[33] CWL identified these lines of energy as the grossest level of matter in the emotional plane. There is, then, according to CWL's perceptions, a seamless connection between physical and psychic life. This subtle energy (called the aura) can be perceived clairvoyantly around living things and during the performance of rituals.

Interestingly, CWL noted similarities between some Christian ceremonies (which after all have perennial origins) and perennial initiations such as K's. For instance, he explained that the ceremony of baptism has also another aspect, as typical of the Initiation towards which it is hoped that the young member of the Church will direct his steps as he grows up. It is a consecration and a setting apart of the new set of vehicles [made up of psychic, ultra-subatomic matter] to the true expression of the soul within, and to the service of the Great White Brotherhood; yet it also has its hidden side with regard to these new vehicles themselves, and when the ceremony is properly and intelligently performed there can be no doubt that its effect is a powerful one. It is distinctly, therefore, what may be called an act of white magic, producing definite results which affect the whole future life of the child.[34]

About the end of the baptism ritual CWL commented (emphasis added):

> As soon as the divine force has been poured in, the Priest proceeds to *close the centres* which he has opened, so that the force may not immediately pass out again, but may abide in the child as a living power, and radiate from him but slowly, and so influence others. Therefore the next step is to take another kind of sacred oil, the chrism, and with that *the centres are closed.*
>
> . . . The four centres which have been opened—the forehead, the throat, the heart and the solar plexus—are now closed by an effort of the will of the Priest. Each centre is still distended, but only a small effective aperture remains, like the pupil of an eye. While it was open it was all pupil, like an eye into which belladonna has been injected. Now the pupil is closed to its normal dimensions, and a large iris remains, which contracts only slightly after the

immediate effect of the ceremony wears off.[35]

The same act of closure takes place at confirmation, according to CWL, when there is presumably a greater opening of the psychic centers, after which they are sealed (emphasis added):

> As in Baptism, there is first an opening up by the force which moves from below upwards; *then there is a filling and a sealing process*, which moves from above downwards.[36]

CWL explained the confirmation ceremony further, from a clairvoyant perspective:

> The effect of this anointing is great, even upon those who are but little evolved. It makes the force-centre into a kind of sieve, which rejects the coarser feelings, influences, or particles; it has been likened to a doorscraper, to remove pollution from the man, or to an acid which dissolves certain constituents in the finer vehicles, while leaving others untouched. If during the day the man has yielded to lower passion of any kind, whether it be anger or lust, this magnetized force-centre seizes upon the excited astral [emotional] particles as they sweep out and will not let them pass until their vibrations are to a certain extent deadened. In the same way if undesirable emotions have been aroused in the man while away from his physical body, the sieve comes into operation in the opposite direction, and slows the vibrations as he passes through it on his way back to waking life.[37]

CWL seems to be suggesting that the ceremonies used in

165

the major religions as well as in many shamanic traditions are mythical intimations of deeper transformative processes that can take place in perennial initiations. His descriptions shed some light on K's painful situation and explain his own puzzlement and concern regarding K's chakra in the head being left "opened." All the available literature on this subject, both ancient and modern, speaks alarmingly about leaving any centers unsealed. Yet according to K, Nitya, and CWL, that is apparently precisely part of the grand experiment on K. That would account for the harrowing pain he experienced all his life. It would also explain the need for uninterrupted protection all his life—and hence for the *uninterrupted presence of the Masters in K's life*.

Critique of Pure Reason

The closure performed at the end of esoteric initiations may have a more mundane counterpart that is perhaps more reasonable and less mysterious in the eyes of those unacquainted with ancient wisdom. This is provided by insights first brought out by Immanuel Kant (1724-1804) in his *Critique of Pure Reason*, which was to become the most influential work in philosophy since its publication.[38] This is particularly intriguing in the light of Blavatsky's comment that Kant had been inspired by perennial influences.[39]

One of the main theses in Kant's work—and one that has had considerable impact on the way we understand the world—is that as humans we have a kind of psychological and perceptual buffer that helps us make sense of the world around us. We are constantly impacted by an overwhelming number of impressions from the world around us. What Kant calls our understanding selects from "the manifold" of those impressions and classifies the selected impressions into a fixed number of categories (twelve). Our organism selects primarily those perceptions that are relevant to our daily life and our welfare, and "tunes out" the vast majority of stimuli.

The selected sensations and perceptions may be somewhat

arbitrary, and the ones that are chosen do not span the entire range of possible selections. However, without the buffer we could go insane; we would be unable to interpret what happens to us and would be unable to have any experience that we could call human. On the other hand, because of it we can never perceive the noumenal—that is, the world "as it is in itself," in Kant's words. We must be content with the phenomenal world given to us by our "forms of sensibility" (space and time), and by our "understanding," which functions in terms of the twelve categories. Science, then, is not an exploration of the world as it is in itself, but is a description and manipulation of the way *we* perceive the world.

For the same reason, according to Kant and other prominent philosophers since his time, it is not possible to do metaphysics. Metaphysics is the attempt to describe *what is* "as it is in itself," and our limitations as living beings do not allow us to do that. What we call metaphysics, then, consists of the futile attempt by the analytical mind to pretend it can describe the noumenal, while its realm is exclusively the phenomenal.

An analogy may be made between the self-protecting selectivity that according to Kant we all employ in order to perceive the world as we do, and the closure that according to Leadbeater takes place at the end of initiatory ceremonies. In both there is a kind of "filter" that protects us from receiving more impressions than we can handle and remain sanely in tune with our experiences. In this context, it is intriguing to note how Gurdjieff used the word *Kundabuffer*—apparently a neologism combining *kundalini* and *buffer*—to refer to a "special organ" that makes it possible for us to perceive as we do.[40]

The Third Eye

Another element contributing to the uniqueness of K's process is that although in the accounts there are numerous references to kundalini rising up his spine, no mention is ever made of the chakras along the spine. Instead, every reference that could be construed as referring to chakras specifies the head as the place where the activity was going on. Since kundalini was awakened, the chakras along the spine were probably vivified as well, given that the movement of kundalini is always said to begin at the base of the spine. So the point is not that there was no activity in the spine; rather, the point is that the "operation" was performed in the head. Whatever part the centers below the head may have played seems to have been relatively insignificant.

To those who know about the chakras through tantric and New Age literature, this may seem odd. However, the teachers in charge of K's process—the same who started the perennial renaissance and who were primarily responsible for most of HPB's writings—apparently worked with a different set of chakras, all of which they described as being in the head. The psychic centers usually referred to as chakras in tantric and New Age literature were called plexuses by HPB's teachers. Considering that the perennial teachers were responsible for most of HPB's writings,[41] the following passage is of particular interest in relation to K's process:

> Our seven Chakras are all situated in the head, and it is these Master Chakras which govern and rule the seven (for there are seven) principal plexuses in the body, and the forty-two minor ones to which Physiology refuses that name. . . . When the time comes, the members of the E.S.T. will be given the minute details about the Master Chakras and taught to use them; till then, less difficult subjects have to be learned.[42]

This passage is deeply intriguing, because the only use it was ever put to is in connection with K's process. Was this meant by the Masters as a veiled reference to the unique experiment they were preparing to perform about forty years later? It appeared in HPB's esoteric *Instructions*, which were originally available only to members of the Esoteric School of Theosophy (E.S.T.), but later were made public at HPB's request. Elsewhere in the *Instructions* HPB's teachers compare their understanding of the chakras and kundalini with that of the Tantrists:

> One [school] is purely psycho-physiological, the other purely psycho-spiritual. The Tantrists do not seem to go higher than the six visible and known plexuses, with each of which they connect the Tattvas [principles in nature, or alternatively, levels of awareness]; and the great stress they lay on the chief of these, the Muladhara chakra (the sacral plexus), shows the material and selfish bent of their efforts towards the acquisition of powers. Their five Breaths and five Tattvas are chiefly concerned with the prostatic, epigastric, cardiac, and laryngeal plexuses. Almost ignoring the Agneya [Ajna, in the forehead], they are positively ignorant of the synthesizing pharyngeal plexus.
>
> But with the followers of the old school it is different. We begin with the mastery of that organ which is situated at the base of the brain, in the pharynx, and called by Western anatomists the Pituitary Body. In the series of the objective cranial organs, corresponding to the subjective Tattvic principles, it stands to the "Third Eye" (Pineal Gland) as Manas [analytical mind] stands to Buddhi [insight-compassion]; the arousing and awakening of the Third Eye must be performed by that vascular organ, that insignificant little body, of which, once again, physiology knows nothing at all. The one is the Energizer of Will, the other that of Clairvoyant Perception.[43]

This assessment points to yet one more reason for not engaging in any form of kundalini yoga except under the direction of a perennial teacher. The "material and selfish . . . acquisition of powers" implied in this practice (common in some New Age circles) seem to refer to psychological dangers that a beginner has no way of fathoming until it is too late. This suggests one more reason why "occultism" is not part of the new perennial approach, as exemplified in K's insights and observations. If clairvoyance and other "faculties" develop as a natural result of the rechanneling of energies at deep levels as implied in dying to the known, it would not cause any harm. But to seek "powers" while one is still a prisoner of closed loops in the brain and of self-centeredness, can be very dangerous.

If nothing else, K's experience of the chakras as exclusively in his head provides continuity and affirmation of this rare teaching on the subject given by HPB's teachers. It is also interesting that as late as 1961, writing in the *Notebook*, K referred to the process as "an operation going on deep within," noting that "the pressure and the strain were from the back of the head, through the palate to the top of the head," and he would wake up "in the middle of the night, shouting and groaning; the pressure and the strain, with its peculiar pain, was intense."[44]

Apparently, physiologists of HPB's time and conventional Tantrists were not the only ones who were not conversant with what the perennial teachers had discovered about the human organism. Even Leadbeater and Besant—who were privy to some of this information—in the few places where they speak of their own experience with chakras, refer exclusively to what HPB's esoteric *Instructions* call plexuses—the centers along the spine. The evidence suggests that CWL simply did not know from personal experience anything about the kind of extremely delicate psycho-biological brain surgery performed in K's head. The fact that it was so different from his own experiences and knowledge is very likely another reason why CWL was so anxious about what was happening to K. This explains why he acknowledged his ignorance and stated there was nothing he could do except "wait and watch."

An important part of this sophisticated form of "brain surgery" must have been the opening of the "third eye." According to Blavatsky's teachers, the pineal gland was originally—millions of years ago—a fully operational physical eye at the back of the head that also allowed the forerunners of the human species to be clairvoyant. However, as ordinary perception became more important for physical survival, the third eye withdrew to the inside of the head.

At the end of the twentieth century—more than a hundred years after HPB's death—physiologists still know little about the functions of the pineal gland, although the little information that is available confirms in every respect statements HPB made on the subject.[45] It is curious that modern physiology has identified the occipital region at the back of the head as the primary visual area of the brain—seemingly a vestige of what HPB and her teachers claimed was its ancient function. Further, one of the few things known about the pineal gland is that its function is related to our responses to light and darkness—also a visual function. Moreover, even physiologists now refer to the pineal gland as the third eye, since they now know that in invertebrates and some lower vertebrates the pineal gland functions as an eye. Thus their observations and even their language are very similar to those in HPB's writings.[46]

Opening the Inner Eye

What HPB's teachers said is that the pineal gland, which is largely inactive and atrophied, can be reactivated, and that as this occurs in an increasing number of people over time, it will slowly regain its importance as an organ of perception for most of us. Compared with the way our ancestors experienced the third eye, in the future its function would be integrated with other capacities that we will have developed in the interim, such as greater mastery over our environment. The physical bodies of the Masters, for instance, are said to have already incorporated some of these changes, which make them able to experience the world differently from the way "ordinary" people do.

The brain of modern humankind is dominated physiologically—and therefore psychologically as well—by the relatively large frontal lobe and by the brain cortex's division (which includes the frontal lobe) into "right" and "left," about which so much has been written.[47] The pineal gland is atrophied. The pituitary body, believed by contemporary physiologists to have originally been a kind of mouth, has now become a regulator for practically everything having to do with our metabolism. A midline view of the brain (dividing it down the middle into left and right) reveals that both the pituitary and pineal glands lie exactly dead center, the former just behind the eyes and the latter slightly above it and further back. According to Blavatsky's teachers, these and other organs are the ones connected with the seven chakras located in the head; in the future, these will become developed in humans, and the cortex will cease to have the prominence it has at present.

This, if it were to happen, would cause radical change, for the prominence of the cortex is implied in the two-valued logic we use to perceive the world in terms of "me" and "not me." To vastly simplify the recent research on cortex dichotomy: the right hemisphere cortex is associated with pattern and context, and the left hemisphere with linearity and detail. The two work together. A pattern or system (right brain) without details would be useless to us, just as linear thinking (left brain) without context would be meaningless. Although it has not been expressed quite this way in the literature, in a sense the right brain is space-dominant and the left brain time-dominant. Perhaps the two working together is what provides our perception of *what is* as if everything takes place in time and space. The two working together also make it possible to perceive the world in terms of "me" and "not me." A linear, time-bound continuity of perception and experience is needed in order to identify "me," but a space-bound context is also needed, in terms of which the world can thus be divided into two.

The development of the brain cortex as a kind of repository for all the pairs of opposites (night-day, black-white, good-evil, me-not me) may be the culmination of a schism that seems to be present throughout nature. Even unicellular organisms seem to respond to their environment in terms of "me" and "not me." The present human frontal lobe may then be a culmination of this schism. If HPB and her teachers were correct, it is in a Master that transcending all dichotomies becomes a permanent factor for the first time in the evolutionary process.

On the other hand, the non-dual factor has also been present all along in the "global" consciousness expressed in life forms. For instance, bacteria seem to behave not as individuals but as a mass, perhaps even as a species. This is evident in a more restricted way in more developed forms, like ants and bees. Even human beings, for whom dichotomy has developed into a sophisticated art form, as it were, thanks to the split brain cortex, have a proven capacity for solidarity, compassion, and other qualities not based on duality. Aesthetic appreciation has this quality. That may be a deep reason why the likes of Pythagoras and Nietzsche, for instance, thought so highly of music.

In the 1970s researchers began concluding that creativity comes from the right hemisphere.[48] If this were so, creativity would be a more limited thing than most of us have thought; for it would always be confined to the time-and-space-bound give-and-take intrinsic to the right-left workings of the brain cortex. The perennial teachings, on the other hand, suggest that the source of creativity is beyond any dichotomies. K, in any case, spoke of the limitations of the bivalent view of the brain and emphasized the intrinsic non-duality of consciousness.[49] To the extent that it is reflected in our physiology, true creativity is more likely connected with areas not limited by recursive patterns such as those associated with the brain cortex.

The awakening and development of some other part of the brain might imply a more synthesizing way of perceiving. Perhaps, as the perennial teaching has said for millennia, the pituitary and pineal glands—which are even physically positioned in the center of the right-left brain dichotomy—can eventually provide the basis for such synthesis. This is a complex and largely unexplored subject, however, and what is said here should be taken as only suggestions for further thought and research.

Whether or not the pituitary and pineal glands are involved, different ways of perceiving the world may be available even now. This is suggested, for instance, by the development of three- and many-valued logics. A logic implies a patterned way of perceiving the world, and as such, its form and the context it provides are identified with the right side of the brain. But the creative source of such a new way of perceiving might be found elsewhere, if the perennial teachings are correct.

Interestingly, alternative logics have actually become necessary to communicate properly about subtle processes of nature, such as those revealed by quantum physics. This new development in logic thus seems to be integral to the numerous transformations that have been adumbrating throughout the twentieth century. Before this, a way of thinking not based on two-valued logic would have been considered science fiction, or only a game. Even the *Encyclopedia of Philosophy*, published in the 1960s, still viewed many-valued logics as a merely theoretical curiosity:

> It is common logical doctrine that every proposition is either true or false and that although there are intermediate possibilities between being certainly true and being certainly false, or between being known to be true and being known to be false, there are none between truth and falsehood themselves. This principle is one version of the law of excluded middle. Nowadays truth and falsehood are commonly described as the two possible truth-values of a proposition, the law of excluded middle, in the form just given, being referred to as the law of bivalence. At various times, however, logicians have entertained the view that there might be other possibili-

ties—that there might be more than two truth-values.[50]

Perhaps the experiment performed on K points to the dawn of a new era in our evolution, a true psycho-biological mutation. However, there may be still another dimension to what was taking place. K commented shortly before he died that throughout his life he had been a vehicle for "an immense energy, an immense intelligence."[51] The experiment might have been to adapt K's brain so it would be in as great a rapport as possible with the brain of the Master of Masters, the Lord Maitreya, whom Christians call Christ. The different physiology of the Masters implies a way of experiencing the world not limited by the two-valued logic implicit in the present domination of the split brain cortex. So now the possible perception of the world would not be limited to the intrinsically adversarial terms exemplified in the time-and-space-bound notions of "me" and "not me." K's message certainly conveyed no compromises with the violence and fear that are always implied in two-valued logic and in this limited, time-and-space-bound perception of the world. He insisted passionately on a holistic, synthesizing, and non-dual view of *what is*.

PART THREE

THE OTHER

CHAPTER SEVEN

The Beloved

INEVITABLY, AS THE YEARS PASSED, MORE AND more people who associated with K came to know of the process yet were unfamiliar with K's perennial pedigree. His early encounters with Pupul Jayakar and her sister in 1947 may have been a first opportunity for K to break new ground, as it were, outside the Theosophical milieu. Jayakar recounted:

> It began on an evening when Krishnaji had been for a walk with us. He started to say that he was not feeling well, and could we go home. When we asked whether he wanted to see a doctor, he said, "No, it is not that." He would not explain further. When we got home he went to his room, telling [Maurice] Friedman that on no account was he to be disturbed; but he asked Nandini and me to come into the room. He closed the door and then told us not to be afraid, whatever happened, and on no account to call a doctor. He asked us both to sit quietly and watch him. There was to be no fear. We were not to speak to him, not to revive him, but to close his mouth if he fainted. On no account were we to leave the body alone.
>
> Although I had been swept away by my meeting with K [on psychological, personal, and philosophical grounds], I had a skeptical mind and observed very intensely the events as they took place.

Krishnaji appeared to be in extreme pain. He complained of severe toothache and an intense pain at the nape of the neck, the crown of the head, and in the spine.

In the midst of the pain he would say, "They are cleansing the brain, oh, so completely, emptying it." At other times he would complain of great heat, and his body would perspire profusely. The intensity of the pain varied as did the area where it was concentrated. At times the pain was located in the head, in the tooth, the nape of the neck, or the spine. At other times he groaned and held his stomach. Nothing relieved the pain; it came and went at will.

When the process was operating, the body lying on the bed appeared a shell; only a body consciousness appeared to be present. In this state the voice was frail, childlike. Then suddenly the body filled with a soaring presence. Krishnaji would sit up cross-legged, his eyes closed, the fragile body would appear to grow and his presence would fill the room; there was a palpable, throbbing silence and an immense strength that poured into the room and enveloped us. In this state the voice had great volume and depth.[1]

"The World Teacher Is Here"[2]

Throughout the manifestations of the process that the sisters witnessed, K referred to the perennial teachers and to the Lord Maitreya, but without naming them. He would make remarks such as the following, recorded by Jayakar:

I know what they are up to. . . . I know when the
limit of pain is reached, they will return. They know
how much the body can stand. . . . They are very
careful with the body. . . . They have burnt me so
that there can be more emptiness. They want to see
how much of him can come.[3]

These sorts of statements are explainable in light of the
understanding, discussed in earlier chapters, that the perennial
teachers were preparing K's body so that the "immense" consciousness of the Lord Maitreya could "overshadow"* it—in K's
own words, "to see how much of him can come. " K made other
comments about the body needing to be prepared and kept ready
for this purpose. For instance, in 1979 he said:

I mustn't do anything that is irrelevant for the body.
I feel it because of what K has to do in the world. I
mustn't get ill because I couldn't talk, so I take as
much care as possible. The body is here to talk; it has
been brought up that way and its purpose is to talk.
Anything else is irrelevant, so the body has to be
protected. Another aspect of this is that I feel there
is another kind of protection which is not mine.
There is a separate form of protection, as if the
future is more or less laid down. A different kind of
protection, not only of the body. The boy was born

---

*In 1882, in one of his letters, the Master KH explained that Gautama
Buddha would no longer incarnate on earth. However, he would "overshadow every decimillennium (let us say and add 'has overshadowed
already') a chosen individual who generally overturned the destinies
of nations." (C. Humphreys and E. Benjamin, eds., *The Mahatma
Letters to A. P. Sinnett from the Mahatmas M and KH*, Adyar:
Theosophical Publishing House, 1962, Letter 17.) The word was later
used by CWL and AB to refer to K's relationship to the Lord Maitreya.
It was originally used in Luke 9:34, King James version.

with that peculiarity—he must have been protected to survive all he did. Somehow the body is protected to survive. Some element is watching over it. Something is protecting it.

. . . The very truth protects itself. Truth itself is undamageable, therefore it protects itself. Goodness needs no protection. In itself it has the quality of protection. Truth has inherent in itself the quality of its own protection; but it is much more than that. Much, much more than that. Here there is not only protection of the body but something much more universal. I cannot tell you more but that is not the end of it.[4]

Anyone who is unacquainted with the perennial philosophy and its teachers or maintains that they are nonexistent is likely to find such statements strange and unacceptable. To say there is no possible explanation and that it is all a mystery is to propose an "explanation " that explains nothing. The unsupported speculations advanced by various authors have been shown inadequate in previous chapters. The only explanation still standing is the one K himself gave, which is outlined in these pages. Thus far, no one has come up with a credible alternative that accounts for all aspects of K's inner life, as well as of his insights and observations. In this way K's inner life itself provides compelling evidence for the reality of the perennial philosophy and its teachers—and of his mission.

K spoke of his inner life with close friends a number of times during the last two decades of his life. However, he tended to avoid speaking as if what he said came from himself. Rather, he would quote CWL or AB, or describe certain events from his youth, or encourage others to try to understand it. Since he was not generally given to creating mystery around his person, his reticence must have been prompted by other reasons. Indeed, he occasionally indicated that he could not say more because of vows of secrecy made to the perennial teachers. He had spoken specifically of vows in the 1920s, when he was surrounded by people who were privy to and appreciated the nature of his relationship with the Masters. In later years he could not be as explicit, since his new friends did not accept anything they thought was "just theosophical." So he would simply say something like "I cannot tell you more," as in the quotation above.

There was another, deeper reason for his silence, related to the presuppositionlessness that was integral to every aspect of his insights and observations. It was, in one sense, a way of making his inner life also a topic of research. He had no objection to others inquiring into the process. In fact, he even encouraged it. Earlier we saw that he had said to Mary Lutyens and Mary Zimbalist in 1979:

> You might be able to [find out about his esoteric life] because you are writing about it. I cannot. If you and Maria [MZ] sat down and said, "Let us enquire," I'm pretty sure you could find out. Or do it alone. . . . You could. You would find a way. The moment you discover something you have words for it. Like a poem. If you are open to enquire, put your brain in condition, someone could find out. But the moment you find it, it will be right. No mystery . . . the mystery will be gone. . . . The sacredness will remain.[5]

K's reticence about his esoteric life was also in keeping with his refusal to promote himself as a spiritual authority. This too was in consonance with what he said in public talks and published writings, where he spoke of the uselessness and danger of following authorities in psychological and spiritual matters. His refusal to say much is also one more item in support of the presence of the Masters in his life, for it may have been a way of protecting these teachers and his own esoteric experiences—by not allowing something he might say to be corrupted as merely his opinion in the perception of his listeners.

Speaking of the Masters without knowing them directly amounts to misinterpreting and misconstruing who they are. People who have not undergone the kind of mutation K spoke of would understand the word *Masters* to mean whatever their conditioning and inner urges demanded. The word would be shallow, empty of substance. As documented below, even HPB, who first acquainted the world with the Masters and their work, came to regret having done so for these reasons. K's reticence was a way of saying that he intended for no one to speak of these things, including himself, without a proper attitude of respect and inner silence. This shows that all of this meant a great deal to him— which supports the fact that for him the perennial teachers and his mission in connection with the Lord Maitreya were a reality.

K's manner of referring to the perennial teachers changed radically over the years. With his later friends he would use terms like *the Presence, It,* and *the other.* For instance, to Mary Lutyens and Mary Zimbalist he spoke of "that thing ":

> That thing is in the room. If you ask it what it is, it wouldn't answer. It would say, "You are too small."
> I think we said the other day that there is a reservoir of good that must manifest. . . . But all this is sacred and I don't know how you will convey not only the sacredness but everything else we have talked about.
> . . . The moment you understand it, it is no longer a mystery. But the sacredness is not a mystery. So we are trying to remove the mystery leading to the source.[6]

"You are too small" refers to the extent that one is still conditioned, untransformed, self-centered—that is, not in a position to address, let alone "know," what the word Master might refer to. One has to earn the right to speak about these things. With the words "all this is sacred," K indicated that these issues were of utmost importance to him. The word *sacred* was a strong word for K; he reserved it to refer to his inner life. In the same conversation with the two Marys K also said:

> Amma [Mrs. Besant] and Leadbeater maintained that a Bodhisattva was to manifest and they must find a body—the tradition of the Avatar manifesting. The Buddha went through all that, the suffering, etc., then threw it aside and became enlightened. What he taught was original but he went through all that. But here is a freak who didn't go through any of it. Jesus may have been a freak too. The power must have watched over this body from the moment it was born. Why? How did it happen? A boy from a family that was nothing special. How did that boy happen to be there? Was it the power wanting to manifest that created the boy or was it that the power saw a Brahmanical family, an eighth child, and said, "That is the boy"?[7]

From the context, and considering that these matters were sacred to K, clearly his reference to himself and Jesus as "freaks" is not meant derogatorily. It is also clear that K is speaking about his inner life here, which is important, because this is one of the few recorded instances where he did not speak about it indirectly or vaguely. The familiarity implicit in using the word "freak" suggests he was speaking from personal knowledge. According to the perennial teachings, Jesus was "overshadowed" by the Christ (the Lord Maitreya)—who was a different member of the perennial brotherhood and whose insights Jesus taught to the world. The Christ is said in the perennial teachings to also stand for all-embracing insight and compassion, and whenever insight-compassion manifests through someone, Christ is said to be born in that person. K was suggesting that he was overshadowed by the same personage or state standing for universal insight and compassion as Jesus.

The fact that K had no tolerance for anyone speaking of anything to do with the Masters without a basis of personal experience suggests that what he did say was a matter of personal experience for him. The fact that there are no records of K speaking of such things between the 1930s and 1960s in one way supports the observation that he was not keen on talking about such subjects. His general reticence about his inner life could also suggest that his connection with the teachers of the perennial philosophy was simply a matter of fact for him, not a subject for dispute or speculation. It is only when the existence of the perennial teachers and K's mission as vehicle for the world teacher are not taken into account that K's reticence can be turned, unnecessarily, into yet another mystery about him.

K and Esoteric Teachings

The widespread belief is that K eschewed all esoteric—often called theosophical—teachings. The archival and biographical evidence shows, however, that he avoided speaking of esoteric matters largely because he considered them too serious to explore with most people. In other words, what he attacked was not the esoteric itself, but the way people took as lightweight and frivolous—as mere belief and opinion—what to him were serious and sacred. He sometimes expressed his attitude about the esoteric publicly, for instance in the talks he gave in Australia in 1970, where he said:

> You know all those things exist. There is thought transference, you know it, don't you? When you are very close to somebody, husband, wife, the wife hasn't to say a thing, and you do it, or you think it, there is immediate transference. There is also extrasensory perception, all kinds of powers as you

begin to investigate yourself deeply. All kinds of capacities come, so-called clairvoyance and other kinds of powers. But a wise man puts aside all those because they are irrelevant. But, people who want excitement, power, position, use those as a means of exploiting. A wise man avoids all this and moves away from all this.[8]

In other words, K's attitude was neither that the esoteric does not exist, nor that it exists but should be avoided. Rather, what is important is to bring about a mutation in oneself. Then esoteric abilities would become a normal part of life. However, one should not think about achieving mutation *in order to* acquire such powers, for mutation is what takes place when the "I" exists no longer, so there is no "one" left to acquire anything.

This is precisely what the early theosophical leaders said. In the *Key to Theosophy*, for instance, HPB said that being a true Theosophist "is a difficult undertaking, as the foremost rule of all is the entire renunciation of one's personality."[9] The critical thing according to Blavatsky is transformation. She said that seeking "powers" is dangerous, not because they are exotic but because it requires the promotion of "me." She called such a "me"-centered pursuit "black magic" and warned against it. In other words, both K and HPB saw the problem as not the esoteric itself, but the dangerous idiocy of someone wanting to acquire esoteric knowledge and powers without transformation. When she was asked whether someone "off the street" could acquire occult abilities, HPB answered (emphasis added):

He may; but there are ten thousand chances against one that he will fail. For one reason out of many others, no books on Occultism or Theurgy exist in our day which give out the secrets of alchemy or medieval Theosophy in plain language. All are symbolical or in parables; and as the key to these has been lost for ages in the West, how can a man learn the correct meaning of what he is reading and studying? Therein lies the greatest danger, one that leads to unconscious *black* magic or the most helpless mediumship. *He who has not an Initiate for a master had better leave the dangerous study alone.*

Look around you and observe. While two-thirds of *civilized* society ridicule the mere notion that there is anything in Theosophy, Occultism, Spiritualism, or in the Kabbalah, the other third is composed of the most heterogeneous and opposite elements. Some believe in the mystical, and even in the *supernatural* (!), but each believes in his own way. Others will rush single-handed into the study of the Kabbalah, Psychism, Mesmerism, Spiritualism, or some form or another of Mysticism. Result: no two men think alike, no two are agreed upon any fundamental occult principles, though many are those who claim for themselves the *ultima thule* of knowledge, and would make outsiders believe that they are full-blown adepts.

Not only is there no scientific and accurate knowledge of Occultism accessible in the West—not even of true astrology, the only branch of Occultism which, in its exoteric teachings, has definite laws and a definite system—but no one has any idea of what real Occultism means. Some limit ancient wisdom to the Kabbalah and the Jewish Zohar, which each interprets in his own way according to the dead-letter of the Rabbinical methods. Others regard Swedenborg or Boehme as the ultimate expressions of the highest wisdom; while others again see in mesmerism the great secret of ancient magic. One and all of those who put their theory into practice are rapidly drifting, through ignorance, into black magic. Happy are those who escape from it, as they have neither test nor criterion by which they can distinguish between the true and the false.[10]

Remarkably, the similarities between K and the original theosophists on this subject have not been noted. This is very likely because those who have written about K seem to have little understanding of or even interest in theosophy, even though they apparently feel justified in belittling theosophists and their work. On the other hand, New Agers, including Theosophists, tend to have the same attitude toward K. Without comprehending what he said, many tend to dismiss him because of the mistaken notion that he denied the esoteric.

The truth of the matter seems to be that K considered the esoteric too serious to discuss publicly. Like Blavatsky, he emphasized that without transformation, nothing else matters. According to HPB and to perennial teachers throughout history, a true student of the esoteric is someone who has been initiated—transformed—first. Theosophy, then, is meant to be learned while one is in theosophical (divine-like) states of awareness.[11]

Those who merely believe in some Theosophical "teaching" are not engaging in theosophy. Without transformation, whatever is studied is not perennial or esoteric but a travesty of such, according to HPB and her teachers. This is what K also said all along, except that he extended it to refer to everyone. That is, K did not make a distinction between initiates or candidates inside the "harmonious circle" (as Gurdjieff called it) and those outside it. Before the new way of expressing the perennial teachings came through K, all perennial schools had made that distinction. And since HPB was making the old perennial teachings known, the distinction comes up in her work as well. Yet even this does not mark a real difference between K and HPB, since K's job was presumably to open up the gates to the perennial temple even wider than HPB had done. So he was merely continuing what she had started. Before this time, the temple, while open for the serious, had always been otherwise sealed hermetically—a word derived from the ancient initiatory mysteries of Hermes, where no outsiders were allowed, under penalty of death.

Who Brings the Truth?

In later years K referred to the entity or condition he had earlier called the Lord Maitreya as "the Presence," "the benediction," "that thing," "the Other," or often simply as "It." For instance, in his entry in the *Notebook* for September 27, 1961, he spoke of "that otherness" and "a benediction" in ways very similar to those he had used in the 1920s when referring to the perennial teachers and the Lord Maitreya. In that entry, which he wrote soon after arriving in Rome, he said:

> Walking along the pavement overlooking the biggest basilica and down the famous steps to a fountain and many picked flowers of so many colours, crossing the crowded square, we went along a narrow one-way street (via Margutta), quiet, with not too many cars; there in that dimly lit street, with few unfashionable shops, suddenly and most unexpectedly, that otherness came with such intense tenderness and beauty that one's body and brain became motionless. For some days now, it had not made its immense presence felt; it was there vaguely, in the distance, a whisper but there the immense was manifesting itself, sharply and with waiting patience. Thought and speech were gone and there was peculiar joy and clarity. It followed down the long, narrow street till the roar of traffic and the over-crowded pavement swallowed us all. It was a benediction that was beyond all image and thoughts.[12]

K may have avoided using the names of the perennial teachers or the Lord Maitreya in order to prevent misinterpretation of who these teachers really are. He shunned the kind of personalization of these teachers that resulted when their existence had been made a public matter previously. Examples of such misunderstanding abound in the history of the world's religions, in many New Age circles, and, according to Blavatsky, in the early years of the Theosophical Society.

Even in the 1920s K did not often mention the perennial teachers in his public talks—although he did so in numerous letters and when speaking to small groups who presumably showed promise for a spiritual life and expressed interest in transformation, which was referred to as "initiation" or the "Path."[13] Perhaps the main reason why he was more open—or rather, more "concrete"—about the perennial teachers at that time was because he was addressing people who accepted and at least had an intellectual grasp of the perennial philosophy and its teachers. Another reason may be that K's brain was probably not transmitting the new perennial message as fully and spotlessly as it would in later years. According to his own statements, his brain underwent transformation throughout his life, and as he grew older, more of the Lord Maitreya could manifest in what he said. This may explain why in one public talk he referred to his person while engaged in teaching as merely a "telephone."[14] (Interestingly, HPB also referred to herself as a "telephone" of the perennial teachers, even though the invention was hardly ten years old and not yet in wide commercial use at the time.)[15]

In a talk K gave in Eerde, Holland—at the time, the international headquarters of the Order of the Star—on August 2, 1927, he spoke extensively of what he called "the Beloved. " In retrospect it becomes apparent that "the Beloved" was a transitional expression between naming the Masters, as he had done before, and using even vaguer expressions than "the Beloved" as he was to do in later years. In the speech he explained why it was important not to make the expression "Maitreya" a concrete thing—that being vague about would it lead to greater clarity about its meaning. His explanation would apply as well to synonyms for "the Beloved" that he used in later years, such as "the Presence," or "It." As this talk is very difficult to find in print except in India—in spite of its importance for understanding Krishnamurti—it is quoted at length here. At the beginning of that talk he explained how he researched within himself:

> I wanted to find out what was meant by the taking of a vehicle by the World-Teacher, and what was meant by His manifestation in the world. *I am going to be purposely vague, because although I could quite easily make it definite, it is not my intention to do so* [emphasis added]. Because once you define a thing it becomes dead. If you make a thing definite—at least that is what I maintain—you are trying to give an interpretation which in the minds of others will take a definite form and hence they will be bound by that form from which they will have to liberate themselves.[16]

Though K set out to be deliberately vague about what he meant by "the Beloved" in this talk, he also equated the Beloved with what could be described as the state of awareness in which the universal teacher manifests under various names. In other words, though he was doing his best to move away from a concrete image that might be fashioned by the mind into a fixed belief, he was more "concrete" than he would be in later years. His later, vaguer ways of speaking would be more faithful to his message, which was not concept-bound and therefore not easily caged by words. He continued:

> I have been asked what I mean by "the Beloved" I will give a meaning, an explanation, which you will interpret as you please. To me it is all—it is Shri

Krishna, it is the Master K.H., it is the Lord Maitreya, it is the Buddha, and yet it is beyond all these forms. What does it matter what name you give? You are fighting over the World-Teacher as a name. The world does not know about the World-Teacher; some of us know individually; some of us believe on authority; others have experience of their own, and knowledge of their own. But this is an individual thing and not a question about which the world will worry. What you are troubling about is whether there is such a person as the World-Teacher who has manifested Himself in the body of a certain person, Krishnamurti; but in the world nobody will trouble about this question. So you will see my point of view when I speak of my Beloved. It is an unfortunate thing that I have to explain, but I must. I want it to be as vague as possible, and I hope I have made it so. My Beloved is the open skies, the flower, every human being.

I said to myself: until I become one with all the Teachers, whether They are the same is not of great importance; whether Shri Krishna, Christ, the Lord Maitreya, are one is again a matter of no great consequence. I said to myself: as long as I see Them outside as in a picture, an objective thing, I am separate, I am away from the centre: but when I have the capacity, when I have the strength, when I have the determination, when I am purified and ennobled, then that barrier, that separation, will disappear. I was not satisfied till that barrier was broken down, till that separateness was destroyed. Till I was able to say with certainty, without any undue excitement, or exaggeration in order to convince others, that I was one with my Beloved, I never spoke.

I talked of vague generalities which every-

body wanted. I never said: I am the World-Teacher;
but now that I feel I am one with the Beloved, I say
it, not in order to impress my authority on you, nor
to convince you of my greatness, nor of the greatness of the World-Teacher, nor even of the beauty of
life, the simplicity of life, but merely to awaken the
desire in your own hearts and in your own minds to
seek out the Truth. If I say, and I will say, that I am
one with the Beloved, it is because I feel and know
it. I have found what I longed for, I have become
united, so that henceforth there will be no separation, because my thoughts, my desires, my long-
ings—those of the individual self—have been
destroyed.

Hence I am able to say that I am one with
the Beloved—whether you interpret it as the
Buddha, the Lord Maitreya, Shri Krishna, the
Christ, or any other name.[17]

The Grand Inquisitor

In the same speech K drew an analogy between his own
case and the situation in the famous passage in Dostoyevsky's *The
Brothers Karamazov* called "The Grand Inquisitor." This story,
which was first translated into English by HPB, was to be widely
discussed in theological and philosophical circles in the twentieth
century.[18] The fact that both HPB and K thought this an important fragment of literature is intriguing in light of how relevant
it became later in fields such as psychology, philosophy, and religion. The passage describes the return of Christ during the heyday of the Inquisition. The Grand Inquisitor has a long talk with
Christ—or rather, engages in a long monologue, since Christ
remains silent throughout. He explains that the masses of people
do not want the freedom Christ offers, with its implications of
responsibility, suffering, and seriousness. What they want is what

the Grand Inquisitor and his Church have to offer: security, the status quo. So long as the Church provides them with the enclosed environment they identify as safety, they will continue speaking of things like "God's love" and "heaven" and "turning the other cheek" while their behavior glaringly contradicts such phrases.

K's comment on the similarity between this story and his own case is significant, even though he is not accurate regarding the specifics of Dostoyevsky's story. For instance, it was the Grand Inquisitor in Spain, not the pope in Rome, who spoke with Christ. And in the novel the Grand Inquisitor explains why he must denounce Christ and kill him once more, even while knowing full well who he is murdering, while Krishnaji refers to merely keeping him in prison:

> For sixteen years you have worshipped the picture which has not spoken, which you have interpreted as you pleased, which has inspired you, given you tranquility, given you inspiration in moments of depression. You were able to hold to that picture because that picture did not speak, it was not alive, there was nothing to be kept alive; but now that the picture, which you have worshipped, which you have created for yourselves, which has inspired you, becomes alive and speaks, you say: Can that picture, which I worshipped, be right? Can it speak? Has it any authority? Has it the power to represent the World-Teacher? Has it the magnitude of His wisdom, the greatness of His compassion, fully developed and can it be manifest in one individual?

> These of course are questions which you must solve for yourselves. You remember the well-known story by Dostoyevsky in which the Christ reappears? He had been preaching and He went at

last to Rome, and the Pope invited Him, and in secrecy fell on his knees and worshipped and adored Him, but kept Him imprisoned. He said: "We worship you in secrecy; we admit that you are the Christ; but if you go outside, you will cause so much trouble; you will create doubts, when we have tried to quell them."

Now that picture is beginning to get alive, and you cannot have anything real, you cannot have anything true, which is not alive. You may worship a tree in the winter-time, but it is much more beautiful in the spring, when the buds, when the bees and the birds, when all the worlds, begin to be alive. Through the years of winter you have been silent and not questioning yourselves very sincerely, it has been comparatively easy; but now you must decide for yourselves what it all means.

Before, it was easy to say that you expected a World-Teacher, and it meant very little; but now you are face to face with the problem of that picture coming to life. Whether you are going to worship continually a mere picture, or worship the reality of that picture, must, of course, be left to the individual. But do not, please, try to use your authority to persuade another, as I do not use mine to convince you of the truth of that picture being alive. To me it is alive.[19]

K was unmistakably equating the Beloved with the World Teacher. As he explained in another passage from the same speech, "I never said [in the past]: I am the World-Teacher; but now that I feel I am one with the Beloved, I say it."[20]

He also said that the way to destroy the World Teacher is to do what the Grand Inquisitor did: to create a religion around him, a system of ideas and practices that provide false security for the fearful; to worship him rather than cleanse our lives of the conditioning with which they are saturated; to make concrete and conceptual everything connected with the sacred. A little later in that speech K said:

> When Krishnamurti dies, which is inevitable, you will make a religion, you will set about forming rules in your minds, because the individual, Krishnamurti, has represented to you the Truth. So you will build a temple, you will then begin to have ceremonies, to invent phrases, dogmas, systems of beliefs, creeds, and to create philosophies. If you build great foundations upon me, the individual, you will be caught in that house, in that temple, and so you will have to have another Teacher come and extricate you from that temple, pull you out of that narrowness in order to liberate you. But the human mind is such that you will build another temple round Him, and so it will go on and on.
>
> But those who understand, who do not depend on authority, who hold all peoples in their hearts, will not build temples—they will really understand. It is because a few have truly desired to help other people, that they have found it simple. Others who have not understood, although they talk a great deal about it, and of how they will interpret the teaching, will have difficulties.[21]

He also made it clear that what he was saying was not meant exclusively for theosophists or members of the Order of the Star, but that he would be teaching the world at large. This strongly suggests that his imminent break with the Theosophists was integral to the development of his work, and was not necessarily a blanket criticism of them. He said:

It is perfectly simple for me to go out into the world and teach. The people of the world are not concerned with whether it is a manifestation, or an indwelling, or a visitation into the tabernacle prepared for many years, or Krishnamurti himself. What they are going to say is: I am suffering. I have my passing pleasures and changing sorrows—have you anything lasting to give? You say you have found Happiness and Liberation—can you give me of that, so that I can enter into your kingdom, into your world? That is all they are concerned about and not the badges, the orders, the regulations, the books.

They want to see the living waters that flow under the bridge of human beings, so that they can swim with those waters into the vast ocean. And what you are concerned with all the time is how you are going to interpret. You have not found the Truth for yourselves, you are limited, and yet you are trying to set other people free. How are you going to do it? How are you going to discover what is true, what is false, what is the World-Teacher, what is reality, if you have not cleared the stagnation from the pool so that it will reflect the Truth?[22]

The Beloved

This speech is without a doubt at least as historically important as K's "Truth Is a Pathless Land" speech in 1929, with which he broke away from the Theosophists. A number of issues are discussed clearly here that were confused in later years by various interpreters of K's inner life. For instance, K says here that part of the meaning of "the Beloved" is "the Teacher." K's unambiguousness here is valuable, since subsequently he would speak of the Beloved in increasingly vague terms, referring to "the Other" or "It" in the same contexts where earlier he had spoken of the Beloved. This is perhaps as it should be, since his later expressions are vaguer in order to be less amenable to exploitation by the conditioned mind. In a deeper sense, the later expressions may actually be more accurate, more clear.

So also, in later years K avoided words such as *Maitreya* in connection with his inner life because such words and their attendant concepts were "too concrete." K's objection to using the word seems to be the fruitlessness of attempting to objectify the *Maitreya*—which implies a deeper dimension of awareness than ordinary use of the word can refer to. In casual usage, the word *Maitreya* refers to an object of thought—thought that is conditioned and full of expectations—or to a person in the conventional sense of the word. This should be kept in mind especially in the present investigation, where the words *Maitreya, perennial teachers*, and *Masters* have been retained provisionally, to avoid awkwardness in communication, in the previous chapters. But in the discussion of the meaning of *Maitreya* in the next two chapters, they are dropped.

In this 1927 speech K spoke in a manner not heard later in his life:

> I have always in this life, and perhaps in past lives, desired one thing: to escape, to be beyond sorrow, beyond limitations, to discover my Guru, my Beloved—which is your Guru and your Beloved, the Guru, the Beloved who exists in everybody, who exists under every common stone, in every blade of grass that is trodden upon. It has been my desire, my longing, to become united with Him so that I should no longer feel that I was separate, no longer be a different entity with a separate self. When I was able to destroy that self utterly, I was able to unite myself with my Beloved. Hence, because I have found my Beloved, my Truth, I want to give it to you.[23]

A careful reading of K's writings and talks from the 1920s
reveals his apparent search for a proper idiom for conveying the
ultimately ineffable phenomenon that was going on within him.
His early forms of expression tended to sound somewhat biblical.
There are many instances of his apparent intention to move away
from the religious associations of the expression "the Beloved,"
which he had borrowed from the biblical *Song of Songs*, a text he
had enjoyed reading as a young man. Yet it is not too difficult to
see a kinship between those early writings and what he wrote and
said in his later years. For instance, in 1927 he wrote in *The
Search*:

Fresh and eager as the wind
That seeketh the hidden places of the valley,
So have I sought
The secret abodes of my soul,
And purged myself of all things,
Past and present.

As, suddenly, the robes of silence
Fall over the noisy world,
So, instantly, have I found Thee,
Deep in the heart of all things and in mine own.

On the mountain path
I sat on a rock,
And Thou wert beside me and in me,
All things being in Thee and in me.
Happy is the man that findeth Thee and me
In all things.
In the light of the setting sun,
Through the delicate lace of a spring tree,
I beheld Thee.
In the twinkling stars
I beheld Thee.
In the swift passing bird,
Disappearing into the black mountain,

I beheld Thee.
Thy glory has awakened the glory in me.[24]

Compare this with the following, the entry for August 13, 1961 in the *Notebook*. The idiom has been cleansed of any conventional religious expression, and the poetry has been dropped—replaced with what could be described as poetical prose. Yet one is touched by the stunning similarity between the two texts.

> As the path that goes up the mountain can never contain all the mountain, so this immensity is not the word. And yet walking up the side of the mountain, with the small stream running at the foot of the slope, this incredible, unnameable immensity was there; the mind and heart was filled with it and every drop of water on the leaf and on the grass was sparkling with it.
>
> It had been raining all night and all the morning and it had been heavy with clouds, and now the sun was coming out over the high hills and there were shadows on the green, spotless meadows that were rich with flowers. The grass was very wet and the sun was on the mountains. Up that path there was enchantment and talking now and then seemed in no way to [word left out] the beauty of that light nor the simple peace that lay in the field. The benediction of that immensity was there and there was joy.
>
> On waking this morning, there was again that impenetrable strength whose power is the benediction. One was awakened to it and the brain was aware of it without any of its responses. It made the clear sky and the Pleiades incredibly beautiful.

And the early sun on the mountain, with its snow, was the light of the world.

During the talk it was there, untouchable and pure, and in the afternoon in the room it came with a speed of lightning and was gone. But it's always here in some measure, with its strange innocency whose eyes have never been touched.

The process was rather acute last night and as this is being written.[25]

It

K often used the expression "It" to refer to the presence, personage, or condition from which his state of grace came. It is documented in works about his life that he said he would die whenever, wherever, and however It would determine. For instance, when he arrived in Los Angeles from India in January of 1986, in a very weakened condition because of the cancer of the pancreas that would finally take him away in February, he was met by his friend Mary Zimbalist.

As soon as they were alone K told her that for the next two or three days she must not leave him or he might "slip away." He said, "*It* doesn't want to inhabit a sick body, one that couldn't function. We must not have an accident, because if I were hurt that would be the end."[26]

Evidently he had no personal concern about dying. His only concern seemed to be to continue providing a body through which his mission could proceed. The clear implication is that the insights did not come from him, but from *It*.

Later, when he was examined by a surgeon and an oncologist on January 23, K felt it was important to explain to the doctor who would be taking care of him—to let the doctor know he would be dealing with a different situation than he was used to:

> After the examination K, according to Scott [Forbes], "began to tell Dr. Deutsch something of what he was. He seemed to need to do this in order to help the doctor know how to take care of him, i.e., that it was not an ordinary body, that *something extraordinary used the body* [italics added], that the body was extraordinarily sensitive, that somehow, regardless of how experienced the doctor was, he had no experience of dealing with what he was now going to deal with."[27]

A Meaningful Puzzlement

Sometime after he came to know he would soon die, K spoke briefly with Mary Zimbalist and Scott Forbes, who were closest to him in those last few days, referring again to his relationship to the being or universal state he had identified as the Lord Maitreya in earlier years:

> When Mary and Scott next went into K's room, K said, "It seems I am going to die," as if he had not expected it so soon but accepted the fact. Later he said, "I wonder why 'the other' doesn't let the body go." He was to wonder this often in the succeeding three weeks. On another occasion he said to Mary, "I'm watching it. It's most curious." And at another time, he remarked, "'The other' and death are having a struggle."[28]

K's puzzlement about why "the other" was not allowing him to die immediately is only understandable if he knew he was working for and with the perennial teachers and that they would not allow him to suffer unnecessarily; for he had said quite often in the last two decades of his life that as soon as the body could no longer be used for his mission he would die, and it was now plain that he could no longer teach. In fact, his perplexity is intriguing, since on the surface it seems to contradict what he always said about being one with *what is*: that it means to have no expectations. The only way to avoid such contradiction in K seems to be to take into account his rich inner life.

As K often questioned out loud in the ensuing three weeks why he was not allowed to die in peace right away, he seems to have been convinced that someone else had control over when and how he would die. Further, he seemed to assume that that someone was compassionate, cared for him deeply, and would not allow him to suffer unnecessarily, that is, he had absolute trust in this someone. Considering all that he had said up to this point and stating it in its most concrete form, it seems that this someone would have been the Lord Maitreya, and the protection was from the perennial teachers. Nevertheless, it is important not to personalize—make concrete—our understanding of who or what these teachers are. As Mary Lutyens said:

> In the same way it had been asked in 1927: did K's consciousness blend with that of the Lord Maitreya or did the Lord's consciousness blend with K's? At any rate, "the other" was not personalised.[29]

On February 7, ten days before he died, he stated again unambiguously that his body was but an instrument, just as CWL and AB had said in the early days. Mary Cadogan of the Krishnamurti Foundation in England had written, asking, "When Krishnaji dies, what *really* happens to that extraordinary focus of understanding and energy that is K?" Krishnaji had excellent mechanical skills all his life and particularly loved cars, and he used an automobile analogy to answer her:

I was telling them this morning—for seventy years that super energy—no—that immense energy, immense intelligence, has been using this body. I don't think people realise what tremendous energy and intelligence went through this body—there's [a] twelve-cylinder engine. And for seventy years—was a pretty long time—and now the body can't stand any more. Nobody, unless the body has been prepared, very carefully, protected and so on—nobody can understand what went through this body. Nobody. Don't anybody pretend. Nobody. I repeat this: nobody amongst us or the public, know what went on. I know they don't. And now after seventy years it has come to an end. Not that that intelligence and energy—it's somewhat here, every day, and especially at night. And after seventy years the body can't stand it—can't stand any more. It can't. . . . You won't find another body like this, or that supreme intelligence operating in a body for many hundred years. You won't see it again. When he goes, it goes. There is no consciousness left behind of *that* consciousness, of *that* state. They'll all pretend or try to imagine they can get into touch with that. Perhaps they will somewhat if they live the teachings. But nobody has done it. Nobody. And so that's that.[30]

This is an apt explanation of the tremendous pain he went through for so many years—a twelve-cylinder engine trying to work through a less powerful vehicle. That he spoke of the manifestation of that immense energy and intelligence as spanning seventy years is telling in itself. K was ninety at the time, so clearly that intelligence did not begin in him when he was born. Seventy years before would have been 1916—the midpoint between his first initiation in 1910 and his grand initiation in

1922. Whichever of these he was referring to, he was clearly speaking of something that began manifesting through him about that time. No credible explanation of this deathbed statement has been offered so far other than what he had said all along: that he had been the vehicle for what in earlier days he had identified as the Lord Maitreya—as Christ, as Shri Krishna.

What happened immediately after this statement, which was tape-recorded, shows the "anti-esoteric" attitude of most of those who surrounded K from the 1940s until he died. Right after K responded to Mary Cadogan's question, Scott Forbes asked him to explain what he meant.

> When Scott asked him to clarify some of what he had said in this statement for fear it might be misunderstood he became "very upset" with him and said, "You have no right to interfere in this."[31]

Forbes was one of just a handful of people who were closest to K at the end. Whatever misunderstanding he may have held regarding K's inner life, that does not change the value of his work, for which anyone interested in K would feel grateful to him. The difficulty of those close to K in understanding the place of the esoteric in his life is understandable. K's work was either completely independent of or strongly opposed to *conceptual* views of the esoteric. Correspondingly, people drawn to his work have tended either to have no interest in things esoteric or to hold strong views against them. Both views assume the esoteric to be a metaphysical—a conceptual—system. This is also understandable, for New Agers and Theosophists have made the same assumptions.

However, as documented throughout this study, for K the esoteric was not only real, it was the core of his work and of who and what he was. This is not the esoteric of metaphysics, systems, and methods typical of the New Age milieu. Rather, it is the esoteric of the perennial schools that have existed for millennia, the

esoteric that has meaning only after initiation, transformation—
what K called mutation—has taken place. If a distinction is not
made between the esoteric of concepts and the esoteric of transformation, confusion will inevitably reign supreme. Yet this distinction has not been made by New Agers, including
Theosophists, nor by sympathizers of K's work, including his
close friends and associates, who therefore tended to be strongly
biased against the esoteric. This attitude may be an important reason why there is relatively little information about his inner life,
even though K spoke about these matters. For instance, in 1977 in
Ojai, he said to a gathering of representatives of the various
Krishnamurti Foundations:

> If people come here and ask, "What was it like to live
> with this man?" would you be able to convey it to
> them? If any of the Buddha's disciples were alive
> would not one travel to the ends of the earth to see
> them, to find out from them what it had been like to
> live in his presence?[32]

Although there may be some question as to whether this
was "the nearest he had ever come to defining his own status," as
Mary Lutyens put it, her comments on K's remark shed additional light:

> K's allusion to the Buddha and his disciples could
> surely mean only one thing? It was the nearest he
> had ever come to defining his own status, yet it is
> impossible to convey to anyone who does not know
> him well how totally without self-importance such a
> comparison was made. Where the self is absent there
> can be no conceit. "This man" K spoke of was not his
> own personality. All the same, how does one recon-
> cile all this with his constant reiteration, before and

since, that no one has any authority to represent him after his death and that the guru-disciple relationship is an abomination to him?

Is it not perhaps quite simple? If anyone close to him ever does undergo a complete psychological transformation will not he or she carry on in the same non-authoritarian way as K himself? In asking the trustees to be with him as much as possible surely he is hoping that at least one or two of them may be granted the depth of perception to bring about a total revolution in the psyche, thus freeing them from their need of him as from all other crutches. This is very different from the guru-worship of disciples. If anyone ever claims after K's death authority to speak for him, one will know that he or she has not been transformed. But here another question arises which may never be answered: if a transformation should take place in anyone close to K would he or she choose to remain under the Krishnamurti aegis?[33]

The evidence points unequivocally to K's acceptance of the presence of the perennial teachers throughout his life, as well as to his role as the vehicle for the Lord Maitreya. Those close to K in his later years, however, by disassociating themselves from any interest in his early, "Theosophical" years, eliminated the possibility of understanding that his life and also his insights and observations were grounded in the perennial philosophy.

On the other hand, it may be wise not to underestimate the human penchant for fantasies such as one can construct around the esoteric. These can distract a person from the one thing of real importance: to bring about a mutation in ourselves and help create a good society and a radically new humanity. In the deft hands of the frivolous and the fearful, concepts that form around words like "Masters" and "Maitreya" become like putty to be fashioned in response to the fears and expectations of the creators. Unfortunately, this is what has happened in existing religions, in various systems of self-transformation, and in numerous New Age activities and organizations. Exploring some implications of this problem is the subject of chapter 8.

CHAPTER EIGHT

Ecce Homo

IF INDEED THE AVATAR FOR THE NEW AGE SPOKE THROUGH
J. Krishnamurti, it would be valuable to look at what this means
in light of his scathing remarks against authority. It should be
made clear at the outset that K recognized a legitimate function
for authority in mechanical fields, such as engineering and cybernetics, and in handling practical issues, such as obeying traffic
laws. Only when authority is misapplied and therefore inappropriate did K rail against it. Such is the case when authority is set
up in areas concerning values and reality, such as ethics, aesthetics, and in the religious or psychological life. Authority has no
place in these areas, according to K. It is only this sense that
authority is discussed in K's work and in this study.

Authority can take many forms. It can appear as a scrip-
ture-bound system—be it political, religious, philosophical, or
any other sort—believed by particular individuals to hold the
answers to questions that matter. It can take the form of a
method—meditational, religious, technocratic, military, or any
other sort—believed to lead to an expected, satisfying result.

Whatever form it takes, authority always includes two elements. First, it has an emotional dimension, which provides the
"satisfaction" component and is the "reason why" people become
devoted to various forms of authority. The emotional dimension
invariably masks the second: the logic-bound, dualistic, linear-
thinking, analytical element. As the following discussion reveals,
behind every devotee of an authority is an even greater devotee
of logic. The positing of an authority always has exactly the form
of a valid argument of two-valued logic. In such arguments, the

premises must always lead to the conclusion. In the same way, the actions of a devotee must always lead (via the means or premises) to the aim expected by the authority.

Ecce Homo

K's own remarks, as well as testimony from those who knew him intimately, reveal his conviction that the keynote teaching for the new age was being given through him. Yet he made it abundantly clear that the message was not associated in any way with following or worshipping anyone, including him. History shows us that the teachers of compassion throughout the world promoted neither the teachings of a given religion nor the founding of a new one. The Christ of the Gospels, for instance, was not a Christian, just as the Buddha of *Jataka* was not a Buddhist. Nevertheless, even while both of these teachers gave a message that is always intrinsically universal and free of cultural trappings, both of them were associated with particular cultures. K's presence in the twentieth century, on the other hand, marked the first time in history that a perennial teacher has truly spoken to the whole world. This may be why the expression "World Teacher" was coined in connection with him.

To identify oneself with a teacher and a body of teachings and to put that teacher up on a pedestal seems a sure way to wash one's hands of responsibility for one's own life. In the New Testament drama, Pontius Pilate presented Christ, crowned with thorns, before the Sanhedrin and then washed his hands, saying *ecce homo*: "Here is your man; I have nothing to do with this." If we consider the mythical dimension of the stories in the Gospels, Pilate's insensitive and irresponsible act can also represent something applicable to all of us. If we put the voice of wisdom and compassion up on a pedestal, crowned as king, we may separate wisdom-compassion from what goes on in our lives from moment to moment. We may alienate Christ from our lives.

This seems to be true as long as Christ is understood as a person, rather than as a dimension, a state of awareness of insight and compassion. People who follow Christ the person, rather than live in Christ-like states of awareness, divide themselves from those who believe otherwise. They also cause fragmentation within themselves. To hold to Christ as a person is an irresponsibly violent act, because it implies that one intends to cling to one's conditioning, instead of dying to it. "Being a Christian" is taken to mean that one must follow certain authorities (the Bible, the minister or priest, certain forms of behavior). But adhering to predetermined patterns is exactly what conditioning is all about, and deeply felt identification with any pattern implies segregation from those who are not so identified. This is an adversarial, violent attitude to have toward others, whether one knows them or not.

Conditioning also implies violence toward oneself. Most of the rules the faithful must follow are impossible rules. That is, in themselves, they have the rigidity of a logical argument. But human beings are not machines that follow given instructions exactly, so the faithful cannot hope to follow the rules to perfection. This means they are *always guilty* of not being "good" followers. The sense of guilt this engenders spells self-inflicted violence, which is likely to manifest in relationship, one way or another.

Clinging to one's conditioning is also a frivolous act, for it implies a refusal to be serious in a deeper sense. That is, one refuses to let truth and compassion lead one by the hand from moment to moment, and insists instead on following a prescribed set of ideas and behaviors. The "seriousness" of the conditioned person is always limited to that which she is serious about. So it always and necessarily implies a refusal to see and accept *what is* totally. "Seriousness" based on conditioning is *always* frivolous in this deeper sense. A Christian who is serious about her Christianity is by that very fact frivolous about living in Christ-like states of awareness, where there are no segregations and fragmentations. And that is the only "Christ" that ultimately matters.

To follow Christ as a person and assert his primacy as "savior" is to promote the values of the Christian subculture over all others. Such a subculture—by definition but also in fact—sees itself as the holder of the true moral values, and universalizes its conception of values as if they applied to every human being. But other religious subcultures interpret moral values differently. Clinging to the morality of the subculture inevitably leads to segregation, and potentially to hatred and even war. Anyone who identifies with a particular organized religious group, then, is supporting fragmentation and conflict. This morality is highly immoral from a more universal and so truer perspective.

A truer morality must be based on unconditional respect for *all* human beings. Identifying with a particular religion and following its morals and teachings is often an exercise in "doing the best one can." Since one cannot be "perfectly good" according to the religion's implicitly logical procedures, "doing the best one can" is often justification for doing whatever one can get away with. This spiritual mediocrity is a travesty of what the great teachers of humanity have taught and lived. It lies at the root of degeneration in society and in our private lives. This is precisely the degeneration Nietzsche predicted, referring to it as the nihilism that results from moralities based on conditioning, not transformation. True fellowship is not possible in the context of the particular and the provincial—corresponding to what we have seen earlier as closed loops in the brain. However, when heartfelt respect evolves into genuine affection for all, one approximates the state of Jesus or Buddha. Only to the extent that this affection for all is a fact in one's daily life can one claim to be moral.

So long as one insists on identification with the particular, one creates division at every level. Even within major religions, there are groups who consider themselves representatives of the true faith and segregate themselves from other members of their own religion. The divergence between Vishnu and Shiva followers in Hinduism and between Orthodox and Reformed Jews are two examples, and further subdivisions exist within each of these. Identification with a particular group is an act against the religious spirit, which seeks unity and wholeness, not fragmentation.

So the person who says *ecce homo* to universal, unconditioned affection is living in fragmentation. But fragmentation, violence, and frivolousness can be found wherever the analytical mind holds sway. Excellent examples can be found in the methods devised all over the world to attain the goals set out by authoritative systems.

The Sound of Two Hands Clapping

Certain practices and methods held a great deal of value before the perennial renaissance and may even have been stepping stones towards developments in that grand contemporary movement. In certain schools of Zen, for instance, a candidate is asked to meditate on a puzzle, called a koan. One of the best-known koans is "What is the sound of one hand clapping?"

The candidate sits in a prescribed way that is said to make alertness easier and insight-compassion an achievable goal. The practice is done every day for many hours at a time until the koan is solved, which usually takes several years and may elude some people permanently. The purpose of the koan is to jolt the logical mind out of its habitual grooves of thought and thus help generate a new, non-linear, more comprehensive level of awareness. This is the realm of insight-compassion. This is what Christianity would call "Christ being born in us."

Despite their unquestionable value, such practices may be more like stumbling blocks in the way of what is needed at present. For any form of practice—whether it is based on Zen, Tibetan Buddhism, Gurdjieff teachings, or any other school considered transformative—in fact involves conditioning at several levels. As such, it is not the kind of radical, total mutation that K suggested and that is required if we are to be integrated as individuals and as a society. Following such practices as a means to attaining insight-compassion has the form of a logical argument—leading from the premises implied in authoritatively prescribed methods to the conclusion implied in "attaining the goal." Realization of the implications of this fact may be what prompted a number of Zen teachers and high lamas of the Vajrayana tradition to attend K's talks—often in street clothes—or to seek him out privately.[1] Perhaps this is also why, in the last two decades of K's life, the heads of several Gurdjieff organizations in Europe and elsewhere attended K's yearly talks in Saanen, Switzerland, in conjunction with annual private meetings of their own.[2]

The same is true of any form of therapy or shamanism or any practice that engages mythology. (For instance, a Muslim saluting prayerfully toward Mecca several times a day, a Hindu performing *puja*, and a Jew reverencing the sabbath are all acting in accord with the mythologies associated with each of their religions.) Though therapy, shamanism, and mythologies have served humanity well in bringing awareness of alternative forms of perception, in terms of K's message they may now turn out to be more an impediment than an aid, if humanity is to truly mutate in order to create a new world. Like following a teacher or a religion, these approaches require commitment to a particular system of thought. They all require unconditional faith in logic, in the analytical mind's efficacy in fields of experience and understanding that matter to human beings. Such approaches can and will produce results: they can produce in certain people states that feel transformative at some level. But—if it may be pointed out respectfully—so can speaking in tongues, taking LSD, or riding a roller coaster.

Practices like drinking alcohol, smoking cigarettes, and taking mind-altering drugs follow the same dynamics, the same patterns of behavior, as those found in therapy, mythology, or shamanism. All of these activities follow logical algorithms that go from the practice to the expected goal. Engaging in any of these, one is saying with one's actions (knowingly or unknowingly) that one wants the world to remain the way it has been from time immemorial—violent, confused, and insensitive—and that one intends no profound mutations in one's life. Otherwise, one would not act as if the things that matter most in life call for engaging in patterns of behavior that attempt to fulfill the mathematical perfection of a logical argument. These patterns of practice do not necessarily result in feelings of guilt stemming from implicit inadequacies, as in some religions. But there is the same faith in the logic-bound analytical mind: all these practices assume that following a set of procedures will lead to a satisfying end. None of them are about transformation in a deeper sense; they only "play at" deeper transformation. Their implicit stumbling block is that they require the practitioner—like a hero of a tragic play—to follow a certain script to achieve the expected goal.

Even therapy "works" like a logical argument. That is, though it cannot claim the rigor of logic, mathematics, or even drama (its cousin), it promises to provide satisfaction at some level. All methods "work" within their bounds. The point is that no such system can bring about mutation at deep levels, for mutation involves seeing that no set of procedures will ever lead to a satisfactory end. This is not to say that if one spends hours a day for several years working on a koan or concentrating on the breath or practicing deity yoga or self-remembering, nothing will happen. Of course something will happen. *Any* method will generate *some* result. As K said while speaking to a college audience in California in the 1960s:

> When you examine a method, a system, what is implied in it? Somebody says "Do these things, practice them day after day, for twelve, twenty, forty years, and you will ultimately come to reality." That is, practise a method, whatever it is, but in practising a method, what happens? Whatever you do as a routine every day, at a certain hour, sitting cross-legged, or in bed, or walking, if you repeat it day after day your mind becomes mechanical. So when you see the truth of that, you see that what is implied in all that is mechanical, traditional, repetitive, and that it means conflict, suppression, control. A mind made dull by a method cannot possibly be intelligent and free to observe.

They have brought Mantra Yoga from India. And you also have it in the Catholic world—*Ave Maria* repeated a hundred times. This is done on a rosary and obviously for the time being quietens the mind. A dull mind can be made very quiet by the repetition of words and it does have strange experiences, but those experiences are utterly meaningless. A shallow mind, a mind that is frightened, ambitious, greedy for truth or for the wealth of this world, such a mind, however much it may repeat some so-called sacred word, remains shallow. If you have understood yourself deeply, learnt about yourself through choiceless awareness and have laid the foundation of righteousness, which is order, you are free and do not accept any so-called spiritual authority whatsoever (though obviously one must accept certain laws of society).

Then you can find out what meditation is. In meditation there is great beauty, it is an extraordinary thing if you know what meditation is—not "how to meditate." The "how" implies a method, therefore never ask "how"; there are people only too willing to offer a method. But meditation is the awareness of fear, of the implications and the structure and the nature of pleasure, the understanding of oneself, and therefore the laying of the foundation of order, which is virtue, in which there is that quality of discipline which is not suppression, nor control, nor imitation. Such a mind then is in a state of meditation.

. . . Now, what is a method, a system? Please follow this closely because by discarding what is false—that is, through negation—one finds out what is true. That is what we are doing. Without negating totally that which is obviously false, one

cannot arrive at any form of understanding. Those
of you who have practised certain systems or forms
of meditation can question it for yourselves. When
you practise something regularly day after day, getting up at two and three in the morning as the
monks do in the Catholic world, or sitting down qui-
etly at certain times during the day, controlling
yourself and shaping your thought according to the
system or the method, you can ask yourself what
you are achieving.

You are, in fact, pursuing a method that
promises a reward. And when you practise a method
day after day, your mind obviously becomes
mechanical. There is no freedom in it. A method
implies that it is a way laid down by somebody who
is supposed to know what he is doing. And—if I may
say so—if you are not sufficiently intelligent to see
through that, then you will be caught in a mechanical process. That is, the daily practising, the daily
polishing, making your life into a routine so that
gradually, ultimately—it may take five, ten or any
number of years—you will be in a state to understand what truth is, what enlightenment and reality
are and so on.

Quite obviously no method can do that
because method implies a practice; and a mind that
practises something day after day becomes mechanical, loses its quality of sensitivity and its freshness.
So again one can see the falseness of the systems
offered. Then there are other systems, including Zen
and the various occult systems wherein the methods
are revealed only to the few. The speaker has met
with some of those but discarded them right from
the beginning as having no meaning.

So, through close examination, understanding and intelligence, one can discard the mere repetition of words and one can discard altogether the guru—he who stands for authority, the one who knows as against the one who does not know. The guru or the man who says he knows, does not know. You cannot ever know what truth is because it is a living thing, whereas a method, a path, lays down the steps to be taken in order to reach truth—as though truth is something that is fixed and permanent, tied down for your convenience. So if you will discard authority completely—not partially but completely, including that of the speaker—then you will also discard, quite naturally, all systems and the mere repetition of words.[3]

Following a system or a method is in many ways like repeating a mantra, such as "Hare Krishna," the *Prajñaparamita Hridaya Sutra*, or the Lord's Prayer, with the intention of coming face to face with God. As K often suggested, if one were to sit down and repeat constantly, hour after hour, and with great intensity any mantra—even "Coca-Cola, Coca-Cola, Coca-Cola"—*something* will happen in the brain synapses, and sooner or later one will feel "different" in some way.[4] Any practice implies a time-bound, recursive-loop, closed-circuit movement in the brain that progresses from the choreographed act to the expected result of that action. This involves the right-left brain dichotomy: the right brain provides the context, the system that "makes sense" out of the specific practices, which are the province of the left brain. The right brain provides the pattern of expectancy, the left brain provides the specific steps to be taken, and a happy meeting of the two spells *satisfaction*.

Great Expectations, Failed Expectations

The "me," with its fears and ambitions, will always be at

the center of recursive loops in the right-left brain. The expectation is that "I," with *my* memories and *my* expectations, will attain liberation, or heaven or holiness, or the complete therapeutic fix, if only "I" can follow the prescribed method to perfection. This closed-circuit pattern seems to be what has contained us in cages of pettiness, violence, and fear as far back as we can collectively recall. However, anything that involves repetition of an act implies following a mechanical algorithm and therefore is not likely to break genuinely new ground. Mutation cannot take place without the unconditional cessation of the pattern of following authority in psychological-spiritual matters.

Specific, repetitive practices are always intrinsic to a conceptual structure that calls for following an authority. And following an authority always implies acceptance of two-valued logic, which arbitrarily divides *what is* into "me" and "not me." That is, the authority or system "I" follow is always outside of "me"; "my" job, or "my" quest is to move from where "I" am to where "not me"—the authority or system—will lead. "I" am *always* (by definition) located at the point in any valid logical argument where the premises can be found. The goal of the system is *always* (by definition) located at the point where the conclusion of any valid logical argument can be found. So moving from the premises to the conclusion implicit in the system-method creates the illusion that "I" am moving from "here" to "there" in time. The logic-bound set of procedures creates the illusion that "I" am getting "closer to the goal" and "making progress" along the lines laid out by the system as premises "I" have not yet fulfilled. However, unfortunately, since the whole scheme has been laid out by the analytical mind, it is impossible to ever reach the conclusion, the goal. In a logical argument, premises are always clearly distinct from the conclusions they are expected to lead to. Similarly, *no matter what I do*, my actions (premises, if you will) cannot become the goal (conclusions).

Despite the illusion that as "I" fulfill more "premises" I am closer to the conclusion, no time is actually involved in the process. The whole set of procedures from "premises" to "conclusion" is timelessly a logical unit. However, the system-method demands that "I" accept the time-dependent process as if it were real. After all, the authority asserts that it is real. This is a fragmentation within myself, and it makes wholeness impossible. And without wholeness there can be no real transformation—or liberation or heaven or holiness. As the etymology of *holiness* suggests, the religious life at its perennial best means "wholiness"—wholeness. Anything short of wholeness is at best only a predetermined, and inevitably failed, attempt at living the religious life in the deeper, perennial sense.

Engaging in specific practices that call for following authority means there is also an element of fear. One holds the picture of the ideal provided by the authority in the mind's eye in order to know what to do. So there is a lurking fear that one may fail to see what is the right thing to do—or worse, that having seen it, one cannot do it. As St. Paul said in a much-quoted passage (which is reminiscent of the Buddha's foundational understanding that "life is suffering, having what one does not want, and wanting what one does not have"):

> For the good that I would, I do not: But the evil which I would not, that I do.[5]

This dichotomy between "what is" and "what should be," with its inescapable implication of fear, K explored again and again over many decades. It is another instance of fragmentation. While such psychological divisions are burning inside a person, wholeness—or true religiousness—is not possible.

Huddling in Groups

Engaging in a practice also means participation in what seem in the end to be the rituals of a tribe. Belonging to an association or tradition that includes generations of now-dead practitioners, the many now living, and generations of future ones gives a feeling of safety. Sanctioning by one's actions such a structure of authority and tribal yearnings implies that one feels "safe" in that environment. Yet this sense of safety is ultimately false. It replicates the time-bound illusion that results whenever actual situations are made to fit into what is essentially the form of a valid logical argument. That false sense of safety disguises one's fear of truly dying to the known—of stepping into the unknown without a safety net at any level.

The sense of false security that comes from identification with a group represents another recursive, closed loop in the brain. Like all valid logical arguments, it moves from "here" to "there"—from the premise to the conclusion. Closed loops preclude wholeness. They provide an anchor for the "me," so freedom from "me," which is the signature of wholeness, becomes impossible. Closed loops characterize the ways we choose to remain where humanity has been for as long as human memory can recall. They are not the stuff that a real new era, the result of transformations at the individual level, is made of.

Proponents of some systems of thought and practice believe that self-knowing and transformation must take place in a group, and that attempts to bring these about by oneself are likely to lead to self-deception. This belief is an expression of the need for huddling together with others. Understanding *what is* does take place in relationship, and, as K pointed out on numerous occasions, when he spoke of aloneness he did not mean isolation. Transformation can only take place in the context of human relationship, since relationship is intrinsic to what a human being is, as discussed in chapter 9. Yet the fact that human life is life in relationship should not be confused with the penchant for tribal huddling, with its fears, hopes, expectations, and faith in some authority.

Major transformations in human life—identified throughout the world and for millennia with birth, sexual ecstasy, and death—do not take place in groups, but in aloneness. We do not experience birth or death together. Even in collective suicide, where people choose to die together, or in multiple births, one's death and birth are still one's own. Sexual experience, which can be a symbol and expression of transformation, does involve another person and as such, points to the fact that human life is lived in relationship. Human life is a series of networks of symbiotic relationships, as discussed in chapter 9. In sexual experience, one person's transformation necessarily touches another. So also, a person's birth or death touches others in various ways. One can discuss death with others or be present at the death of another.

Yet the act of transformation itself is an individual, not a group, experience. For instance, while discussing death with others and being present at someone's death have value, meeting death face to face—realizing the reality and proximity of one's own death—is what is critical. What matters is confronting the *mysterium tremendum et fascinans*. So also, mutation, by its very nature, is not a group effort. Discussing it with others can be of immense value. However, the moment meeting with others becomes routine or psychological necessity or a field for expectations or an arena for locking horns with others or a palliative for loneliness or a way to feel good about oneself by "doing good" or any other pattern that implies recursive loops, meeting becomes another realm for degeneration. The same may result from watching Krishnamurti videos or studying his work in groups. Such activities are not in themselves related to actual mutation.

The importance of meeting with others on a more or less regular basis (with grand religious, philosophical, or psychological expectations) may in fact be exaggerated. Existing religious organizations meet regularly, yet this does not seem to help much in keeping the various faithful from being at each others— throats, or stopping their members from feeling internal conflict over not being "good enough" practitioners. Groups in themselves are not necessarily transformative. Criminal gangs would be an extreme example of this point. Corporate boards of directors and political bodies also meet as a group, yet this does not make them more sensitive to the needs of humanity or the planet.

To meet with a purpose in mind is to project from where one is "now" to where one wants to be "later." A good example may be budget projection discussions at board meetings of large corporations and political subcommittees. Meeting with a future purpose in mind involves the "I," with its notions of "growing" and "getting better" through (re)actions performed in the context of "time." Such a perspective implies an insensitivity to *what is* at this very moment. It assumes arbitrarily, and based on presuppositions, what will be best. This insensitivity to the present seems to be at the root of all violence, whether it comes from a banana republic dictator, an abusive spouse, a CEO, a politician—or a spiritual discipline.

Searching in Wrong Places

Our quest for *what is*—that is, for the sacred—through any of innumerable systems, methods, and practices is reminiscent of a Sufi story of the *mula* Nassr Eddin. Once the *mula* was on his hands and knees, searching intently for something on the ground. A friend came by and inquired what the *mula* was searching for. Nassr Eddin said he had lost his key. The friend asked him whether he had lost it right where he was looking. Nassr Eddin replied, "No, I lost it over there. But it is easier to search for it here, where there is more light."

Perhaps we have searched for *what is* in so many ways and in all the wrong places because we do not trust our own capacity to explore and find it out for ourselves.

We do not seem to trust that the universe may already be put together in such a way that insight and compassion are intrinsic to it. Perhaps our "problem"—our seriously misplaced sense of where to search—amounts to a lack of faith, in a deep sense of the word. All methods, systems, and religions have been devised by human beings. Even if truly divinely inspired, they still were formulated by human brains, and human brains understand and follow them. Whatever may be of value—whatever is transformative—in any system or method is within our reach as individuals; for transformation may flourish even in the arid soil provided by systems and methods. Yet putting the emphasis of our trust in a system or method, or in an authority—rather than in transformation—is a way of avoiding the real search. Choiceless awareness from moment to moment is more difficult than following a method, just as Nassr Eddin thought it would be harder to find his key where it was, in the dark. But in fact, that may be the only place where the key to real transformation may be found.

The Theosophical classic *Light on the Path*—said to have been translated by one of the European perennial teachers connected with the Theosophical Society from an ancient manuscript used in India and Egypt—expresses it thus:

> Within you is the light of the world—the only light that can be shed upon the Path. If you are unable to perceive it within you, it is useless to look for it elsewhere.[6]

The human situation at the turn of the twenty-first century and beyond, with so many systems and methods now widely available (and new ones ever waiting in the wings), is reminiscent of a famous sermon of the Buddha recorded in the *Majjhima Nikaya*. As long as mutation has not taken place, the various systems may be distractions from the real problem, which is to remove the poison of conditioning from our being. As the Buddha said in response to a disciple who demanded analytical justifications for "questions that matter":

> It is as if, Malunkyaputta, a man had been wounded by an arrow thickly smeared with poison, and his friends and companions, his relatives and kinsfolk, were to procure for him a physician or surgeon; and the sick man were to say, "I will not have this arrow taken out until I have learnt whether the man who wounded me belonged to the warrior caste, or to the

Brahman caste, or to the agricultural caste, or to the menial caste."

Or again he were to say, "I will not have this arrow taken out until I have learnt the name of the man who wounded me, and to what clan he belongs. . . ."

That man would die, Malunkyaputta, without ever having learnt this.[7]

Similarly, a person who insists on continuing with certain types of practice and belief independently of mutation will most likely continue to degenerate. Steadfastly participating in a practice may give the impression of making progress because one is faithfully following the internal logic of the practice. But this may be because, for a conditioned brain, *any* logical structure is potentially pleasurable in that it can satisfy simultaneously the needs of the right and left brain. It leads to the "satisfaction" of "achieving a goal." So although the many practices that call for repetition have some value, they can mislead as long as yearning for satisfaction remains at some level. As K said:

> To possess and to be possessed is considered a form of love. This urge to possess, a person or a piece of property, is not merely the demands of society and circumstances but springs from a far deeper source. It comes from the depths of loneliness. Each one tries to fill this loneliness in different ways, drink, organized religion, belief, some form of activity and so on. All these are escapes but it's still there.
>
> To commit oneself to some organization, to some belief or action is to be possessed by them, negatively; and positively is to possess. The negative and positive possessiveness is doing good, changing the world and the so-called love. To control another,

to shape another in the name of love is the urge to possess; the urge to find security, safety in another and the comfort. Self-forgetfulness through another, through some activity makes for attachment. From this attachment, there's sorrow and despair and from this there is the reaction, to be detached. And from this contradiction of attachment and detachment arises conflict and frustration.

There's no escape from loneliness: it is a fact and escape from facts breeds confusion and sorrow.

But not to possess anything is an extraordinary state, not even to possess an idea, let alone a person or a thing. When idea, thought, takes root, it has already become a possession and then the war to be free begins. And this freedom is not freedom at all; it's only a reaction. Reactions take root and our life is the ground in which roots have grown. To cut all the roots, one by one, is a psychological absurdity. It cannot be done. Only the fact, loneliness, must be seen and then all other things fade away.[8]

The crises facing humanity at the turn of the twenty-first century and beyond seem to call for a deep, comprehensive transformation. Algorithms, whether of the past or the present, cannot bring about that kind of all-encompassing transformation, however much fleeting satisfaction they may bring at the individual or group levels. Though they may seem attractive, they all imply repetitive loops in the brain in terms of the logic-and-time-bound expectations of particular cultures, systems, or methods, and the acceptance of authority.

Of Blood-Rich Turnips

In case the above leaves the impression that there is

absolutely no place for approaches that use myths, systems, or methods, or promise therapeutic results, let it be said that these approaches may still have a place, though a limited one. A careful reading of the above will reveal that no blanket denial of their value has been made at any point. Contrary to the proverbial saying, it *is* possible to draw blood out of a turnip.

This is an era of major transitions. The perennial teachers have made the epoch-making decision to lay out in the open much that used to be hermetically sealed. Millions of people who otherwise would have had no inkling of anything perennial now have the opportunity to encounter it and appreciate its value—hence the current popularity of formerly secret approaches, such as meditation and the internalized appreciation for the real value of myth. Even drama, which began as a perennial mystery play to induce cathartic transformation in participants, is now widely available as a form of entertainment. In their original perennial context, these approaches were meant to invite transformation in various ways; but, as noted in chapter 1, the perennial teachers have now abandoned these as too limited. Now movement in a totally different direction is called for. There is now a sense of urgency for an all-encompassing transformation, given the present possibilities for global destruction.

In this context, the old approaches have value to a certain point, but they cannot bring about the kind of mutation the human condition presently requires. There is certainly no place for the old approaches in K's insights and observations. However, they may have a place as a transition from the overtly self-centered mainstream to the pursuit of radical mutation K spoke of.

An alchemical analogy may be appropriate here. Especially given that alchemy had mythological, meditational, therapeutic, and mystical connotations, besides scientific ones, the old perennial practice of alchemy may be able to help us find the best that might be drawn out of the old practices. In alchemy, *all* the lead put through the alchemical process is expected to turn to gold. So also, the whole "leaden" personality is expected to die to the known in order to give way to the "gold" of the ineffable. No alchemical text says that the lead is preserved intact while a layer of gold appears on the outside only. Yet any approach to transformation that falls short of total mutation seems to be settling for just that—a merely gilded brick of lead. But what the human condition is crying out for at the turn of the twenty-first century is the kind of radical dimensional switch Krishnamurti spoke of. As he put it in the *Notebook*, in a language intriguingly reminiscent of Wittgenstein:

> That which is sacred has no attributes. A stone in a temple, an image in a church, a symbol is not sacred. Man calls them sacred, something holy to be worshipped out of complicated urges, fears and longings. This "sacredness" is still within the field of thought; it is built up by thought and in thought there's nothing new or holy. Thought can put together the intricacies of systems, dogmas, beliefs, and the images, symbols, it projects are no more holy than the blueprints of a house or the design of a new aeroplane. All this is within the frontiers of thought and there is nothing sacred or mystical about all this. Thought is matter and it can be made into anything, ugly—beautiful.
>
> But there's a sacredness which is not of thought, nor of a feeling resuscitated by thought. It is not recognizable by thought nor can it be utilized by thought. Thought cannot formulate it. But there's a sacredness, untouched by any symbol or word. It is not communicable. It is a fact.
>
> A fact is to be seen and the seeing is not through the word. When a fact is interpreted, it ceases to be a fact; it becomes something entirely different. The seeing is of the highest importance. This seeing is out of time-space; it's immediate,

instantaneous. And what's seen is never the same again. There's no again or in the meantime.

This sacredness has no worshipper, the observer who meditates upon it. It's not in the market to be bought or sold. Like beauty, it cannot be seen through its opposite for it has no opposite.[9]

Mutation Calls for Discipline

Total mutation calls for seriousness and discipline. But there is a difference between this discipline, and discipline in the usual sense, which is not unlike the discipline of the military or martial arts. Discipline in the usual sense is an attempt to follow the logic-bound injunctions of a particular approach, to repeat given patterns, to follow algorithms of thought and behavior as faithfully as one can. The discipline required for total mutation, however, calls for constant awareness—being constantly on the alert, constantly learning, constantly researching into *that which is.*

This sort of intensity and one-pointedness may be reminiscent of Gurdjieff's Haida Yoga, which he reserved for special times, or the "week of weeks" known as Rohatsu in Zen monasteries.[10] However, these are mechanical disciplines, as noted above. Also, Haida Yoga and Rohatsu call for high levels of stress over short periods of time, whereas choiceless awareness is not subject to a context of either stress or no stress. Nor is its pursuit time-bound. No emotional pressure is needed for its manifestation. Emotional pressure involves a "me" experiencing the pressure and hoping to be released from it, either through achieving the intended result or through the practice simply ending. True, confronting the *mysterium tremendum et fascinans* is highly stressful, since one comes face to face with awesomeness. But this is not a contrived, thought-out stress such as that found in the formulas of systems and methods. Rather, it takes place unannounced, like a bolt from the sky.

It should be clarified that dying to the known is not an
attempt to be ruthlessly heroic with oneself. Any discipline of
heroism implies a seed of "I" who conceives of that discipline as
heroic. But dying to the known is a process in which the "I" fades
out. There is no sense of "me" attaining anything. There is the
insight that the observer *is* the observed, the thinker *is* the
thought—that the notion of "me" has been an illusion all along.
The illusion is related to the analytical mind's relentless assumption that *everything* follows the pattern of a logical argument.
When that illusion is seen for what it is, there is no longer an "I."
Such an insight implies choiceless awareness from moment to
moment. This is *not* an algorithm.

On the other hand, choiceless awareness from moment to
moment is an arduous thing. It is not dependent on associating or
not associating with others, or on following or not following a
practice. Dependence of any kind means there are recursive loops,
choreographed algorithms, patterns such as that of a logical argument. In choiceless awareness there is no dependency on anything at any level, so there is no moment at which time-bound
algorithms and formulas could arise. No quantity of following
methods or observing rules will ever do that for us. Nor will
"choiceless awareness" dispel the problem—if by that one means
a concept one has created in order to follow some practice one has
arbitrarily assumed corresponds with it. The word is not the
thing, K might say.

There is no blueprint for making the ways of choiceless
awareness amenable to the conditioned, self-centered mind.
Choiceless awareness can only take place in the context of mutation. It does not depend on the relatively easy path of following a
pattern. Choiceless awareness from moment to moment is the
most rigorous discipline there is. In fact, it redefines what discipline is really about.

Mutation Calls for Maturity and Seriousness

Krishnamurti's message asks us to bring a level of seriousness into our lives that most of us refuse to even consider. This may be the main reason why, in spite of his increasing influence in philosophical, educational, psychological, and religious circles, he has yet to make a greater impact. Most of us seem to want to have our cake and eat it too. We do not want to give up a certain amusement-park attitude toward life.

On the other hand, most of us want to be considered serious, particularly regarding our spiritual and philosophical standpoints. The idea that adhering to a particular spiritual or philosophical stance is by definition frivolous and violent is totally unacceptable to a mind that demands to be entertained, and to be considered serious for it. Yet this is precisely the definition of frivolous violence.

Our human situation, both individual and global, requires maturity if we are to live harmoniously within ourselves, with each other, and with this planet. Yet, as K pointed out, maturity does not come cheaply. Before real maturity is possible, one must die to the known at great depths:

> There is no end to depth; the essence of it is without time and space. It's not to be experienced; experience is such a tawdry thing, so easily got and so easily gone; thought cannot put it together nor can feeling make its way to it. These are silly and immature things. Maturity is not of time, a matter of age, nor does it come through influence and environment. It's not to be bought, neither the books nor the teachers and saviours, the one or the many, can ever create the right climate for this maturity. Maturity is not an end in itself; it comes into being without thought cultivating it, darkly, without meditation, unknowingly. There must be maturity, that ripening in life; not the ripeness that is bred out of disease and turmoil, sorrow and hope. Despair and labour cannot bring this total maturity but it must be there, unsought.

For in this total maturity there is austerity. Not the austerity of ashes and sackcloth but that casual and unpremeditated indifference to the things of the world, its virtues, its gods, its respectability, its hopes and values. These must be totally denied for that austerity which comes with aloneness. No influence of society or of culture can ever touch this aloneness. But it must be there, not conjured up by the brain, which is the child of time and influence. It must come thunderingly out of nowhere. And without it, there's no total maturity. Loneliness—the essence of self-pity and self-defence' and life in isolation, in myth, in knowledge and idea—is far away from aloneness; in them there is everlasting attempt to integrate and ever breaking apart. Aloneness is a life in which all influence has come to an end. It's this aloneness that is the essence of austerity.

But this austerity comes when the brain remains clear, undamaged by any psychological wounds that are caused through fear; conflict in any form destroys the sensitivity of the brain; ambition with its ruthlessness, with its ceaseless effort to become, wears down the subtle capacities of the brain; greed and envy make the brain heavy with content and weary with discontent. There must be alertness, without choice, an awareness in which all receiving and adjustment have ceased. Over-eating and indulgence in any form makes the body dull and stupefies the brain.

There is a flower by the wayside, a clear, bright thing open to the skies; the sun, the rains, the darkness of the night, the winds and thunder and the soil have gone into making that flower. But the flower is none of these things. It is the essence of all flowers. The freedom from authority, from envy,

fear, from loneliness will not bring about that aloneness, with its extraordinary austerity. It comes when
the brain is not looking for it; it comes when your
back is turned upon it. Then nothing can be added to
it or taken away from it. Then it has a life of its own,
a movement which is the essence of all life, without
time and space.

That benediction was there with great
peace.[11]

Perennial Transformation

The single most important object of the perennial teachers
for millennia has been to bring about a planetary transformation
based on individual mutation. Everything now known about the
ancient stalwarts of the perennial philosophy suggests that the
purpose of initiations—which are acts of dying to the known, that
is, to particular cultures, personal associations, and accepted patterns of belief—was to bring about this transformation. HPB's
teachers said that human consciousness is now ready for mutation on a grand scale, in accord with the condition of the human
psyche at this cyclical moment. That is, human grand cycles are
said to come about organically, as a result of great crises that cry
out for transformation. Human beings have shown throughout
history the resiliency to withstand many forms of oppression, as
well as the patience to put up with the notorious inadequacies of
systems. They have also shown they will tolerate oppressive inadequacies for just so long. At some point, they get "mad as hell and
won't take it any more." It is from the energy of that human
response that grand transformations come, according to HPB and
her teachers. It is in such a context that the Theosophical Society
was founded, to spark the perennial renaissance.

When the Theosophical Society was established in 1875, its
main object was "To form a nucleus of the universal brotherhood
of humanity, without distinction of race, creed, sex, caste, or

color." It should now be obvious that such a human fellowship is impossible without the kind of transformation that Krishnamurti spoke about. Global transformations in human consciousness happen as a result of mutations in individuals. As HPB said in her classic on the essence of esoterism:

> Let them know at once and remember always, that true Occultism or Theosophy is the "Great Renunciation of SELF," unconditionally and absolutely, in thought as in action. It is ALTRUISM, and it throws him who practises it out of calculation of the ranks of the living altogether. "Not for himself, but for the world he lives. . . . " No sooner is he accepted than his personality must disappear, and he has to become a mere beneficent force in Nature.[12]

Radha Burnier, seventh president of the Theosophical Society, expressed the need for transformation in the context of the organization's first object thus:

> There is a mystic quality in the realization of brotherhood; it is not an ordinary experience. When some people say that the Theosophical Society's object of universal brotherhood is obsolete, they do not know what they are saying. They look at it in a very ordinary sort of way, not understanding the depth and truth contained in this aim. They think there are many organizations which stand for international relations. The United Nations is meant to bring all the nations together. There are other humanistic movements. The idea has spread everywhere, so this object can be shunted away.
>
> But from the deeper point of view, universal brotherhood is far from realized, and nowhere do

we see brotherhood in action. Unless we see that this object implies a deep psychological revolution, we will not be able to carry out the work of the Society with the requisite energy. When human consciousness becomes free of its biases and barriers, if it ceases to separate itself from everything else, a new world of beauty, freedom and goodness will materialize at the physical and subtler levels. Krishnaji states, "Where the self is, beauty does not exist," the beauty that is goodness, peace and bliss. So, when we reflect well, it should not be difficult to realize that universal brotherhood without distinctions of any kind is a revolution in consciousness. It is the one thing which will change humanity, and bring it to a new level of existence.[13]

Further, the Society's motto, "There is no religion higher than truth," suggests that involvement in particular religions or other systems may be a distraction from a more authentic religious life. This was expressed unequivocally by the Master KH in a letter written in 1882:

Ignorance created Gods and cunning took advantage of the opportunity. Look at India and look at Christendom and Islam, at Judaism and Fetishism. It is priestly imposture that rendered these Gods so terrible to man; it is religion that makes of him the selfish bigot, the fanatic that hates all mankind out of his own sect without rendering him any better or more moral for it. It is belief in God and Gods that makes two-thirds of humanity the slaves of a handful of those who deceive them under the false pretence of saving them.

Is not man ever ready to commit any kind of evil if told that his God or Gods demand the crime—voluntary victim of an illusionary God, the abject slave of his crafty ministers? The Irish, Italian and Slavonian peasant will starve himself and see his family starving and naked to feed and clothe his padre and pope. For two thousand years India groaned under the weight of caste, Brahmins alone feeding on the fat of the land, and today the followers of Christ and those of Mahomet are cutting each other's throats in the names of and for the greater glory of their respective myths.

Remember the sum of human misery will never be diminished unto that day when the better portion of humanity destroys in the name of Truth, morality, and universal charity, the altars of their false gods.[14]

Each person shares in the responsibility for the condition of humankind and the planet. To remind us of this fact is said to be a main reason why there is a periodic avataric manifestation. But, as noted above, this happens only as a consequence of major human crises. As K put it most poignantly, shortly before he died:

The tears of all the world have produced the World Teacher.[15]

The presence of a world teacher always occurs at a landmark moment in the human psyche: there is a symbiotic relationship between the two (this is explored further in chapter 9). In that moment, humanity cries out for guidance, and guidance comes in the form of a world teacher. But, as noted in chapters 1 and 5, a teacher can only point the way. The arduous, mature, serious work of mutation implied in the teacher's message is each individual's responsibility.

Krishnamurti's message may well represent the finest expression so far of the true ends of the perennial philosophy throughout the ages. If he was the spokesperson for a major avataric moment in the human psyche, this clearly does not mean we should become his followers, place him on a pedestal, or create temples in his name. Worshipping him or his teaching, like worshipping anyone else, would be our own way of saying *ecce homo* and washing our hands of responsibility for the work that urgently needs to be done. K's insights and observations show that he was interested in helping bring about a new, transformed human being, one who would not set him or herself apart on account of race, sex, nationality, or religion, or become identified with certain teachers or ideologies—including the oxymoron that a Krishnamurti ideology would be.

CHAPTER NINE

Maitreya

MUCH OF WHAT HAS BEEN SAID IN THIS BOOK MAY be transcended. Particularly worthy of at least a second look is the notion of the perennial teachers, or Masters, especially in light of K's reluctance to use the terminology found in theosophical and theosophy-derived perennial renaissance sources, even though the Masters were a presence in his own life.

Masters

K's scathing attacks against the *notion* of Masters, in whatever form, is almost a trademark of his expositions. At the same time, with the passing of years his tendency to depersonalize and demythologize the Masters increased. His discussions of the subject late in his life were relatively few and took place only with very close friends and associates. What may not be as well known is that HPB behaved in a similar way in her attempts to tell her Victorian—and thus pre-Gurdjieff, pre-Alan Watts, pre-Zen, pre-Vajrayana, pre-Jung, and, lest we forget, pre-Krishnamurti—audience that thinking of the Masters as personas was a grievous error. She found that people had personalized the Masters, attempting to fit notions about them into conventional patterns of thinking and behavior. And she expressed regret for having spoken of what are actually non-conditioned states of awareness—which we all partake of at some level—as if those states referred to persons. So, even though she was the first to make the world aware of the existence of Masters who were not identified with a particular region or religion, she commented later:

[T]he reader must realize that the present writer entertains no desire to force such a belief on any one unwilling to accept it, let him be a layman or a theosophist. The attempt was foolishly made a few years back in all truth and sincerity, and—it has failed. More than this, the revered names were, from the first, so desecrated by friend and foe, that the once almost irresistible desire to bring the actual truth home to some who needed living *ideals* the most, has gradually weakened since then. It is now replaced by a passionate regret for having ever exhumed them from the twilight of legendary lore, into that of broad daylight.

The wise warning:

> Give not that which is holy unto the dogs,
> Neither cast ye your pearls before swine
> (Matt., vii, 6)

is now impressed in letters of fire on the heart of those guilty of having made of the "Masters" public property. Thus the wisdom of the Hindu-Buddhist allegorical teaching which says, "There can be no Mahatmas, no Arhats, during the Kaliyuga," is vindicated. That *which is not believed in, does not exist.* Arhats and Mahatmas having been declared by the majority of Western people as nonexistent, as a *fabrication*—do not exist for the unbelievers.[1]

We may understand better the efforts of both K and HPB to depersonalize the notion of the perennial teachers if we examine what a Master might be. In the process, we may also gain a different perspective on other perennial renaissance teachings and practices.

Examination of the nature of a Master may be enhanced by

first considering what a human being is, and so we will begin there. Aristotle's suggestion that humans are social animals may be richer than it appears on the surface.[2] Human beings may be related to one another in a way similar to ocean waves: they are separate from another yet also share a common substrate. If so, what we are calls for a more careful look than our usual conditioning leads us to believe. We tend to take for granted a kind of chasm between what we call "me" and what we assume to be "not me." And yet that alleged line of demarcation is very hard to find.

Considering ourselves simply as biological beings: In order to live we must inhale oxygen and other gases, drink liquids, and consume food. Are these substances part of "me" or part of "not me"? Whichever answer we come up with implies that we are different from what we normally think we are. If we answer that yes, they are part of "me," then "I" is, at minimum, part and parcel of the earth's biosphere. If the answer is no, we are saying either that there is no such thing as "me," or that "me" is not as "clear" a term as previously thought, since I can only exist dependent on those substances.

Language Limitations

The same apparent paradox seems to arise in every other aspect of human life. What seem to be paradoxes and contradictions may result from accepting two-valued logic as the only judge, and subject-predicate grammar as the only way of viewing, considering, and speaking about the world. Subject-predicate grammar has been analyzed and discussed rather intensely by philosophers, especially after G. W. Leibniz (1646-1716), and more particularly in the twentieth century. Their concern with this issue has not been with the fine points of syntax. Rather, they have been passionately interested in understanding what is the relationship, if any, between the way we organize our language and thoughts, and the way the world is put together. Aristotle (384-322 BC), for instance, assumed that because our thoughts are expressed in words (*logoi*) with logical connotations, therefore the world itself is put together "logically." That is, just as a logical argument moves from premises to conclusion, for Aristotle everything in the universe moves toward its "final cause"—that which each thing was meant to "fulfill."[3]

By the twentieth century all such metaphysical attributions to the logical structure of our grammar, and to words themselves, had been shown to have been either ludicrously false or, at best, grossly exaggerated. At the pinnacle of this movement was Ludwig Wittgenstein (1889-1951), for whom "the meaning of a word is its use."[4] That is, in order to know what a word means, the dictionary is—at best—of very limited use: one must actually "look" and see how the word is used. No word ever has either a univocal or a universal meaning. This is precisely part of what K meant when he said that "the word is not the thing"—an expression he used quite often.[5] That is, words do not have the grand metaphysical connotations generally attributed to them by those who have not *seen* ("looked," Wittgenstein would say) the value of words. As K said in a talk to school children:

> The word, the symbol has become an extraordinarily destructive thing for most of us, and of this we are unaware. Do you know what I mean by the symbol? The symbol is the shadow of truth. . . . The word, the symbol, the image, the idea is not the truth; but we worship the image, we revere the symbol, we give great significance to the word, and all this is very destructive; because then the word, the symbol, the image becomes all-important. That is how temples, churches, and the various organized religions with their symbols, beliefs, and dogmas, become factors which prevent the mind from going beyond and discovering the truth. So do not be caught up in words, in symbols, which automatically cultivate habit. Habit is a most destructive factor, because when you want to think creatively, habit comes in the way.[6]

Lack of awareness in the use of words gets in the way of creativity and spells degeneration. Similarly, the habitual use of subject-predicate sentences without awareness of their connotations creates further obstacles to seeing more clearly. Every sentence—every thought—implies the existence of a subject and a predicate. That is, a sentence always takes for granted that I—or you or they—is an actual, distinct entity, and that that entity performs some act that affects someone or something separate from that entity, something that is "not I."

The internal logic of subject-predicate discourse affirms a sense of division between "me" and "not me." If it were possible to think and communicate using a different universe of discourse with a different set of assumptions, we might see the apparent dichotomy for what it is: a particular logical way of structuring the world. Perhaps then the notion of a separation between "me" and "not me" would not have such a stranglehold on the understanding of *what is* for most human beings at this time.

Part of the problem may be that subject-predicate grammar will make sense and feel right as long as the split-brain dichotomy, with its numerous self-enclosed loops, continues to be dominant. Without a mutation away from accepting a subject-predicate grammar as applying to our psychological reality, the right-left brain dominance will continue to be *what is* for us. There will be no way out of the various predicaments—whether individual or global—that arise from unquestioned acceptance of a subject-predicate orientation.

For instance, is my field of perception (what I see, touch, hear, smell, my kinesthetic reactions, and so forth) part of "me" or not? If the answer is no, then there is either no such thing as "I," or else it refers to something more "fuzzy" than previously thought, for what I perceive would not be at all a part of what I am. It does not seem possible for "I" to exist except including my psychological state when I perceive. This sort of dualism between "perceiver" and "field of perception" leads us inevitably to blind alleys, as philosophers of many schools have discovered. It is a problem raised by philosophers from Descartes to Hume, and still very much with us.

The dualism of perceiver and perceived as a philosophical assumption has been largely based on a Newtonian model of the universe. But that model is now considered a special case within the larger purview of the universe as understood through quantum physics. The new model rejects dualism outright and asserts that the observer is an integral component of whatever observations are made. (This point, incidentally, is what prompted physicist David Bohm to seek out Krishnamurti. He was intrigued by K's assertion that the observer is the observed from a psychological standpoint, which was so similar to the insights of quantum physics.)

If one says that the observer is none other than the observed, one seems to be making the remarkable statement that there is no seam between what are considered "me" and "not me." This implies the provisional suspension, or "bracketing off," of some of the presuppositions of subject-predicate grammar, and is in keeping with the phenomenological approach. If there are no perceptions at any level, there seems to be no sense in which "me" has any meaning. On the other hand, acknowledging that there are perceptions in the context of the observer being the observed implies a lack of division, such as the one artificially created by the use of subject-predicate language. This in turn may be intimately related to the primacy of the brain's right-left dichotomy discussed in earlier chapters.

Perhaps as long as the assumptions of subject-predicate grammar are not questioned, the appearance of a "me" will continue, and that "me" will act as if hypnotized by the purely arbitrary notion that there is a separation between "me" and "not me." As in the double images used in psychological studies of perception and some of the images in M. C. Escher's art, what one sees may depend on what one concentrates upon.[7]

Perhaps all it takes to see that the observer is the observed is to switch to a mode of perception in which one is aware that the field of perception is within "me"—in fact, is "me." In this mode of perception, there is no "I" watching something "outside." Instead, there is a single, unitary field of being, as well as of perception. In that moment, the hypnotic-like mode of perception to which "I" am accustomed may disappear. It is possible to deepen this manner of perceiving such that not only the field of perception but other aspects of *what is*—aspects that are normally ignored—may become part of that seamless field.[8]

Memory Limitations

One may still insist on asserting the alleged reality of the separate entity "I." One can argue that "only *I* was born in a particular place and time, and only *I* have certain memories of experiences *I* have had; this makes *me* a separate entity." Yet memories are recollections of numerous instances when the field of observer-observed was present, and as we have seen, that field is in fact seamless, non-dual. Further, if the brain is trained—hypnotized—into accepting the notion of "me" versus "not me," from that unquestioned presupposition may come the notion that "my" memories may be different from "yours."

The way we talk about memories—the way we use language—also serves to affirm that "my" memories are "my own." Language is a communal medium; it has no meaning except as a social tool. A private language is not a language in any meaningful sense of the word, as Wittgenstein showed.[9] This brings us back to Aristotle's statement that humans are social animals. Ortega y Gasset expressed it this way: "I am I and my circumstances"—and my circumstances may include the entire universe as it is when I am.

The way we identify with our memories may also be related to the structure of the brain. Briefly, the brain is divided into right and left hemispheres, each of which has been divided by physiologists into four "lobes": the frontal, parietal, temporal, and occipital. Clinical studies have shown that most of our memory is located in the brain cortex (the brain "bark" or surface), and some of it is in the hippocampus, which is more interior and is part of the bilateral temporal lobes. The location of our memory grids makes them important components of the split brain, with its dichotomies and recursive loops and expectations that the world is necessarily divided into "me" and "not me."

If there were any truth to astrology, then each entity—human or otherwise—is born with an imprint determined by the position of the heavenly bodies at a particular time and place. But it is not necessary to appeal to the principles of a practice considered controversial, such as astrology; a metaphor of those principles would still be true. Each of us is a co-conspirator and co-creator with the rest of the universe by being born at the particular place and time and in the particular modality that will come to be known as "me." It can be said that we all live in a vast amniotic sac that makes life in the universe what it is from moment to moment. Or, from a different perspective, the universe is a vast network, in which every element is interdependent and co-creative with all the others in order to be what it is and do what it is there to do.

The Cell and I

William Irwin Thompson makes the same observation in his magnificent discussion of the origins of life in *Reimagination of the World*. In a brief comment on biologist Lynn Margulis's film on spirochetes (a type of bacteria) Thompson remarks on the origins of the cell as a separate entity as determined by its membrane—just as we might think of ourselves as separated from the environment by our skin:

> The origins of life require a membrane for the cell. . . . But how did the first cell in the origins of life achieve its membrane? It did so in concert with the entire surrounding environment, be it ocean, clay bed, or atmosphere. We know now, through the work of bacteriologists like Sorin Sonea at

Montreal, that bacteria are not really individuals in the way we think of individuals. They are social entities. In fact, Sonea prefers to call them a "super-organism," even "a planetary bioplasm."

Clearly, the membrane is a provisional and fuzzy definition of individuality; it is simply the locus of a chemical conversation. When you attempt to isolate a membrane, you find, once again, that it is fuzzy, porous and permeable, and "empty." Think of the Tao Te Ching: "Four walls bound a room. / But the purpose of the room / comes from the space that is not." We cannot conceive of the origins of life in an American way: that one day long ago an enter-prising fellow surrounded his private property with a fence to keep his neighbors out. We have to see life as a planetary concert.[10]

Like an individual bacterium—or a subatomic particle in a plasma physics chamber—the human self may be more "fuzzy" than the logic-bound requirements of the analytical mind demand. If so, the expectation that one can *define* the self in neat, dualistic categories—mind/matter, perceiver/perceived, phenom-enal/noumenal—may be as doctors say, "dead on arrival." Like other "things that matter" (to use Wittgenstein's expression), perhaps this issue cries out for total abandonment of any logic-bound, analytical expectations. As Thompson put it:

However, the fact that individuals always exist in relationships does not mean we should jump over to the flip side of rugged individualism to some kind of New Age fascism that says individuals will all be melted down into one gigantic planetary cell of the coming global brain. Long ago, the great Buddhist philosopher Nagarjuna corrected these errors of oscillating from absolutism to nihilism, from individualism to collectivism. What we see in Lynn's film is precisely what Nagarjuna explained as *pratityasamutpada*, or "dependent co-origination." The web of relationships among beings in Being is built out of real individuals, just as large numbers are founded on the very necessary value of the number one.[11]

Perhaps what is required in order to understand the self is not an analytical algorithm; Nagarjuna showed all these to be intrinsically inadequate.[12] It seems that nothing short of transformation in K's comprehensive sense can yield such deeper understanding.

A Symbiotic Universe

It seems possible that at least certain human beings might be able to live from moment to moment fully aware of the universe as a vast network of symbiotic relationships. For them, the time-bound notion of "me" as a separate entity would have no place. The world of discrete existences might be but one of many ways of being—and not the most fulfilling one at that. To return to an image used earlier, this comprehensive state of awareness would be like identifying with the entire ocean, including its depths and undercurrents, rather than with a particular wave on its surface, which would be the ordinary state of most people. The nature of this comprehensive awareness of *what is* from moment to moment cannot be adequately expressed in language, which is conditioning-bound and based on subject-predicate grammar.

According to the *Stanzas of Dzyan*, an ancient perennial text for which HPB's *Secret Doctrine* is largely a commentary, in this divine-like (theosophical) state of awareness

Time was not, for it lay asleep in the infinite bosom of duration.

Universal mind was not, for there were no ah-hi (celestial beings) to contain it.

The seven ways to bliss (nirvana, moksha) were not. The great causes of misery (nidanas) were not, for there was no one to produce and get ensnared by them.

The causes of existence had been done away with; the visible that was, and the invisible that is, rested in eternal non-being—the one being.

Alone, the one form of existence stretched boundless, infinite, causeless, in dreamless sleep; and life pulsated unconscious in universal space, throughout that all-presence, which is sensed by the opened eye of dangma (the highest adept).[13]

A Hero with a Thousand Faces

Even to call this "entity" who sees comprehensively "the highest adept" would seem to be a mistake since, at least from the standpoint of that entity, there would be no "me" to identify with. The psychological nature of such a being would possibly be closer to that of a network. And if one uses conventional language to speak of this being, the plural form might not be incorrect. David Spangler's discussion of this point is most enlightening:

> I have been speaking of incarnations as if they were specific points such as particles, atoms, entities, selves. That they possess such specificity is apparent. We live in a world of diversity, and each of us is a unique manifestation of that diversity. We are individuals.

However, we are also patterns of connection and interaction. Where do our selves begin and end? Many of the boundaries we imagine are cultural; some are biological; some are psychological. But each boundary can be transcended or, perhaps more appropriately, can be permeable to an exchange of being that turns it from a barrier into part of the architecture of a greater incarnation, a greater uniqueness.

We are what I call co-incarnates. Ultimately, only one thing really incarnates, and that is the multiverse itself; or, we might say that only God incarnates. Everything else is an aspect of that Incarnation. Or we could say we are all co-incarnating the ground of all being.

More specifically, each of us is who we are because of the contributions of many other people and beings with whom our lives have intersected. They have contributed to the overall pattern that we call ourselves. We are bundles of crossroads, each one a point at which some new or unexplored or unexpected aspect of ourselves emerged and became incorporated into our sense of identity. We would not exist as we are were it not for these contributions from others. They have co-incarnated us, and we have done the same for them.[14]

A similar view is found in José Argüelles's magnificent presentation of Mayan science. He reveals Quetzalcoatl not as an individual being, but as a plurality that found expression even in the culture-destroying conquistador Hernán Cortés:

It was clear that Quetzalcoatl was not just a god, but a multiple god; not just a man, but many men, not just a religion but a mythic complex, a mental structure. And it was also clear that this constellation of features, this multiple presence, informed almost every aspect of ancient Mexican and even Mayan Civilization. Not just the arts, but astronomy and the calendar were affected by Quetzalcoatl, who was strongly associated with the morning and evening star, the planet Venus.

Astronomical, celestial associations, as much as his role as a religious figure of the stature of a Moses or a Christ, brought Quetzalcoatl into prophetic prominence. So it was that the tenth-century 1 Reed, Quetzalcoatl, presumed founder of the City of Tula and revitalizer of Chichen Itza in Yucatan, having prophesied his return on the day 1 Reed, in the year 1 Reed, was vindicated by the arrival of Cortés on that very day, Good Friday on the Christian calendar, AD 1519.[15]

Similar myths of individuals manifesting themselves as a plurality can be found in other civilizations, for instance Proteus in ancient Greece (who could take on any form) and Krishna in the Hindu tradition (who might manifest as a lovely maiden, or as a deer). Of particular interest to Christians, Muslims, and Jews is the fact, revealed by HPB in several places and supported by rabbinical and Cabalistic scholarship, that the Hebrew word *Elohim*, translated as "God" in Christian and Jewish scripture, is in fact both feminine and plural.[16] The Bible thus should begin: "In the beginning, the female divinities created the heavens and the earth."

In one sense the notion of someone being simultaneously an individual and a network should not be difficult to understand, since the human body is precisely that—a collection of biological networks, each involved in its own processes. Here we are considering the possibility that someone—that is, a non-self-centered, unified field of awareness—could not only be more or less simultaneously aware of the many physiological networks that compose the organism, as it were, but also *be* such networks psychologically and spiritually. In that sense, it might be incorrect—or at least imprecise and misleading—to speak of *the* Master KH or *the* Lord Maitreya.

In a remarkable passage in the *Notebook* Krishnamurti addresses this very question, not as a speculation or proposition to consider, but as a reality in his own life:

> We [K and a friend] were going up the path of a steep wooded side of a mountain [in Switzerland] and presently sat on a bench. Suddenly, most unexpectedly that sacred benediction came upon us, the other felt it too, without our saying anything. As it several times filled a room, this time it seemed to cover the mountainside across the wide, extending valley and beyond the mountains. It was everywhere. All space seemed to disappear; what was far, the wide gap, the distant snow-covered peaks and the person sitting on the bench faded away. There was not one or two or many but only this immensity. The brain had lost all its responses; it was only an instrument of observation, it was seeing, not as the brain belonging to a particular person, but as a brain which is not conditioned by time-space, as the essence of all brains.[17]

Obviously, reading, talking, or thinking about this—as we are doing now—may be useful to a point, but is not of great help for deeper understanding. Such activities tend to imply unquestioned acceptance of subject-predicate grammatical forms and two-valued logic—such as observer/observed, me/not me—as if these reflected metaphysical realities. From such a self-enclosed perspective, it would seem contradictory or nonsensical to speak of someone being simultaneously a separate entity and a network. Analytical ballast imposes enormous psychological weight. Jettisoning that analytical ballast generates great energy and clarity, and with these resources research into deeper issues, such as what the *word* "Master" refers to, becomes a possibility—*but not before*. Concepts and reasoning are helpful only to the point where the mind sees its own incapacity and gives up on itself, thus allowing other, human-*cum*-universal resources to take over the task of understanding. After all, insight and understanding are nonverbal and so do not conform to the logic of subject-predicate strictures—even though the explanations that may come *after* the moment of understanding would use language.

This issue is at the heart of why the scientific community initially had a difficult time accepting quantum physics, for conceptualizing about the implications of quantum physics requires setting aside two-valued logic. For instance, according to quantum theory, the existence of any given particle cannot be absolutely determined; it can only be considered in terms of averages, since it is always part of an inseparable network of energy plasma. Thus, a particle can be in more than one place at a time, or can appear and disappear in a seemingly random manner—which are contradictory from the perspective of two-valued logic and subject-predicate grammar.

Words

It is very easy to assume one has a good understanding of what K meant by "the Beloved" or "Maitreya," or what HPB meant by "the Masters" by taking the words and explaining them according to preconceived notions and in terms of the conventions of ordinary language. An example of this occurs in Ingram Smith's short memoir of his association with K, *Truth Is a Pathless Land*. Like other writers about Krishnamurti who have prejudged anything theosophical about K's life, Smith recounts an incident in the belief that it demonstrates K's unqualified denial of the Masters' existence:

One evening Gordon Pearce came with us in the car. He had known Krishnaji from boyhood; indeed, ever since his uniqueness had been discovered, and he had lived in the Theosophical Society headquarters at Adyar. Pearce was in the front seat during the drive out of town, and there had been talk about those early days. Then, twisting right around to face Krishnaji in the back seat, he asked, "During that time with CWL, did you actually see the Master KH? Did you ever talk with Kuthumi?" I was greatly surprised when Krishnamurti replied, "Yes, I did." And so was Gordon Pearce, both of us having heard Krishnamurti discount Masters and teachers and gurus. And here he was admitting to an old and trusted friend that he had actually seen the Master Kuthumi, a nonphysical being. "Did you actually talk with him?" Gordon asked. "Yes," he answered, "sometimes during the early morning meditation."

Krishnaji went on to say that under Leadbeater's direction he rose at four o'clock in the traditional manner and meditated, and that sometimes Kuthumi was present and a conversation took place. Then one morning just after sunrise—Krishnamurti was seated in the lotus posture facing east—Kuthumi appeared in the doorway. Until that day, talking with KH had been enough. "That day I wanted more than talk. I wanted not only to feel his presence, hear his voice, but to actually touch him, to make sensual contact. Until that day he had been a voice, a presence standing in the doorway. It was a morning when the sun came clear into the room. Kuthumi was standing with his back to the light. I got up, walked to him and through him. I turned. There was no one there. He had disappeared. There was nothing there. And . . . I did not ever see him again."[18]

Incidentally, no theosophist or other person on record as having met KH and the other Masters or having received their letters ever said they were nonphysical beings, as Smith does in this passage. Making such a claim falls in the same category as saying that somebody one is talking to on the telephone is a nonphysical being because the person is not visible. Masters are said to be human beings with highly developed yogic abilities, such as telepathic audiovisual communication. Classic works on yoga, such as Patanjali's *Yoga Sutras* explain how these abilities may be acquired.

Smith uses this story to point out that K was denying the existence of Master KH, even though K said "Yes [he had met KH]." However, the way Smith has used the story tells more about Smith's presuppositions about the Masters than about K's perception of what actually took place. Smith may have been unaware that K had recounted this experience in one of his poems from the late 1920s. K's version has a very different sense:

> He was at the door of my room,
> I passed through Him.
>
> Purified, with a new song in my heart,
> I remain.
>
> He is before me forever.
> Look where I may, He is there.
> I see all things through Him.
>
> His glory has filled me and awakened a
> glory that I have never known.
>
> An eternal peace is my vision,
> Glorifying all things.
> He is ever before me.[19]

Smith's anecdote illustrates K's genuine lack of interest in persuading people to change the way they think, even regarding

misinterpretations of details about his own inner life. It also
shows how easily an unquestioning adherence to closed-loop,
conditioned thinking can betray, twist, or corrupt an intended
meaning.

Maitreya

It is interesting to consider the way K himself spoke about
Maitreya. He may have done this only once after the 1920s, since
he was generally emphatic about not describing or defining
aspects of his inner life—presumably to avoid providing grist for
the mind's mill. K was speaking with a Varanasi pandit friend,
professor Jagannath Upadhyaya of Benares Hindu College. The
professor mentioned that according to Swami Vishudhanand, a
prominent tantrika who had lived in Varanasi in the early 1900s,
there was an intimate relationship between secret tantric teachings and the inner teaching of the Theosophical Society. The professor said that soon after K's "discovery" the swami had spoken
to Annie Besant

> of the imminent coming of the Maitreya Bodhis-
> attva and his manifestation in a human body;
> according to the swami, the body chosen was that of
> Krishnamurti.[20]

In response, K said:

> The Maitreya cannot manifest, it would be like the
> sky manifesting. It is the teaching that manifests.[21]

K could not have made such a statement unless he felt
strongly that he knew who or what Maitreya is. His response is
also strikingly similar to a statement by HPB from the esoteric
Instructions:

"Planetary Spirits" [such as Maitreya] . . . incarnate
no longer in the universe [but nevertheless] . . .
appear on earth as Avataras [emphasis added].[22]

K's response is reminiscent of his early poetic writings, in
which he spoke of the Beloved as—much like the sky—seeming
to have a center everywhere and a circumference nowhere. He did
not say that there is no Maitreya or no Beloved, just as he was not
saying that there is no sky. In *The Immortal Friend* he described
the Beloved in a way reminiscent of Argüelles's description of
Quetzalcoatl as both singular and plural.

In the vale where the cloud hangs in loneliness
Searching the mountain for rest,
In the still smoke climbing heavenwards,
In the hamlet towards the setting sun,
In the thin wreaths of the fast disappearing clouds,
There thou will meet with my Beloved.

. . . The thunder among the mountains
Fills thy soul
With the strength
Of His voice.
In the roar of a vast city,
Through the shrill moan of swift passing vehicles,
In the throb of a distant engine,
Through the voices of the night,
The cry of sorrow,
The shout of joy,
Through the ugliness of anger,
Comes the voice of my Beloved.[23]

So the Beloved as described by K is "everywhere" while being "here." An important reason for such imprecision is that the moment one provides a description, what is said becomes fixed, a frozen, inert image, whereas what is described may be profoundly alive, in constant motion, multifaceted, and even multidimensional. This is much like the Buddhist saying: "If you see the Buddha on the road, kill him," or the similar but much less known statement from the Christian mystics: "If you see the Virgin, spit on her face." One of Hegel's most famous catch phrases might apply here: "All determination is negation."[24] Wittgenstein, in the process of creating a completely new way of doing philosophy, expressed it thus:

> There are, indeed, things that cannot be put into words. They make themselves manifest. They are what is mystical.
>
> ... My propositions serve as elucidations in the following way: anyone who understands me eventually recognizes them as nonsensical, when he has used them—as steps—to climb up beyond them. (He must, so to speak, throw away the ladder after he has climbed up it.)
>
> He must transcend these propositions, and then he will see the world aright.[25]

Inquiries into "things that matter" ultimately call for a mutation, in K's sense of the word, in the researcher. There does not seem to be any way around this. Language, concepts, and argumentation of any sort are ultimately not relevant to the investigation, and in fact will obstruct and prevent understanding. Such research calls for a spirit of tentativeness in which one does not know one's way about; the analytical mind cannot be part of it; tremendous restraint and discipline are required before one can even consider such an investigation. Perhaps the best that can be done in terms of language would be to keep in mind—paraphrasing Wittgenstein—that "Whereof one does not see, thereof one should not speak."[26]

The Avatar, Mutation, and Kundalini

At the beginning of a discussion with a small group in Brockwood Park in 1975—recorded in a brief passage in *Truth and Actuality*—Krishnamurti summarized his own understanding of the issues discussed in the present work. Mary Lutyens' first volume of memoirs on K had just come out, and someone commented that it "has caused much confusion and quite a lot of questions." This is understandable, since Lutyens' book contains numerous references to K's esoteric life, and most people interested in his work had thought he had nothing whatsoever to do with esoterism, either publicly or privately. K responded to the comment:

> Basically the question is: what is the relationship between the present K and the former K? (*laughter*). I should think very little. The basic question is, how was it that the boy who was found there, "discovered" as it was called, how was it that he was not conditioned at all from the beginning, though he was brought up in a very orthodox, traditional Brahmin family with its superstitions, arrogance and extraordinary religious sense of morality and so on? Why wasn't he conditioned then? And also later during those periods of the Masters, Initiations and so on—if you have read about it—why wasn't he conditioned? And what is the relationship between that person and the present person? Are you really interested in all this?

Audience: Yes.

K: I am not. The past is dead, buried and gone. I
don't know how to tackle this. One of the questions is about the Masters, as they are
explained not only in Theosophy but in the
Hindu tradition and in the Tibetan tradition,
which maintain that there is a Bodhisattva; and
that he manifests himself rarely and that is
called in Sanskrit Avatar, which means manifestation. This boy was discovered and prepared for that manifestation. And he went
through all kinds of things. And one question
that may be asked is, must others go through
the same process. Christopher Columbus discovered America with sailing boats in dangerous seas and so on, and must we go through all
that to go to America? You understand my
question? It is much simpler to go by air! That
is one question. How that boy was brought up
is totally irrelevant; what is relevant is the present teaching and nothing else.

There is a very ancient tradition about the
Bodhisattva that there is a state of consciousness, let me put it that way, which is the
essence of compassion. And when the world is
in chaos that essence of compassion manifests
itself. That is the whole idea behind the Avatar
and the Bodhisattva. And there are various
gradations, initiations, various Masters and so
on, and also there is the idea that when he
manifests all the others keep quiet. You understand? And that essence of compassion has
manifested at other times. What is important
in all this, if one may talk about it briefly, is:
can the mind passing through all kinds of expe-

riences, either imagined or real—because truth has nothing to do with experience, one cannot possibly experience truth, it is there, you can't experience it—but going through all those various imagined, illusory, or real states, can the mind be left unconditioned? The question is, can the mind be unconditioned always, not only in childhood. I wonder if you understand this question? That is the underlying problem or issue in this.

So as we say, all that is irrelevant. I do not know if you know anything about the ancient tradition of India and Tibet and of China and Japan, about the awakening of [a] certain energy, called Kundalini. There are now all over America, and in Europe, various groups trying to awaken their little energy called Kundalini. You have heard about all this, haven't you? And there are groups practising it. I saw one group on television where a man was teaching them how to awaken Kundalini, that energy, doing all kinds of tricks with all kinds of words and gestures—which all becomes so utterly meaningless and absurd. And there is apparently such an awakening, which I won't go into, because it is much too complex and probably it is not necessary or relevant.

So I think I have answered this question, haven't I?[27]

Perhaps the most outstanding quality of K's response is that, while confirming the richness of his inner life as document-ed in *The Years of Awakening*, K does not appeal to the expecta-tions of the mind or the emotions. He does not sensationalize his experiences related to the process—the awakening of kundalini, the initiations, or his mission as mouthpiece for Maitreya. His statement also shows his remarkable utter lack of interest in promoting himself, even while spelling out his position in the history of the perennial philosophy, and therefore in human history. Because it does not appeal to the mind or emotions, the statement must be read very carefully for what is it says and does not say. This would have been an excellent opportunity for K to deny any connection with the many esoteric happenings related in *The Years of Awakening*. Instead, he tacitly confirms them all, as he had done all along. And significantly, K made this statement publicly. It was not a conversation with close friends and associates, like many of his statements quoted in previous chapters.

K's response to the question provides a concise exposition of all the major issues examined at more length in the present work. He says that he did go through the initiations. This implies the reality of the perennial teachers and Maitreya—since they were the initiators—and his intimate relationship with them, as discussed in chapters 3 and 4. This implies further that he considered the Masters responsible for starting the theosophical movement.

His statement affirms that the Masters were in charge of his early psychological-spiritual experiences. This being so, then he is also saying that the Masters were a real presence in that period of the Theosophical Society's history, and that CWL and AB did commune with them. After all, CWL "discovered" K under the direction of the Masters and the Lord Maitreya. The first person to speak of the Masters was HPB, who was in contact with them for at least forty years, as documented in her biography and elsewhere. Over a period of fifty years, other people claimed to have had contact with the Masters, and many of these contacts were confirmed by HPB. Therefore, K's remarks help corroborate that the teachers of the perennial philosophy did create the theosophical movement in order to spearhead the many transformations that were to take place in the twentieth century.

The manifestation of the avatar would have been consid-

ered the centerpiece of those transformations. Leadbeater and
Besant spoke about it extensively as the first item on their agen-
da for theosophical work. They said that they promoted the coming of the avatar because the perennial teachers had asked them
to do so. Blavatsky also spoke and wrote about the coming of the
avatar in the twentieth century in order to usher in a new era—
though astonishingly, most theosophists seem not to be aware of
this. This, however, is an extensive subject requiring its own treat-
ment elsewhere.

K also states matter-of-factly that the boy Krishna had
been prepared for the manifestation of the avatar. Here he makes
no attempt to disconfirm the numerous statements in *The Years
of Awakening*—some of them in his own words—that he was the
vehicle for Maitreya. He also confirms what he had said elsewhere and what is noted in the present work: that an avatar may
be a manifestation that takes place at cyclically critical times in
response to the degenerated condition of humanity and the need
for regeneration.

K further mentions the awakening of kundalini as an integral part of his inner process. He makes a sharp distinction
between his own experience and what is usually marketed under
that name. This is reminiscent of a similar distinction HBP and
her teachers made in the esoteric *Instructions*, as discussed in
chapter 6, between their understanding of kundalini and what is
taught in tantric circles.

Also of interest is K's response to the question of the
relationship between the youth Krishna and the mature
Krishnamurti: that there was absence of conditioning from the
beginning of his life to the end. His statement that we need not
go through the arduous preparations and initiations that he and
countless others before him did also indicates that he considered
his experiences a landmark event in the history of the perennial
philosophy—which occurred, significantly, in the twentieth
century.

K also states unambiguously that the most important thing
is the transformation of our lives. He manages to communicate all

this in the imprecise (and therefore eminently clearer) language he typically used whenever he spoke of these matters. He appeals to a fact-finding faculty in us, rather than to the "me"-enhancing expectations of the dualistic brain cortex.

K states that discussion of all those psychic experiences is irrelevant—not that they did not happen. Unfortunately, this simple distinction has eluded the majority of people interested in K's life and work, including those who have written about them.

This statement of K's is also highly significant from the perspective of the history of the perennial philosophy, as well as the place of the perennial renaissance in the twentieth century and beyond. When he draws the analogy between his own case and Columbus's rough voyage and says it is no longer necessary for others to do the same, he is stating unequivocally that he *was* prepared for the mission as vehicle for the Lord Maitreya. Formerly, any candidate had to go through the cumbersome preparations and practices of initiation. But now, in the "new dispensation," all that has changed, and transformation can take place in a swifter manner.

K comments that when the avatar is manifesting no other teachings should be promoted, out of respect for the sacred presence of the perennial leadership. This implies a possible conflict between the work of the avatar and the teachings of the many gurus who have populated the twentieth century. Some of these gurus have claimed to be the avatar, sometimes even calling themselves "the World Teacher"—notwithstanding that this expression was coined in the theosophical milieu to refer exclusively to K's work. If the avatar was indeed giving out the keynote teaching of the new dispensation through Krishnamurti—as he himself stated—then anyone simultaneously teaching something else was obstructing the work of the perennial teachers by creating unnecessary distractions.

On the other hand, the work of such gurus and New Agers'even when it might seem misdirected in some respects—has contributed to an environment of interest in perennial issues that has allowed the cyclic avataric work to be carried out simultaneously worldwide. So they all have had a place. If "Maitreya" refers indeed to a cyclical moment in the consciousness of humanity and not exclusively to an individual, this would be true in a further sense: From the perspective of Maitreya as "a hero with a thousand faces," everyone living on earth during the avataric moment partakes of Maitreya in one form or another. So in a sense, the many "avatars" who have flourished since the first quarter of the twentieth century are indeed manifestations of Maitreya. Some might say that the Lord does indeed work in mysterious ways.

K's remarks confirm the main revelations of the present exploration, but he accomplishes this in a deliberately imprecise though simple and direct way. There is no emotionalism in his remarks, no sensationalism, even though what he was saying was astonishing. This manner of presentation is a trademark of his statements on the esoteric. He avoids pointing to something overtly or appealing to logical categories and the expectations of the conditioned mind, since these always yield confusion—never clarity—regarding deeper issues. This was discussed in chapter 8.

Spiritual Quicksand

Making things clear to the mind of course has its place and its value. But there is also a danger in spelling things out, for one may then believe that because something is clear to the analytical mind, one has a true and thorough understanding. That may be very far from the case.

Thus, while necessary in order to understand more clearly who Krishnamurti was, inquiries such as this one present a risk of stepping into a kind of spiritual quicksand. One must be careful not to construct a new point of view around which a religion or cult can form. Strange as it may sound, in some ways it may be better to examine the facts in the privacy of one's own understanding and not engage in discussions about them at all; for discussions tend to turn rapidly into fodder for the analytical mind's insatiable appetite. In terms of what really matters, an investigation of who K really was pales before the question of whether transformation is taking place in one's life.

The dangers implied in an exploration such as this one apply to anything that comes from the analytical mind. And *any* point of view concerning K's inner life is likely to come from such a mind. Assumptions that K did not have an esoteric life at all or that the Masters and Maitreya were merely visions come out of commitment to the conditioned mind, not to the facts. These opinions differ from the documented material provided here in that they have no basis in fact, for they ignore what K himself said about his esoteric life and the Masters. Hopefully the present study will be part of a new era of research into these issues, free of presuppositions one way or another. This study has been driven by a passion for the facts. If any presuppositions have inadvertently crept in, they can be corrected through constructive criticism of this research.

Regarding K's inner life, this study has been almost exclusively in the nature of reporting what took place as relayed by witnesses, including K prominently. An exception to this is that sometimes clarifications were called for and so were added, largely in the form of marshaling further facts the reader may not have been aware of. Despite the fascinating nature of what the facts reveal, no attempt has been made here to advance any *theory* about what it all might mean. If the facts presented here happen to clash with one's preconceptions, one will inevitably conclude that a theory is being advanced in this study. This may especially seem so in Part III. The careful reader will note, however, that the attempt here has been to try to understand the very strange phenomenon that K's life was. No assertions are made at any point pro or con any view or theory. A serious attempt to understand does not a theory make.

This discussion also is not intended to promote the notion that K actually was the vehicle for the manifestation of the avatar. Rather, its purpose is to make clear what K himself said about it. That investigation has led to the attempt to understand the notions of the Masters, Lord Maitreya, the perennial philosophy, theosophical history, the possible significance of the perennial renaissance, and what all this may mean for the future of humanity. Whether K was or was not the vehicle for Maitreya is a separate question, to be discussed elsewhere.

Maitreya: The Future of Humanity

Perhaps a word such as "Maitreya" refers more adequately not to an entity, whether networked or not, but to a cyclic moment of planetary history that is determined by what is going on in the network of human life. K seemed to suggest this in the passage from *Truth and Actuality* quoted above. And HPB observed:

> Cycles and epochs depend on consciousness. . . .
> Cycles are measured by the consciousness of
> humanity and not by Nature.[28]

This may be another way of saying that each of us has the potential to manifest anything that is humanly possible, including Maitreya. To the extent that there is movement away from the universe of subject-predicate discourse and toward unconditioned research into *what is*, perhaps a "manifestation" or expression of the world of Maitreya—of Christ, of Sri Krishna, of Quetzalcoatl—is possible in one's life, and therefore in the world at large. Perhaps moving in that direction is indispensable for understanding questions about the Masters and Maitreya. If so, moving toward this understanding means a radical mutation in the life of the researcher—and then questions and answers would seem of little value in the end. Such an understanding and the mutation it implies, which are what Krishnamurti suggested throughout his long life of teaching, seem to contain the key to a meaningful future for humanity.

We can easily see that identification with a particular race, ideology, or method is the definition of degeneration; so trying to convince others that what we identify with is "better" is actually an attempt to spread a psychological-spiritual cancer to all of humanity. If we put an emotional investment on a specific culture, there is degeneration *now*. If we identify with a particular religion, we are contributing to further segregation among us and to psychological turmoil within. That too is degeneration now. Because we continue to insist on such closed-loop identifications, the planet seems to be cracking and degeneration seems rampant all around us. The degeneration, Krishnamurti would point out, is our responsibility, and no one else's.

Any hope for a redeemed humanity can only come from a radical mutation away from all that. It seems it will not do to leave it for tomorrow, for our children to deal with. If there is no mutation *now*, our children's problems will be even greater. Like an avalanche, degeneration seems to follow the law of inertia and only increases in intensity and extent. The future of humanity turns out to be not a titillating intellectual theory about what will happen to us; rather it depends on what each of us does right now. If closed-loop identifications continue in our daily lives, then the future of humanity is further degeneration. The seeds of regeneration for humanity lie in radical extirpation of all forms of closed-loop identification in every aspect of our existence.

Perhaps the deeper meaning of Maitreya is also to be found in regeneration and its states of awareness.

NOTES

CHAPTER ONE: *The Perennial Philosophy*

1. Pupul Jayakar, *Krishnamurti: A Biography*, San Francisco: Harper & Row, 1986, pp. 46-47.

2. Stuart Holroyd, *Krishnamurti: The Man, the Mystery, and the Message*, Rockport, MA: Element, 1991, p. 18.

3. Jayakar, *Krishnamurti*, p. 57.

4. K. Paul Johnson, *The Masters Revealed: Madame Blavatsky and the Myth of the Great White Lodge*, Albany: State University of New York Press, 1994.

5. Henry Steel Olcott, *Old Diary Leaves: The True Story of the Theosophical Society*, 6 vols., Adyar: Theosophical Publishing House, 1941-1975 [1895-1935].

6. For Olcott's work as a psychic researcher, see Henry S. Olcott, *People from the Other World*, Rutland, VT: Charles E. Tuttle Co., 1972 [1875].

7. Geoffrey A. Barborka, *The Mahatmas and Their Letters*, Adyar: Theosophical Publishing House, 1973.

8. H. P. Blavatsky, *The Key to Theosophy*, Pasadena, CA: Theosophical University Press, 1947 [1889], p. 288.

9. Blavatsky, *The Key to Theosophy*, pp. 288, 289.

10. Gottfried de Purucker and Katherine Tingley, *H. P. Blavatsky: The Mystery*, San Diego: Point Loma Publications, 1974, pp. 12-14.

11. Philip Novak, *The Vision of Nietzsche*, Rockport, MA: Element, 1996, pp. 18-19. Nietzsche passages quoted are from Friedrich Nietzsche, *On the Genealogy of Morality: A Polemic*, translated by Maudemarie Clark and Alan J. Swensen, Indianapolis/Cambridge: Hackett, 1998 [1887], 1.10, 2.2, 2.24; and *The Gay Science*, translated

with commentary, by Walter Kaufmann, New York: Vintage, 1974 [1882], 285.

12. Rudolf Steiner, *Friedrich Nietzsche ein Kämpfer gegen seine Zeit*, Dornach: Rudolf Steiner, 1983 [1895].

13. Mary Lutyens, *Krishnamurti: The Years of Awakening*, New York: Farrar, Straus, and Giroux, 1975, p. 120.

14. Christmas Humphreys and Elsie Benjamin, eds., *The Mahatma Letters to A. P. Sinnett from the Mahatmas M. and K. H.*, transcribed and compiled by A. T. Barker, Adyar: Theosophical Publishing House, 1962 [1923], pp. 32-33.

15. James Webb, *The Occult Establishment*, La Salle, IL: Open Court, 1976, pp. 43-46, 53. See also Martin Green, *Prophets of a New Age: The Politics of Hope from the Eighteenth through the Twenty-First Centuries*, New York: Charles Scribner's Sons, 1992, pp. 64-65.

16. For HPB's influence in bringing about the New Age movement and her influence on culture in general, see her biography (which also provides an excellent introduction to the perennial philosophy and to HPB's influences after her death) by Sylvia Cranston, *HPB: The Extraordinary Life and Influence of Helena Blavatsky, Founder of the Modern Theosophical Movement*, New York: Tarcher/Putnam, 1993, particularly part 7, "The Century After"; see also the works of James Webb, *The Occult Underground*, La Salle, IL: Library Press/Open Court, 1974; *The Occult Establishment*, La Salle, IL: Open Court, 1976; and *The Harmonious Circle: The Lives and Work of G. I. Gurdjieff, P. D. Ouspensky, and Their Followers*, Boston: Shambhala, 1987.

17. Mohandas K. Gandhi, *An Autobiography: The Story of My Experiments with Truth*, Boston: Beacon Press, 1957 [1927, 1929]. See especially p. 68.

18. Aldous Huxley, *The Perennial Philosophy*, New York: Harper & Row, 1944.

19. Blavatsky, *Key to Theosophy*, pp. 4, 5.

20. Blavatsky, *Key to Theosophy*, pp. 7, 8-9.

21. Ken Wilber, *Grace and Grit: Spirituality and Healing in the Life and Death of Treya Killam* Wilber, Boston and London: Shambhala Publications, 1991, pp. 77-78.

22. J. Krishnamurti, *The Awakening of Intelligence*, New York:

Harper & Row, 1973, pp. 140, 141.

23. For the ages of the earth according to HPB and her scientist contemporaries, see Geoffrey Barborka, *The Peopling of the Earth: A Commentary on Archaic Records in the Secret Doctrine*, Wheaton, IL: Theosophical Publishing House, 1975, pp. 203, 205; and H. P. Blavatsky, *The Secret Doctrine*, 6 vols., Adyar: Theosophical Publishing House, vol. 4, p. 264.

24. Marilyn Ferguson, *The Aquarian Conspiracy*, Los Angeles: J. P. Tarcher, 1980.

25. Countess Constance Wachtmeister, for instance, gave many witnessed instances of *The Secret Doctrine* being written by someone other than HPB (who stayed with the Countess for several months, at the time of the writing). See Countess Constance Wachtmeister et al., *Reminiscences of H. P. Blavatsky and the Secret Doctrine*, Wheaton, IL: Quest, 1976. Other instances may also be found in Olcott's *Old Diary Leaves* (which, in a way, is itself a long, well-documented confirmation of such help); in Barborka, *The Mahatmas and Their Letters*; and in Cranston, *HPB*.

26. Alcyone [J. Krishnamurti], *At the Feet of the Master*, Wheaton, IL: Theosophical Publishing House, 1974 [1910], p. 1.

27. Mary Lutyens, *The Open Door*, London: John Murray, 1988, p. 148.

28. Holroyd, *Krishnamurti: The Man, the Mystery and the Message*; Peter Michel, *Krishnamurti—Love and Freedom: Approaching a Mystery*, Woodside, CA: Bluestar, 1995.

29. Evelyne Blau, *Krishnamurti: 100 Years*, New York: Stewart, Tabori, & Chang, 1995, p. 270.

30. For a good discussion of Otto's notion of the *mysterium tremendum et fascinans* in the context of twentieth-century theology, see Merold Westphal, *God, Guilt, and Death: An Existential Phenomenology of Religion*, Bloomington: Indiana University Press, 1987 [1984].

31. Mary Lutyens, *Krishnamurti: The Years of Fulfilment*, New York: Farrar, Straus, & Giroux, 1983, pp. 224-25.

32. Lutyens, *Years of Fulfilment*, pp. 228-29.

33. For a more thorough exploration of the transformative

essence of the teaching of Theosophy, see Aryel Sanat, *The Secret Doctrine, Krishnamurti, and Transformation*, Arlington, VA: Fenix, 2000, [1993]; and Aryel Sanat, *Transformation: Vital Essence of the Secret Doctrine*, Arlington, VA: Fenix, 2000 [1998].

CHAPTER TWO: *A New Perspective*

1. See, for instance, Laurence J. Bendit and Phoebe D. Bendit, *The Etheric Body of Man: The Bridge of Consciousness*, Wheaton, IL: Quest, 1982 [1977]; H. Tudor Edmunds, ed., *Psychism and the Unconscious Mind: Collected Articles from the Science Group Journal of the English Theosophical Research Centre*, Wheaton, IL: Quest, 1968; Nicholas M. Regush, ed., *The Human Aura*, New York: Berkley, 1974; Andrija Puharich, *Beyond Telepathy*, Garden City, NY: Anchor, 1973 [1962]; Shafica Karagulla, M.D., *Breakthrough to Creativity: Your Higher Sense Perception*, Santa Monica, CA: DeVorss, 1973 [1967]; and Anodea Judith, *Wheels of Life: A User's Guide to the Chakra System*, St. Paul, MN: Llewellyn, 1989 [1987].

For earlier expositions on the subject, see Dr. Walter J. Kilner, *The Aura*, (originally *The Human Atmosphere*), illustrated, New York: Weiser, 1973 [1911]; A. E. Powell, *The Etheric Double* and *Allied Phenomena*, Wheaton, IL: Quest, 1969 [1925]; and A. E. Powell, *The Astral Body*, Wheaton, IL: Quest, 1972 [1927].

The best contemporary exposition of the subject can be found in Dora van Gelder Kunz, *The Personal Aura*, Wheaton, IL: Quest, 1991.

The classic that started all of this literature was C. W. Leadbeater's illustrated *Man Visible and Invisible: Examples of Different Types of Men as Seen by Means of Trained Clairvoyance*, Wheaton, IL: Quest, 1971 [1902].

2. For references to the chakra-kundalini energy patterns (under different names and conceptual frameworks, of course) in all the major civilizations, see, for instance, Rosalyn L. Bruyere, *Wheels of Light: A Study of the Chakras*, edited by Jeanne Farrens, Sierra Madre, CA: Bon, 1989. For the teaching in China, see Lu K'uan Yu, (Charles Luk) *Taoist Yoga: Alchemy and Immortality*, New York: Weiser, 1973 [1970]. For the teaching in Egypt, see the very extensive work of R. A. and Isha Schwaller de Lubicz, such as *Sacred Science: The King of Pharaonic Theocracy*, Rochester, VT: Inner Traditions International, 1981; and *Her-Bak: The Living Face of Ancient Egypt*, Rochester, VT: Inner Traditions International, 1981; see also C. W. Leadbeater, *The*

Hidden Life in Freemasonry, Adyar: Theosophical Publishing House, 1963 [1926]. For references in ancient North America, see Frank Waters, *Book of the Hopi*, New York: Penguin, 1985. For the teaching among the Mayans, see José Argüelles, *The Mayan Factor: Path Beyond Technology*, Santa Fe, NM: Bear & Co., 1987. For the teaching in sixteenth and seventeenth century Europe, see C. W. Leadbeater, *The Chakras: A Monograph*, Wheaton, IL: Quest, 1974 [1927].

3. Unfortunately, the subject of the reality of kundalini and the chakras has been obscured and confused by the rampant gullibility and exploitation connected with this and related subjects. Christopher Hills addresses this issue most eloquently in his sobering "Is Kundalini Real?" in *Nuclear Evolution*, Boulder Creek, CA: Trees Press, 1977; reprinted in John White, ed., *Kundalini, Evolution, and Enlightenment*, New York: Paragon House, 1990 [1979]. White's anthology is essential reading for anyone interested in these topics.

4. See, for instance, Carol Ritberger, *Your Personality, Your Health: Connecting Personality with the Human Energy System, Chakras, and Wellness*, Carlsbad, CA: Hays House, 1998.

5. For subtle material patterns of thought and emotions as seen by a trained clairvoyant, see, for instance: Annie Besant and C. W. Leadbeater, *Thought Forms*, Wheaton, IL: Quest, 1971 [1901].

6. Arthur Avalon (Sir John Woodroffe), *The Serpent Power: Being the Sat-Cakra-Nirupana and Paduka-Pancaka* (Two works on laya-yoga, translated from the Sanskrit, with introduction and commentary), New York: Dover, 1974 [1919], p. 326.

7. Avalon, *The Serpent Power*, pp. 346-47.

8. For excellent expositions of the Chinese understanding of subtler energies, see any of the many works by Dr. Yang Jwing-Ming, all published by Yang's Martial Arts Association in Jamaica Plain, MA (except as noted), including *The Eight Pieces of Brocade (Ba Duann Gin): A Wai Dan Chi Kung Exercise Set for Improving and Maintaining Health*, 1988; *The Root of Chinese Chi Kung: The Secrets of Chi Kung Training*, 1989; *Chi Kung Health and Martial Arts*, 1988 [1985]; and *Yang Style Tai Chi Chuan*, Burbank, CA: Unique Publications, 1982.

9. See, for instance, Manfred Porkert with Christian Ullmann, *Chinese Medicine*, New York: Henry Holt, 1990 [1982]; see also Harriet Beinfield and Efrem Korngold, *Between Heaven and Earth: A Guide to Chinese Medicine*, New York: Ballantine, 1991.

10. For the effectiveness of Chinese healing where medicine based on European metaphysics (such as that practiced in America) has failed, see the works of Dean Black, such as *Health at the Crossroads*, Springville, UT: Tapestry Press, 1988, which includes good additional references.

11. For Taoist yoga, see, for instance, Lu K'uan Yu (Charles Luk), *Taoist Yoga*; see also the numerous works by Mantak and Maneewan Chia, such as *Chi Nei Tsang: Internal Organs Chi Massage*, Huntington, NY: Healing Tao Books, 1991 [1990].

12. See, for instance, Mantak and Maneewan Chia, *Chi Nei Tsang*, and other works. See also the works by Dr. Yang Jwing-Ming cited above.

13. C. W. Leadbeater and Annie Besant, *The Lives of Alcyone: A Clairvoyant Investigation of the Lives throughout the Ages of a Large Band of Servers*, Adyar: Theosophical Publishing House, 1924.

14. Annie Besant and C.W. Leadbeater, *Occult Chemistry*, London: Theosophical Publishing House, 1919.

15. E. Lester Smith and V. Wallace Slater, *The Field of Occult Chemistry*, 2nd ed., London: Theosophical Publishing House, 1954, pp. 59-60.

16. Stephen M. Phillips, *Extrasensory Perception of Quarks*, Wheaton: Theosophical Publishing House, 1980.

17. Article by Stephen M. Phillips in *The Theosophist*, October 1978.

18. J. Moss and K. L. Johnson, quoted in *Communion*, September 1974, p. 2. For more recent research into the aura, see, for instance, Kunz, *The Personal Aura*, which includes a bibliography.

19. For an example of the worldwide appeal of CWL's way of explaining these subtler energies, see, for instance, Ustad Saheb Beramshaw N. Shroff, *Khvarenangh Khoreh Aura*, vol. 4 of *What Every Zarathustrian Should Understand, Advanced Series*, Bombay: Mazdayasnie Monasterie, 1980. This work (as well as others in the series) includes reproductions of CWL's descriptions of the aura, as well as theosophical explanations of the subtler energies and comparisons with non-Zoroastrian ways of describing them, such as the Chinese and the Hindu. The Parsees, like the Hindus and the Buddhists, experienced a renaissance at the end of the nineteenth century and well into the

twentieth, as a result of the work of HPB and of those who followed in her footsteps.

20. Leadbeater, *The Chakras*, pp. 1-4.

21. For CWL's influence on Kandinsky, see, for instance, Wassily Kandinsky, *Concerning the Spiritual Art: And Painting in Particular*, New York: George Wittenborn, 1963 [1912]. For Agnes Pelton (as well as the major figures in twentieth-century art), see Gail Levin and Marianne Lorenz, *Theme and Improvisation: Kandinsky and the American Avant-Garde 1912-1950 (An Exhibition Organized by the Dayton Art Institute)*, Boston, Toronto, and London: Bulfinch Press, 1992. See also Kathleen Regier, *The Spiritual Image in Modern Art*, Wheaton, IL: Quest, 1987.

22. For clairvoyants subsequent to Leadbeater who have corroborated substantial aspects of his perceptions, see the numerous works by Geoffrey Hodson, all published by the Theosophical Publishing House, Adyar, including *The Miracle of Birth: A Clairvoyant Study of Prenatal Life*, 1960 [1929]; *The Kingdom of the Gods*, 1972 [1952]; *Music Forms: Superphysical Effects of Music Clairvoyantly Observed*, 1976. For more recent research, see works by Dora van Gelder Kunz, such as *The Chakras and the Human Energy Fields* (with Shafica Karagulla), Wheaton, IL: Quest, 1989.

23. White, *Kundalini, Evolution, and Enlightenment*, p. 21.

24. See Bruyere, *Wheels of Light*, and Judith, *Wheels of Life*.

25. Leadbeater, *The Chakras*, pp. 27-31.

26. Communications from several of those present, including Dr. David Bohm.

27. Mary Lutyens, *Krishnamurti: The Years of Awakening*, New York: Farrar, Straus, and Giroux, 1975, p. 21.

28. For Kunz's diagnostic work with doctors, see, for instance, Karagulla, *Breakthrough to Creativity* where she is called "Diane" to protect Kunz's privacy.

29. Dora Kunz, "The Early Leaders of the Theosophical Society," *The American Theosophist*, Late Summer 1995.

CHAPTER THREE: *Mutation*

1. Mary Lutyens, *Krishnamurti: The Years of Fulfilment*, New

York: Farrar, Straus, and Giroux, 1983, p. 225.

2. For Besant on transformation, see Mary Jane Newcomb, *Personal Transformation in the Tradition of Annie Besant: A Study Course*, Wheaton: Department of Education, Theosophical Society in America, 1990, which also includes an extensive bibliography.

3. J. Krishnamurti, *The Collected Works of J. Krishnamurti*, 15 vols., Dubuque, IA: Kendall/Hunt, vol. 1, 1933-1934, p. 172.

4. Mary Lutyens, *Krishnamurti: The Years of Awakening*, New York: Farrar, Straus, and Giroux, 1975, p. 147.

5. Lutyens, *Years of Awakening*, p. 152.

6. J. Krishnamurti, *Krishnamurti's Notebook*, New York: Harper & Row, 1976, p. 16.

7. Krishnamurti, *Notebook*, p. 9.

8. Pupul Jayakar, *Krishnamurti: A Biography*, San Francisco: Harper & Row, 1986, p. 242.

9. Lucy Lidell, with Narayani and Giris Rabinovitch, *The Sivananda Companion to Yoga*, New York: Simon & Schuster, 1987 [1983], p. 71.

10. Jayakar, *Krishnamurti*, p. 243.

11. Lutyens, *Years of Fulfilment*, pp. 107-8.

12. For an account of K's abilities as a healer, see Vimala Thakar, *On an Eternal Voyage*, Ahmedabad: New Order, 1969.

13. J. Krishnamurti and David Bohm, *The Future of Humanity: A Conversation*, San Francisco: Harper & Row, 1986, pp. 2-3.

14. Deepak Chopra, *Ageless Body, Timeless Mind: The Quantum Alternative to Growing Old*, New York: Harmony, 1993, p. 244.

15. James Lovelock, *The Ages of Gaia: A Biography of Our Living Earth*, New York: Bantam, 1990 [1988], p. 153.

16. For outlines of some of the research into cycles, see, for instance, Gay Gaer Luce, *Body Time: Physiological Rhythms*, New York: Pantheon, 1971; Ritchie R. Ward, *The Living Clocks*, New York: Mentor, 1972 [1971]; and Michel Gauquelin, *The Cosmic Clocks*, Chicago: Henry Regnery, 1967.

17. John White, ed., *The Meeting of Science and Spirit: Guidelines for a New Age*, New York: Paragon, 1990, pp. 13-14.

18. Chopra, *Ageless Body, Timeless Mind*, pp. 4-6.

19. For HPB on new and important cycles beginning in the twentieth century, see, for instance, H. P. Blavatsky, *The Secret Doctrine*, 6 vols., Adyar: Theosophical Publishing House, 1971 [1888], vol. 1, pp. 64-65, vol. 2, pp. 335-337, and vol. 5, pp. 465-66; see also H. P. Blavatsky, *Collected Writings*, vol. 8, Adyar: Theosophical Publishing House, 1960, p. 174 fn.; vol. 12, Wheaton, 1980, p. 384 and pp. 600-1; and H. P. Blavatsky, *The Original Programme of the Theosophical Society and Preliminary Memorandum of the Esoteric Section*, Adyar: Theosophical Publishing House, 1966 [1886, 1888], p. 71. See also Christmas Humphreys and Elsie Benjamin, eds., *The Mahatma Letters to A. P. Sinnett*, transcribed and compiled by A. T. Barker, Adyar: Theosophical Publishing House, 1962 [1923], 3rd and rev. ed., p. 145, and numerous other references.

20. Annie Besant, *A Study in Consciousness: A Contribution to the Science of Psychology*, Adyar: Theosophical Publishing House, 1972 [1904], p. 171.

21. For the central place of transformation (another way of saying "dying to the known") in the original theosophical teaching, see Aryel Sanat, T*he Secret Doctrine, Krishnamurti, and Transformation*, Arlington, VA: Fenix 2000, [1993]; and Aryel Sanat, *Transformation: Vital Essence of the Secret Doctrine*, Arlington, VA: Fenix, 2000 [1998].

22. For an excellent example of the conceptual nature of theosophy as it was understood at the time, see, for instance, the series of lectures delivered in 1909 and later published by C. Jinarajadasa, *First Principles of Theosophy*, Adyar: Theosophical Publishing House, 1967 [1921], particularly the chapters "The Inner Government of the World," "The Path of Discipleship," and "God's Plan, Which is Evolution"; for a later exposition of the conceptual understanding of theosophy, see, for instance, Geoffrey A. Barborka, *The Divine Plan*, Adyar: Theosophical Publishing House, 1972 [1961].

23. Krishnamurti and Bohm, *The Future of Humanity*, p. 3.

24. Krishnamurti, *Notebook*, p. 11.

25. Krishnamurti, *Notebook*, p. 6.

26. For K on the writing of *At the Feet of the Master*, see Rom

Landau, *God is My Adventure*, London: Faber and Faber, 1941, pp. 262-63.

27. Alcyone [J. Krishnamurti], *At the Feet of the Master*, Wheaton: Theosophical Publishing House, 1974 [1910], pp. 12-13.

28. Gopi Krishna, *Kundalini: The Evolutionary Energy in Man*, Berkeley: Shambhala, 1971.

29. On children developing clairvoyance spontaneously: personal communication from Geoffrey Hodson.

30. See C. W. Leadbeater, *The Chakras: A Monograph*, Wheaton: Quest, 1974 [1927], p. 117.

31. Lutyens, *Years of Awakening*, p. 158. The original texts of this description of the process by K and the account by his brother Nitya quoted later in this chapter are in the Adyar Archives, but reference is made to either Lutyens or Jayakar, since these sources are readily accessible.

32. Radha Rajagopal Sloss, *Lives in the Shadow with J. Krishnamurti*, London: Bloomsbury, 1991.

33. See Erna Lilliefelt, *KFA History: Report on the Formation of Krishnamurti Foundation of America and the Lawsuits Which Took Place between 1968 and 1986 to Recover Assets for Krishnamurti's Work*, Ojai: Krishnamurti Foundation of America, 1995; and Mary Lutyens, *Krishnamurti and the Rajagopals*, Ojai, CA: Krishnamurti Foundation of America, 1996. Transcripts of two tape-recorded conversations between Krishnamurti and KFA trustees, on January 9 and March 1, 1972, are available at the Krishnamurti Archives, Ojai, Krishnamurti Foundation of America. The main points of these references are summarized in *Statement by the Krishnamurti Foundation of America about the Radha Sloss Book, Lives in the Shadow with J. Krishnamurti*, Ojai: Krishnamurti Foundation of America, 1995 (no author).

34. Lutyens, *Krishnamurti and the Rajagopals*, p. 16.

35. Lutyens, *Krishnamurti and the Rajagopals*, p. 16.

36. H. P. Blavatsky, "On Pseudo-Theosophy," *Lucifer*, vol. IV, No. 19 (March 1889) pp. 1-12; see also *Collected Writings*, vol. 11, pp. 55-56.

37. C. W. Leadbeater, *The Inner Life*, 2 vols., Wheaton: Theosophical Publishing House, 1967 [1911], vol. 2, p. 132.

38. For K's discussions of the relationship between a thinker and thought, see the following works by J. Krishnamurti: *The First and Last Freedom*, San Francisco: HarperSanFrancisco, 1975 [1954], pp. 30-33, 108-10, 140-42; *Commentaries on Living: From the Notebooks of J. Krishnamurti*, second series, Wheaton: Quest, 1981 [1958], pp. 25-27, 63-67; and *The Awakening of Intelligence*, New York: Harper & Row, 1973, pp. 30-33. For the observer being the observed, see *First and Last Freedom*, pp. 170-171, 174-176; *Commentaries*, second series, pp. 116-18; and *The Only Revolution*, London: Victor Gollancz, 1970, pp. 107-14.

39. See, for instance, J. Krishnamurti and David Bohm, *The Ending of Time*, San Francisco: Harper & Row, 1985; also available on audiotapes as *Krishnamurti and Dr. David Bohm: 1980 Dialogues*, Krishnamurti Foundation of America, 1980.

40. J. Krishnamurti, *The Wholeness of Life*, New York: Harper & Row, 1979, pp. 114-16; also available on the videotape series *The Transformation of Man*, Ojai: Krishnamurti Foundation of America, 1976.

41. Lutyens, *Years of Awakening*, pp. 156-57. See also endnote 31.

42. Mary Lutyens in *Krishnamurti: With a Silent Mind*, a film by Michael Mendizza on videotape, Ojai: Krishnamurti Foundation of America, 1989.

CHAPTER FOUR: *Initiation*

1. For different names for the same avatar, see, for instance, "Kalki Avatar" in H. P. Blavatsky, *The Theosophical Glossary*, Los Angeles: The Theosophy Company, 1966 [1892].

2. See for instance, James Webb, *The Occult Underground*, La Salle, IL: Library Press/Open Court, 1976 [1974]; and *The Harmonious Circle: The Lives and Work of G. I. Gurdjieff, P. D. Ouspensky, and Their Followers*, Boston: Shambhala, 1987.

3. See James Webb, *Occult Establishment*, La Salle, IL: Library Press/Open Court, 1976.

4. Martin Heidegger, *Being and Time*, translated by John Macquarrie and Edward Robinson, San Francisco: Harper San Francisco, 1962 [1927]. His discussion of inauthenticity runs through the whole

text, but see especially pp. 175-78.

5. For America's perennial roots from secret societies such as the Rosicrucians in Europe and the original Americans, notably the Iroquois, see, for instance, Robert Hieronimus, *America's Secret Destiny: Spiritual Vision and the Founding of a Nation*, Rochester, VT: Destiny Books, 1989, which includes an excellent bibliography.

6. For evidence of perennial work in Europe during the Renaissance, the Reformation, and the Enlightenment in preparation for the creation of the new society, see for instance, the works of Frances A. Yates, such as *The Rosicrucian Enlightenment*, London and New York: Ark Paperbacks, 1986 [1972]; and *Giordano Bruno and the Hermetic Tradition*, New York: Vintage Books, 1969 [1964]. See also Peter Dawkins, *The Great Vision*, Coventry: Francis Bacon Research Trust, 1985.

7. For K's discussion of the need to create a good society, see for instance his 1979 Oak Grove Talks, available on audio cassettes, Krishnamurti Foundation of America, Ojai, California.

8. HPB even had scars from wounds received at the battle of Mentana while riding with Giuseppe Garibaldi, who had perennial connections. See Sylvia Cranston, *HPB: The Extraordinary Life and Influence of Helena Blavatsky, Founder of the Modern Theosophical Movement*, New York: Tarcher/Putnam, 1993, pp. 78-79.

9. Edwin Bernbaum, *The Way to Shambhala*, Garden City, NY: Anchor, 1980, p. 82.

10. H. P. Blavatsky, "Forlorn Hopes," *Lucifer*, vol. 7, no. 4, December, 1890, p. 268; H. P. Blavatsky, *Collected Writings*, vol. 12, 1987 [1980], p. 387. For HPB's discussion of the relevance of the *Vishnu Purana* to the perennial teaching on the world teacher, see H. P. Blavatsky, *The Secret Doctrine*, vol. 5, Adyar: Theosophical Publishing House, 1971, pp. 336-39.

11. For the "seven keys" in which the teaching is given, see for instance H. P. Blavatsky, *Isis Unveiled*, Pasadena: Theosophical University Press, 1960 [1877], vol. 2, p. 461; see also Blavatsky, *The Secret Doctrine*, vol. 1, p. xxxviii.

12. J. Krishnamurti, *Krishnamurti's Notebook*, New York: Harper & Row, 1976, p. 14.

13. For Pythagoras, see Kenneth Sylvan Guthrie, comp. and

trans., *The Pythagorean Sourcebook and Library: An Anthology of Ancient Writings Which Relate to Pythagoras and Pythagorean Philosophy*, edited by David R. Fideler, Grand Rapids, MI: Phanes Press, 1987 [1920].

14. For pragmatism, see, for instance, William James, *The Varieties of Religious Experience: A Study in Human Nature*, edited by Martin E. Marty, New York: Penguin, 1985 [1902]; and John Dewey, *Reconstruction in Philosophy*, Boston: Beacon, 1957 [1920]. For existentialism, see, for instance, F. H. Heinemann, *Existentialism and the Modern Predicament*, New York: Harper Torchbooks, 1958 [1953]. For logical positivism, see, for instance, A. J. Ayer, ed., *Logical Positivism*, New York: Free Press, 1959, especially chapters 2-5 and 12-14. For deconstructionism, see, for instance, John D. Caputo, ed., *Deconstruction in a Nutshell: A Conversation with Jacques Derrida*, New York: Fordham University Press, 1997, which also provides an excellent bibliography. For neo-pragmatism, see Richard Rorty, *Contingency, irony, and solidarity*, Cambridge: Cambridge University Press, 1997 [1989].

See also Richard Garner's magnificent discussion of the point made here about ethics and what I am calling "trans-ethics" in the context of Eastern and Western philosophy in *Beyond Morality*, Philadelphia: Temple University Press, 1994.

15. For discussions of Wittgenstein's views on ethics, see, for instance, Garner, *Beyond Morality*; see also Allan Janek and Stephen Toulmin, *Wittgenstein's Vienna*, Chicago: Elephant Paperbacks, 1996 [1973], especially chapters 5-7.

16. For Nietzsche on revaluing all values, see, for instance, Friedrich Nietzsche, *Beyond Good and Evil: Prelude to a Philosophy of the Future*, translated by Walter Kaufmann, New York: Vintage, 1966 [1886], especially sections 186, 210, and 211; see also Nietzsche, *The Will to Power*, translated by Walter Kaufmann and R. J. Hollingdale, New York: Vintage, 1968 [1901], especially sections 972 and 979. See also Richard Schacht, *Making Sense of Nietzsche: Reflections Timely and Untimely*, Urbana and Chicago: University of Illinois Press, 1995.

17. See, for instance, J. Krishnamurti, *The Awakening of Intelligence*, New York: Harper & Row, 1973.

18. For documentation of Jung's esoteric pedigree, see Webb, *Occult Establishment*, particularly chapter 6, "The Hermetic Academy"; see also references to Jung in Cranston, *HPB*.

19. For the genuineness of HPB's knowledge of Tibetan esoteric doctrines, see W. Y. Evans-Wentz, comp. and ed., *The Tibetan Book of the Dead or The After-Death Experiences on the Bardo Plane*, London, Oxford, and New York: Oxford University Press, 1971 [1927], p. 7, f.n. Evans-Wentz used portions of HPB's translation of the ancient *Book of the Golden Precepts* as a *terma* (a newly discovered, long-lost text of esoteric Buddhism); see W. Y. Evans-Wentz, *Tibetan Yoga and Secret Doctrines: Or Seven Books of Wisdom of the Great Path*, London, Oxford, and New York: Oxford University Press, 1975 [1935]; see also H. P. Blavatsky, trans., *The Voice of Silence: Being Chosen Fragments from the "Book of the Golden Precepts" for the Daily Use of Lanoos (Disciples)*, London: Theosophical Publishing Company, 1889.

20. For sacrifice in theosophical sources, see, for instance, Annie Besant, *The Ancient Wisdom: An Outline of Theosophical Teachings*, Adyar: Theosophical Publishing House, 1966 [1897], particularly chapter 10, "The Law of Sacrifice"; see also C. W. Leadbeater and C. Jinarajadasa, *The Law of Sacrifice*, Adyar: Theosophical Publishing House, 1951 [1894]. For sacrifice in Gurdjieff's work, see references to sacrifice and suffering in P. D. Ouspensky, *In Search of the Miraculous: Fragments of an Unknown Teaching*, New York: Harcourt, Brace & World, 1949; and J. G. Bennett, Gurdjieff: *Making a New World*, New York: Harper & Row, 1973.

21. Carl G. Jung, "Psychological Commentary," in Evans-Wentz, ed., *The Tibetan Book of the Dead*, pp. xxxix-xli.

22. Marvin C. Shaw, *The Paradox of Intention: Reaching the Goal by Giving Up the Attempt to Reach It*, American Academy of Religion Studies in Religion, number 48, Atlanta: Scholars Press, 1988, pp. 1, 2-3.

CHAPTER FIVE: *Process and Authority*

1. For Sutcliffe's comments on the astrology of this initiation, see *The Theosophist*, December, 1909.

2. C. W. Leadbeater, *How Theosophy Came to Me*, Adyar: Theosophical Publishing House, 1948 [1930], pp.152-53.

3. C. W. Leadbeater, *The Masters and the Path*, Adyar: Theosophical Publishing House, 1959 [1925], pp.178-79.

4. Leadbeater, *How Theosophy Came to Me*, pp.154-55.

5. Pupul Jayakar, *Krishnamurti: A Biography*, San Francisco: Harper & Row, 1986, pp. 47-48.

6. Leadbeater, *Masters and the Path*, pp.175-77.

7. Jayakar, *Krishnamurti*, p. 54.

8. *Jataka* in Henry Clarke Warren, comp. and trans., *Buddhism in Translations*, New York: Atheneum, 1968 [1896], p. 74. The joy expressed by other initiates at the end of the Buddha's forty-nine day meditation marked it as an initiation; see Christmas Humphreys, *Buddhism*, Baltimore: Penguin, 1962 [1951], p. 33. For HPB's comment on the meditation under the Bo Tree as esoterically significant, see H. P. Blavatsky, "The Origin of Evil," *Lucifer* 1:2 (October 1887) p. 112; see also H. P. Blavatsky, *Collected Writings*, vol. 8 (Adyar: Theosophical Publishing House, 1960), p. 155; see especially the footnotes in both citations.

9. For a more contemporary discussion of the perennial significance of cycles in terms of numbers (such as seven) see John Addey, *Selected Writings*, Tempe, AZ: American Federation of Astrologers, 1976, particularly the last six chapters.

10. W. Y. Evans-Wentz, comp. and ed., *The Tibetan Book of the Dead or The After-Death Experiences on the Bardo Plane*, London, Oxford, and New York: Oxford University Press, 1971-72 [1927], pp. 6-7.

11. For the dates in question, see Jayakar, *Krishnamurti*, pp. 47, 55.

12. Sidney Field, *Krishnamurti: The Reluctant Messiah*, edited by Peter Hay, New York: Paragon House, 1989, pp. 65-66.

13. Jayakar, *Krishnamurti*, p. 438.

14. Mary Lutyens, *Krishnamurti: The Years of Fulfilment*, New York: Farrar, Straus, & Giroux, 1983, p. 30.

15. For K's attitude towards the question of authorities in psychological and spiritual areas, see, for instance, the chapter "Why Spiritual Teachers?" in J. Krishnamurti, *The First and Last Freedom*, New York: Harper & Row, 1954, pp. 150-53.

16. For one of K's statements (among many) on the need for a teacher as someone who points out, see, for instance, his conversation with Swami Venkatesananda in Krishnamurti, *The Awakening of*

Intelligence, pp. 139-41.

17. For a reference to the Masters, the Lord Maitreya, and K's place as an avatar, according to him, see the reference (discussed in chapter 9), in J. Krishnamurti, *Truth and Actuality*, New York: Harper & Row, 1978, pp. 86-89.

18. David Bohm in *Krishnamurti: With a Silent Mind*, a film by Michael Mendizza on videotape, Ojai: Krishnamurti Foundation of America, 1989.

19. Lutyens, *Years of Fulfilment*, p. 207.

20. There are numerous works that deal with the evidence for the presence of the perennial teachers in the early decades of the theosophical movement. Apart from others cited earlier, among the best are Cranston, *HPB*; and Henry Steel Olcott, *Old Diary Leaves, The True Story of the Theosophical Society*, 6 vols., Adyar: Theosophical Publishing House, 1941-1975 [1895-1935].

CHAPTER SIX: *The Experiment*

1. Pupul Jayakar, *Krishnamurti: A Biography*, San Francisco: Harper & Row, 1986, p. 50.

2. Mary Lutyens, *Krishnamurti: The Years of Awakening*, New York: Farrar, Straus, and Giroux, 1975, pp. 35-36.

3. J. Krishnamurti, *Krishnamurti's Notebook*, New York: Harper & Row, 1976, p. 14.

4. Jayakar, *Krishnamurti*, p. 50.

5. Jayakar, *Krishnamurti*, p. 57.

6. For K being close to dying, see, for instance, Mary Lutyens, *Krishnamurti: The Years of Fulfilment*, New York: Farrar, Straus and Giroux, 1983, pp. 50, 235; see also Mary Lutyens, *Krishnamurti: His Life and Death*, New York: St. Martin's Press, 1990, pp. 100-101, 121.

7. Jayakar, *Krishnamurti*, p. 53.

8. For the perennial teaching on "bodies" or "levels," see Annie Besant, *The Ancient Wisdom: An Outline of Theosophical Teachings*, Adyar: Theosophical Publishing House, 1966 [1897]; see also Annie Besant, *Man and His Bodies*, Theosophical Manual no. 7, London:

Theosophical Publishing Society, 1914; see also Ken Wilber, *The Spectrum of Consciousness*, Wheaton, IL: Quest, 1993 [1973].

9. For an excellent yet simple explanation of the place of these elementals in the life of the perennial candidate, see Alcyone [J. Krishnamurti], *At the Feet of the Master*, Wheaton: Quest, 1974 [1910], pp. 5-27. See also C. W. Leadbeater, *The Hidden Side of Things*, Adyar: Theosophical Publishing House, 1974 [1913], pp. 54-55.

10. Jayakar, *Krishnamurti*, p. 199.

11. See, for instance, Fritjof Capra, *The Tao of Physics*, New York: Bantam, 1977; see also Karl Pribram, *Languages of the Brain*, Englewood Cliffs, NJ: Prentice Hall, 1971.

12. J. Krishnamurti, *Commentaries on Living*, second series, New York: Harper & Row, 1958; *Think on These Things*, New York: Harper & Row, 1964.

13. Lady Emily Lutyens, *Candles in the Sun*, London: Hart-Davis, 1957.

14. For the *Candles in the Sun* episode, see Mary Lutyens, *Krishnamurti: The Years of Fulfilment*, New York: Farrar, Straus and Giroux, pp. 82-90.

15. For transformations in K's language, see Yvon Achard, *Le langage de Krishnamurti: l'évolution spirituelle de Krishnamurti et l'évolution de son langage*, Paris: Le Courrier du Livre, 1970; translated into Spanish as *El Lenguaje de Krishnamurti. La Evolución Espiritual de Krishnamurti y la Evolución de su Lenguaje*, México: Editorial Orión, 1975.

16. Jayakar, *Krishnamurti*, pp. 292-93.

17. Jayakar, *Krishnamurti*, p. 293.

18. Jayakar, *Krishnamurti*, p. 293.

19. Jayakar, *Krishnamurti*, p. 439.

20. Lutyens, *Years of Fulfilment*, p. 234.

21. Lutyens, *Years of Fulfilment*, p. 236.

22. Mary Lutyens, *The Open Door*, London: John Murray, 1988, p. 56; see also Lutyens, *Years of Fulfilment*, pp. 229-31.

23. For the theory of morphic resonance, see Rupert Sheldrake,

The Presence of the Past: Morphic Resonance and the Habits of Nature, London: Collins, 1988; see also Rupert Sheldrake, *The Rebirth of Nature: The Greening of Science and God*, New York: Bantam, 1992 [1991].

24. For group souls see, for instance, C. Jinarajadasa, *First Principles of Theosophy*, Adyar: Theosophical Publishing House, 1921, pp. 115-118; see also Annie Besant, *A Study in Consciousness: A Contribution to the Science of Psychology*, Adyar: Theosophical Publishing House, 1972 [1904], p. 96.

25. For K's statement on the teacher not manifesting again until about five hundred years hence, see Doris Pratt in *Krishnamurti: With a Silent Mind*, a film by Michael Mendizza on videotape, Ojai: Krishnamurti Foundation of America, 1989.

26. Jayakar, *Krishnamurti*, pp. 53-55.

27. C. W. Leadbeater, *The Masters and the Path*, Adyar: Theosophical Publishing House, 1959 [1925], p. 213.

28. Jayakar, *Krishnamurti*, p. 57.

29. Lutyens, *Years of Awakening*, pp. 193-4.

30. Lutyens, *Years of Awakening*, p. 182.

31. Lutyens, *Years of Awakening*, p. 171.

32. Jayakar, *Krishnamurti*, pp. 55-56.

33. Stephen M. Phillips, *Extrasensory Perception of Quarks*, Wheaton: Theosophical Publishing House, 1980.

34. C.W. Leadbeater, *The Science of the Sacraments*, Adyar: Theosophical Publishing House, 1957 [1920], p. 292.

35. Leadbeater, *Science of the Sacraments*, pp. 303, 305.

36. Leadbeater, *Science of the Sacraments*, pp. 318-19.

37. Leadbeater, *Science of the Sacraments*, pp. 304-5.

38. Immanuel Kant, *Critique of Pure Reason*, translated by Norman Kemp Smith, New York: St. Martin's, 1965 [1781].

39. For Kant's perennial influences according to HPB, see, for instance, Blavatsky, *Secret Doctrine*, vol. 2, pp. 325-28.

40. For references to Kundabuffer, see G.I. Gurdjieff, *Beelzebub's Tales to His Grandson: An Objectively Impartial Criticism of the Life of*

Man, New York: Dutton, 1978 [1950]; for an index with the specific references, see *Guide and Index to G.I. Gurdjieff's All and Everything: Beelzebub's Tales to his Grandson*, Toronto: Traditional Studies Press, 1973 [1971].

41. For the authorship of HPB's works, see Boris de Zirkoff, *Rebirth of the Occult Tradition: How the Secret Doctrine of H. P. Blavatsky Was Written*, Adyar: Theosophical Publishing House, 1977; see also Boris de Zirkoff, "How 'Isis Unveiled' Was Written," introductory essay to *Isis Unveiled*, vol. 1 of H. P. Blavatsky, *Collected Writings*, 15 vols., Adyar: Theosophical Publishing House, 1960.

42. H. P. Blavatsky, *Collected Writings*, 15 vols., Adyar: Theosophical Publishing House, 1987 [1980], vol. 12, pp. 619, 620; H. P. Blavatsky, *The Secret Doctrine*, 6 vols., Adyar: Theosophical Publishing House, 1971 [1888], vol. 5, pp. 483, 484; H. P. Blavatsky, *The Esoteric School of Theosophy Instructions*, Glasgow: William McLellan & Co., 1921, pp. 92, 93.

43. Blavatsky, *Collected Writings*, vol. 12, pp. 616-617; *Secret Doctrine*, vol. 5, pp. 480-81; Blavatsky, *Instructions*, pp. 89-90.

44. Krishnamurti, *Notebook*, pp. 16, 14, 15.

45. For HPB's priority in assessing some functions of the pineal gland, see HPB's statements in her esoteric *Instructions* in light of, for instance, Philip Lansky, "Neurochemistry and the Awakening of Kundalini," in John White, ed., *Kundalini, Evolution, and Enlightenment*, New York: Paragon House, 1990 [1979].

46. For reference to the pineal gland as the third eye in medical literature, see, for instance, Edwin B. Steen and Ashley Montagu, *Anatomy and Physiology*, vol 2, New York: Barnes & Noble, 1959, p. 90.

47. See Sally Springer and Georg Deutsch, *Left Brain, Right Brain*, New York: W. H. Freeman, 3rd ed., 1989 [1981].

48. See Springer and Deutsch, *Left Brain, Right Brain*.

49. For K on split-brain speculations, see his 1979 Ojai talks, available on audio cassettes, Ojai: Krishnamurti Foundation of America, 1979.

50. Paul Edwards, ed., *The Encyclopedia of Philosophy*, vol. 5 New York, London: Macmillan, 1967, s.v., "logic, many-valued."

51. Mary Lutyens, *Krishnamurti: The Open Door*, London: John

Murray, 1988, p. 149.

CHAPTER SEVEN: *The Beloved*

1. Pupul Jayakar, *Krishnamurti: A Biography*, San Francisco: Harper & Row, 1986, p. 125.

2. The quotation is taken from Annie Besant's statement to the Associated Press in 1927, and reflects a perception concerning Krishnamurti that she never changed. Despite that, after her death the leaders and the majority of the membership of the Theosophical Society cut off, as much as possible, all connection with K, in glaring contradiction with Besant's perceptions and declarations; see Mary Lutyens, *Krishnamurti: The Years of Awakening*, New York: Farrar, Straus, & Giroux, 1975, p. 241.

3. Jayakar, *Krishnamurti*, pp. 126-28.

4. Mary Lutyens, *Krishnamurti: The Years of Fulfilment*, New York: Farrar, Straus, & Giroux, 1983, pp. 234, 235.

5. Lutyens, *Years of Fulfilment*, pp. 228-29.

6. Lutyens, *Years of Fulfilment*, pp. 230-31.

7. Lutyens, *Years of Fulfilment*, p. 230.

8. J. Krishnamurti, *Talks and Dialogues: Authentic Reports*, Sidney, Australia: Krishnamurti Books, 1970, p. 64.

9. H. P. Blavatsky, *The Key to Theosophy*, Pasadena, CA: Theosophical University Press, 1947 [1889], p. 20.

10. Blavatsky, *Key to Theosophy*, pp. 21-22.

11. For evidence that transformation is the central teaching of theosophy, see Aryel Sanat, *The Secret Doctrine, Krishnamurti, and Transformation*, Arlington, VA: Fenix 2000, [1993]; and Aryel Sanat, *Transformation: Vital Essence of the Secret Doctrine*, Arlington, VA: Fenix, 2000, [1998].

12. Krishnamurti, *Notebook*, p. 126.

13. For an excellent example of his work with small groups who seemed to "show promise," see J. Krishnamurti, *Towards Discipleship (A series of informal addresses to aspirants for Discipleship)*, Chicago: The Theosophical Press, 1926.

14. On K describing himself as a "telephone," see *Krishnamurti: With a Silent Mind,* a film by Michael Mendizza on videotape, Ojai: Krishnamurti Foundation of America, 1989.

15. For HPB describing herself as a "telephone," see *The Letters of H. P. Blavatsky to A. P. Sinnett and Other Miscellaneous Letters,* transcribed and compiled by A. T. Barker, Pasadena, CA: Theosophical University Press, 1973 [1924], p. 174.

16. J. Krishnamurti, *Who Brings the Truth?* Zwolle, Holland: Firma H. Tulp, 1927, pp. 1-2.

17. Krishnamurti, *Who Brings,* pp. 3-5.

18. For HPB's translation of "The Grand Inquisitor," which according to the evidence available was suggested by Master KH, see H. P. Blavatsky, *A Modern Panarion: A Collection of Fugitive Fragments,* London: Theosophical Publishing Society, 1895, p. 410; see also *The Theosophist,* Nov. and Dec., 1881. HPB's introduction to her translation is given in H. P. Blavatsky, *Collected Writings,* 15 vols., Adyar: Theosophical Publishing House, 1968, vol. 3, p. 324.

19. Krishnamurti, *Who Brings,* pp. 5-7.

20. Krishnamurti, *Who Brings,* p. 5.

21. Krishnamurti, *Who Brings,* pp. 8-9.

22. Krishnamurti, *Who Brings,* pp. 9-10.

23. Krishnamurti, *Who Brings,* p. 10.

24. J. Krishnamurti, *The Search,* Eerde, Holland, and London: Star Publishing Trust and George Allen & Unwin, 1927, pp. 14-15; see also J. Krishnamurti, "The Search," in *From Darkness to Light: Poems and Parables,* vol. 1 of *The Collected Works of Krishnamurti,* San Francisco: Harper & Row, 1980, pp. 24-25.

25. Krishnamurti, *Notebook,* pp. 46-47.

26. Mary Lutyens, *The Open Door,* London: John Murray, 1988, p. 132.

27. Lutyens, *Open Door,* p. 134.

28. Lutyens, *Open Door,* p. 135.

29. Lutyens, *Open Door,* p. 8.

30. Lutyens, *Open Door*, pp. 148-49.

31. Lutyens, *Open Door*, p. 149.

32. Lutyens, *Years of Fulfilment*, p. 216.

33. Lutyens, *Years of Fulfilment*, p. 216.

Chapter Eight: *Ecce Homo*

1. Among such prominent teachers was the late Chogyam Trungpa Rinpoche, whose language in all the books he wrote after the late 1960s (subsequent to his first encounters with K) sounds similar to Krishnamurti's *unique* formulation of the perennial teaching; see, for instance, *Cutting through Spiritual Materialism*, Berkeley: Shambhala, 1973, and note the similarity of the language Rinpoche uses with that in any Krishnamurti book. In this select group of Buddhist teachers shines particularly Toni Packer, author of the magnificent exposition of Zen, *The Work of This Moment*, Boston & Shaftesbury: Shambhala, 1990. Packer's work in Zen has been inspired by K for many years.

2. Personal communications from participants; for a brief account of Gurdjieff in the context of theosophy and Krishnamurti's work, see Harry Benjamin, *Basic Self-Knowledge: An Introduction to Esoteric Psychology*, New York: Samuel Weiser, 1976 [1971].

3. J. Krishnamurti, *You are the World*, New York: Harper & Row, 1972, pp. 92-93, 149-50.

4. For reference to repetition of the word "Coca-Cola," see, for instance, Krishnamurti, *You are the World*, p. 148.

5. Romans 7:19 (King James version).

6. M.C., *Light on the Path: A Treatise written for the personal use of those who are ignorant of the Eastern wisdom and who desire to enter within its influence*, Adyar: Theosophical Publishing House, 1961 [1885], p. 16, Fragment 12.

7. Henry Clarke Warren, *Buddhism in Translations: Passages Selected from the Buddhist Sacred Books and Translated from the Original Pali into English*, New York: Atheneum, 1968 [1896], pp. 120, 121.

8. J. Krishnamurti, *Krishnamurti's Notebook*, New York: Harper & Row, 1976, p. 17.

9. Krishnamurti, *Notebook*, pp. 15-16.

10. For Haida Yoga, see, for instance, James Moore, *Gurdjieff: The Anatomy of a Myth*, Shaftesbury: Element, 1991, pp. 172ff. For Rohatsu, see, for instance, Janwillem van de Wetering, *The Empty Mirror: Experiences in a Japanese Zen Monastery*, Boston: Houghton Mifflin, 1974 [1972], pp. 76ff.

11. Krishnamurti, *Notebook*, pp. 59-61.

12. H. P. Blavatsky, *Practical Occultism and Occultism versus the Occult Arts*, Adyar: Theosophical Publishing House, 1981 [1888], pp. 43-44; see also Blavatsky, *Collected Writings*, vol. 9, 1974 [1962], p. 254.

13. Radha Burnier, *Human Regeneration: Lectures and Discussions*, Amsterdam: Uitgeverij der Theosofische Vereniging in Nederland, 1990, p. 21.

14. Christmas Humphreys and Elsie Benjamin, eds., *The Mahatma Letters to A. P. Sinnett*, transcribed and compiled by A. T. Barker, Adyar: Theosophical Publishing House, 1962 [1923], 3rd and rev. ed, p. 58.

15. Quoted by Doris Pratt in *Krishnamurti: With a Silent Mind*, a film by Michael Mendizza on videotape, Ojai: Krishnamurti Foundation of America, 1989.

CHAPTER NINE: *Maitreya*

1. H. P. Blavatsky, *Collected Writings*, 15 vols., Adyar: Theosophical Publishing House, 1973. vol. 11, pp. 292-93.

2. The actual quote is "man is a political animal," but Aristotle then adds that man is more "gregarious" than bees, "the only animal endowed with the gift of speech," and that "the state is by nature clearly prior to the family and to the individual, since the whole is of necessity prior to the part." Clearly, he uses the word translated as "political" in the sense of "social." *Politics, in The Basic Works of Aristotle*, edited and with an introduction by Richard McKeon, New York: Random House, 1941, Book 1, Chapter 2, § 252-53, p. 1129.

3. For Leibniz, see Bertrand Russell, *A Critical Exposition of the Philosophy of Leibniz: With an Appendix of Leading Passages*, London: George Allen & Unwin, 1964 [1900], especially chapters 1-4. For Aristotle, see Aristotle, *Organon* (the collection of his logical treatises)

and *Metaphysics* in *The Basic Works of Aristotle*, edited and with an introduction by Richard McKeon, New York: Random House, 1941. See also Timothy A Robinson, *Aristotle in Outline*, Indianapolis, Cambridge: Hackett, 1995.

4. Ludwig Wittgenstein, *Philosophical Investigations*, translated by G. E. M. Anscombe, New York: Macmillan Co., 1968 [1953], § 43, p. 20e.

5. See, for instance, J. Krishnamurti, *Talks in Europe, 1968*, Amsterdam: Servire/Wassenaar, 1969, p. 18.

6. J. Krishnamurti, *Life Ahead*, New York and Evanston: Harper & Row, 1963, p. 121-22.

7. For Escher, see Douglas R. Hofstadter, *Gödel, Escher, Bach: An Eternal Golden Braid*, New York: Vintage, 1980. See particularly Hofstadter's notion of "Strange Loops" and how it relates to the present discussion.

8. Some aspects of this discussion of perception as choiceless awareness, and related matters, are considered from a completely different point of view in David Edward Shaner, *The Bodymind Experience in Japanese Buddhism: A Phenomenological Study of Kukai and Dogen*, Albany: State University of New York Press, 1985.

9. See Wittgenstein, *Philosophical Investigations*, § 269, § 275, pp. 94e, 96e.

10. David Spangler and William Irwin Thompson, *Reimagination of the World: A Critique of the New Age, Science, and Popular Culture*, Santa Fe: Bear & Company, 1991, pp. 106-7.

11. Spangler and Thompson, *Reimagination of the World*, p. 107.

12. For Nagarjuna, see his *Mulamadhyamakakarika* in *The Fundamental Wisdom of the Middle Way: Nagarjuna's Mulamadhyamakakarika*, translated by Jay L. Garfield, New York and Oxford: Oxford University Press, 1995.

13. H.P. Blavatsky, *The Stanzas of Dzyan*, Wheaton: Theosophical Press, n.d. [1888], pp. 21-22; see also H. P. Blavatsky, *The Secret Doctrine*, 6 vols., Adyar: Theosophical Publishing House, 1971 [1888], vol 1, pp. 101-2.

14. Spangler and Thompson, *Reimagination of the World*, p. 144.

Notes

15. José Argüelles, *The Mayan Factor: Path Beyond Technology*, Santa Fe, NM: Bear & Co., 1987, p. 29.

16. See any of numerous references to Elohim in all of HPB's major writings, for instance, in the *Collected Writings*, 1985, vol. 14, pp. 210-11.

17. J. Krishnamurti, *Krishnamurti's Notebook*, New York: Harper & Row, 1976, p. 25.

18. Ingram Smith, *Truth is a Pathless Land: A Journey with Krishnamurti*, Wheaton: Quest, 1989, pp. 20-21. The story is also repeated by Smith in *Krishnamurti: With a Silent Mind*, a film by Michael Mendizza on videotape, Ojai: Krishnamurti Foundation of America, 1989.

19. J. Krishnamurti, "The Immortal Friend," in *From Darkness to Light: Poems and Parables*, vol. 1 of *The Collected Works of Krishnamurti*, San Francisco: Harper & Row, 1980, pp. 56-57.

20. Pupul Jayakar, *Krishnamurti: A Biography*, San Francisco: Harper & Row, 1986, p. 31.

21. Jayakar, *Krishnamurti*, p. 31.

22. Blavatsky, *Collected Writings*, vol. 12, p. 600; *Secret Doctrine*, vol. 5, p. 465; *Instructions*, p. 74.

23. Krishnamurti, "The Immortal Friend," in *From Darkness to Light*, pp. 60, 61.

24. G.W.F. Hegel, *The Logic of Hegel*, translated from *The Encyclopaedia of the Philosophical Sciences*, by William Wallace, London: Oxford University Press, 1972 [1817], p. 171. Though the expression is generally attributed to Hegel, it actually comes from Spinoza's *Omnis determinatio est negatio*; see Letter L in *The Chief Works of Spinoza*, translated from the Latin and with an introduction by R. H. M. Elwes, New York: Dover, 1955 [1883, 1674], p. 370.

25. Ludwig Wittgenstein, *Tractatus Logico-Philosophicus*, translated by D. F. Pears and B. F. McGuinness, with an introduction by Bertrand Russell, Atlantic Highlands, N.J.: Humanities, 1974 [1921], 6.522, 6.54, pp. 73, 74. For an excellent discussion of Krishnamurti, Wittgenstein, and Alan Watts, see Alan Keightley, *Into Every Life a Little Zen Must Fall: A Christian Philosopher Looks to Alan Watts and the East*, London: Wisdom Publications, 1986.

26. Wittgenstein's famous expression, which is meant to summarize his *Tractatus* and is the last sentence of the work, reads: "Whereof one does not know, thereof one should not speak." Wittgenstein, *Tractatus*, p. 74, though this particular edition, which is the most readily available, offers the much less interesting translation: "What we cannot speak about we must pass over in silence."

27. J. Krishnamurti, *Truth and Actuality*, New York: Harper & Row, 1978, pp. 86-89.

28. H. P. Blavatsky, *The Inner Group Teachings of H.P. Blavatsky to Her Personal Pupils (1890-91)*, reconstructed by H. J. Spierenburg, San Diego: Point Loma, 1985 [1890-91], pp. 51-52.

Selected Bibliography

Krishnamurti's Life

Though an unbiased, fully researched biography of K still remains to be published, the following personal memoirs are extremely useful:

Jayakar, Pupul. *Krishnamurti: A Biography*. San Francisco: Harper & Row, 1986. Despite its very strong anti-Theosophical bias and the author's lack of knowledge or understanding of Theosophy, its history and its leaders, this is a most valuable book. The reader may safely skip altogether Part I, "The Young Krishnamurti 1895-1946," which is full of errors and anti-Theosophical innuendo. But the rest of the book, which is the author's memoir, shows with unusual sensitivity the deeper side of K in his relationship to (mostly) his Indian friends, and his life in India while on constant lecture tours. Also, it documents fully the mystical and the esoteric sides of K, even while attempting to quell its significance.

Lutyens, Mary. *Krishnamurti: The Years of Awakening*. New York: Farrar, Straus, and Giroux, 1975. Originally commissioned by K himself, this was the first work ever published with details about his inner life. Though faulty in its understanding of the perennial philosophy, and therefore of K's background, this and Lutyens' three other works on K's life, cited below, are also recommended.

————. *The Years of Fulfilment*. New York: Farrar, Straus, and Giroux, 1983. K's life from 1930 through 1980.

————. *The Open Door*. London: John Murray, 1988. The last six years of K's life, with emphasis on his approach to his own death (the open door).

————. *Krishnamurti: His Life and Death*. New York: St. Martin's Press, 1990. A further exploration into K's approach to death (especially his own), and a more sustained attempt at understanding who or what K was.

The following are highly recommended:

Krohnen, Michael. *The Kitchen Chronicles: 1,001 Lunches with J. Krishnamurti*. Ojai: Edwin House, 1997. To my mind, this is the best book on K's life published to date. There are no speculations here, only facts about what it was like to live close to K intermittently for many years. Yet it is magnificently well-written, betraying Krohnen's background as a poet.

Mendizza, Michael. *Krishnamurti: With a Silent Mind*, a film on videotape. Ojai: Krishnamurti Foundation of America, 1989. Given the strangeness of K's life, and the subtlety and depth of his insights and observations, this film is a truly remarkable achievement, since it covers K's life, his researches into what is, insightful comments by friends and people who knew him, and videotaped excerpts from his talks in different parts of the world. It is a precious film exquisitely crafted.

KRISHNAMURTI'S WORK

The following are books I recommend for someone unacquainted with K's insights and observations:

Krishnamurti, J. *Education and the Significance of Life*. New York: Harper & Brothers,1953. A revolutionary manifesto on the deeper significance of education, and on bringing about a good society.

———. *The First and Last Freedom*, with an Introduction by Aldous Huxley. San Francisco: HarperSanFrancisco, 1999 [1954]. This is probably the best single-volume introduction to K's insights and observations, even though it dates from just before the time when his audiences got more sophisticated (therapists, philosophers, Zen, Vajrayana and Gurdjieff practitioners, college students and faculty).

———. *Commentaries on Living. First Series*. Wheaton, IL: Quest, 1984 [1956]. The three volumes in this series consist of vignettes of K's observations on nature, his own meditational states, and poignant descriptions of numerous people from all walks of life and every part of the world who come to see him, usually either for advice on some serious personal crisis, or to challenge him. These volumes contain some of the most insightful observations on religion, politics, education, cultural mores, and the human psyche in general that one is likely to find anywhere.

————. *Commentaries on Living. Second Series*. Wheaton, IL: Quest, 1981 [1958].

————. *Commentaries on Living. Third Series*. Wheaton, IL: Quest, 1981 [1960].

————. *The Awakening of Intelligence*. New York: Harper & Row, 1973. An extraordinary series of dialogues with philosophers, mystics, scientists, gurus, and small groups, with a well-chosen selection of talks K gave in different parts of the world. This is probably the most complete single-volume presentation of K's work.

————. *The Only Revolution*. London: Victor Gollancz, 1970. Possibly the best book on what meditation is.

————. *Krishnamurti's Notebook*. A revealing look at K's meditational directions in his daily life, including references to the process and "the presence" or "benediction." Contains some of the deepest remarks to be found in K's work, and mystical descriptions not found elsewhere.

————, and David Bohm. *The Ending of Time*. San Francisco: Harper & Row, 1985. A sustained, keen discussion on the significance of psychological time. Invaluable for anyone engaged in meditation, as well as for psychologists and philosophers.

THE PERENNIAL PHILOSOPHY

Barborka, Geoffrey A. *The Divine Plan*. Adyar: Theosophical Publishing House, 1972 [1961]. Largely a commentary of HPB's *Secret Doctrine*, despite its denseness, this work has become very popular because it gives a grand conceptual, metaphysical understanding of the perennial philosophy.

Besant, Annie. *The Ancient Wisdom: An Outline of Theosophical Teachings*. Adyar: Theosophical Publishing House, 1966 [1897]. A classic presentation of the perennial teachings as understood by Theosophists, prior to K's new perspective.

Blavatsky, H.P. *The Secret Doctrine. The Synthesis of Science, Religion and Philosophy*, 6 vols. Adyar: Theosophical Publishing House, 1971 [1888]. HPB's *magnum opus*, the foundational text for the perennial renaissance. Except for the most hardy, this comprehensive work is primarily either for the very serious student of the perennial philosophy, or to be used as a reference work. It is full of really interesting material in every conceivable area of human interest.

————. *The Key to Theosophy. Being a Clear Exposition, in the Form of Question and Answer, of the Ethics, Science, and Philosophy for the Study of Which The Theosophical Society Has Been Founded*. Pasadena, CA: Theosophical University Press, 1946 [1889]. Despite its being dated in some ways, this is still the best introduction to the perennial philosophy. This is must reading for anyone serious about understanding what Theosophy is.

Guthrie, Kenneth Sylvan, comp. and trans. *The Pythagorean Sourcebook and Library: An Anthology of Ancient Writings Which Relate to Pythagoras and Pythagorean Philosophy*. Edited by David R. Fideler. Grand Rapids, MI: Phanes Press, 1987 [1920]. Excellent single-volume source for Pythagoras as the founder of the Western esoteric lineage, and of the university as an institution open to all serious students of *what is*.

Hieronimus, Robert. *America's Secret Destiny: Spiritual Vision and the Founding of a Nation*. Rochester, VT: Destiny Books, 1989. Excellent introduction to America's perennial sources in perennial schools, both from Europe and the original Americans, particularly the Iroquois.

Huxley, Aldous. *The Perennial Philosophy*. New York: Harper & Row, 1944. The work in which the expression "perennial philosophy" was coined, to refer to what HPB had called by many other names, such as "theosophy" and "wisdom-religion."

Jinarajadasa, C. *First Principles of Theosophy*. Adyar: Theosophical Publishing House, 1972 [1921]. An excellent, easy-to-understand presentation of Theosophy when understood as a conceptual teaching.

Sanat, Aryel. *The Secret Doctrine, Krishnamurti, and Transformation*. Arlington, VA: Fenix, 2000 [1993]. Newly revised version of an abstract of some of the main connections between HPB's *mag-*

num opus, Buddhism after Nagarjuna, and Krishnamurti.

———. *Transformation: Vital Essence of the Secret Doctrine.* Arlington, VA: Fenix, 2000,[1998]. Combines a revised version of two papers originally read at the Third Symposium on *The Secret Doctrine,* held in Oklahoma City in 1998. Shows how metaphysical or conceptual theosophy is not what HPB and her teachers wereinterested in. It documents how, according to them, real theosophy is that which takes place in theosophical (divine-like) states of awareness.

The Perennial Renaissance

Cranston, Sylvia. *HPB: The Extraordinary Life and Influence of Helena Blavatsky, Founder of the Modern Theosophical Movement.* New York: Tarcher/Putnam, 1993. Apart from its being the definitive biography of HPB (and there have been quite a few), this work documents the sources of much of the perennial renaissance in HPB's work.

Ferguson, Marilyn. *The Aquarian Conspiracy.* Los Angeles: J.P. Tarcher, 1980. Though Ferguson does not mention HPB despite her being the foundational source for much of the perennial renaissance documented in Ferguson's book, it is intriguing in that it shows —in an easy-to-read manner—how those engaged in the perennial renaissance must act as "conspirators" because of the pressures and expectations of the mainstream Establishment.

Spangler, David, and William Irwin Thompson. *Reimagination of the World: A Critique of the New Age, Science, and Popular Culture.* Santa Fe, NM: Bear & Company, 1991. Book version of a seminar the authors conducted, with truly insightful observations on the title subjects.

Webb, James. *The Occult Underground.* La Salle, IL: Library Press/Open Court, 1974. Although Webb tends to speak in a derogatory way about Theosophy and related movements, this is an extremely thorough, scholarly documentation of how much of twentieth-century culture had its origins in the "occult underground," of which HPB's work was the centerpiece, focusing largely on nineteenth-century influences.

————. *The Occult Establishment.* La Salle, IL: Open Court, 1976. A continuation of the above, it documents with equal scholarly thoroughness the theosophical origins of numerous twentieth-century movements and currents in mainstream society, such as psychoanalysis and other psychological schools, the Boy Scout movement, mythology, feminism, and the Irish literary renaissance.

————. *The Harmonious Circle: The Lives and Work of G.I. Gurdjieff, P.D. Ouspensky, and Their Followers.* Boston: Shambhala, 1987. Documents, with Webb's exceptional thoroughness and scholarly rigor, critical Theosophical sources for the work of Gurdjieff and other "progressive" (culturally leading edge) aspects of the perennial renaissance.

White, John, ed. *The Meeting of Science and Spirit: Guidelines for a New Age.* New York: Paragon, 1990. Provides an excellent comprehensive understanding of the perennial renaissance as a whole, with emphasis on its scientific dimensions.

THE BEGINNING OF A NEW ERA

Harman, Willis. *Global Mind Change: The New Age Revolution in the Way We Think.* New York: Warner Books, 1990 [1988]. Harman, who was a professor at Stanford and president of the prestigious Institute of Noetic Sciences (founded by cosmonaut Edgar Mitchell), provides a sustained, well-documented argument for why the twentieth century marked the beginning of a new era, with sensible suggestions on what to do to help this transformation come about in a way meaningful globally and individually.

Roszak, Theodore. *Unfinished Animal: The Aquarian Frontier and the Evolution of Consciousness.* New York: Harper Colophon, 1977 [1975]. Shows why and how the radical transformations of the twentieth century have evolutionary significance.

TRANSFORMATION-INITIATION

Blavatsky, H.P., translator. *The Voice of the Silence: Being Chosen Fragments from the "Book of the Golden Precepts" for the Daily*

Use of Lanoos (Disciples). London: Theosophical Publishing Company, 1889. Ancient text of esoteric Buddhism on transformation in daily life, using stunning spiritual poetry.

Evans-Wentz, W.Y,. comp. and ed. *The Tibetan Book of the Dead or the After-Death Experiences on the Bardo Plane*. London, Oxford, and New York: Oxford University Press, 1971 [1927]. A magnificent commentary and discussion of initiation as the act of dying to the known, with insightful comments by Carl Jung.

Krishnamurti, J. *Freedom From the Known*. New York: Harper & Row, 1969. Outstanding selection of K's talks on the issue of transformation, sensitively edited by Mary Lutyens.

———. *The Transformation of Man*. A series of five videotaped discussions between K and Drs. David Shainberg and David Bohm, Ojai: Krishnamurti Foundation of America,1976.

———. (Alcyone) *At the Feet of the Master*. Wheaton, IL: Quest, 1974 [1910]. The actual instructions received by K from the Master KH to prepare him for his first initiation, as recollected laboriously by K, according to witnesses who saw him write this little book, which has been translated in many languages, and of which millions of copies have been printed.

Leadbeater, C.W. *The Masters and the Path*. Adyar: Theosophical Publishing House,1959 [1925]. The classic on perennial initiation, as understood prior to K's work, and according to CWL's perspective.

Shaw, Marvin C. *The Paradox of Intention: Reaching the Goal by Giving Up the Attempt to Reach It*. American Academy of Religion Studies in Religion, number 48, Atlanta: Scholars Press, 1988. Excellent, book-length discussion of the reversal of standpoint that transformation-initiation calls for, although Shaw makes no reference to initiation or explicitly to perennial sources as such. Instead, he focuses on how critical such a reversal is for any genuinely religious person.

THE SUBTLE ENERGIES

Besant, Annie, and C.W. Leadbeater. *Thought Forms*. Wheaton, IL: Quest, 1971[1901]. Two clairvoyants give thorough descriptions, with illustrations, of what the subtler matter of thoughts and emotions looks like to a sensitive.

Hodson, Geoffrey. *Music Forms: Superphysical Effects of Music Clairvoyantly Observed*. Adyar: Theosophical Publishing House, 1976. A trained clairvoyant shows through paintings what the energy fields look like when music is played.

————. *The Kingdom of the Gods*. Adyar: Theosophical Publishing House, 1972 [1952]. Profusely illustrated descriptions of how a clairvoyant sees otherwise invisible entities, such as angels and fairies.

Jwing-Ming, Yang. *Chi Kung Health & Martial Arts*. Jamaica Plain, MA: Yang's Martial Arts Association, 1988 [1985]. Keen descriptions of the flow of energy through the body for health and martial arts purposes, and how to guide that energy.

Karagulla, Shafika, M.D. *Breakthrough to Creativity: Your Higher Sense Perception*. Santa Monica, CA: DeVorss, 1973 [1967]. A neurosurgeon explores the field of extrasensory perception. Dora Kunz is featured (among other sensitives) under the pseudonym of "Diane," giving very accurate medical diagnoses of cases that doctors had been unable to diagnose.

Kunz, Dora van Gelder. *The Personal Aura*. Wheaton, IL: Quest, 1991. Excellent, updated presentation of the aura, profusely illustrated, and informed by Kunz's extensive experience with medical diagnosis over several decades.

————, and Shafika Karagulla, M.D. *The Chakras and the Human Energy Fields*. Wheaton, IL: Quest, 1989. Probably the best presentation of the subject to date, by a trained clairvoyant and a neurosurgeon.

Leadbeater, C.W. *Man Visible and Invisible: Examples of Different Types of Men as Seen by Means of Trained Clairvoyance*. Wheaton, IL: Quest, 1971 [1902]. CWL's pioneering work, in which he created the language and conceptual way of describing the aura that everyone else has copied. Profusely illustrated.

————. *The Chakras: A Monograph*. Wheaton, IL: Quest, 1974 [1927]. The illustrated classic that created a new way of speaking about the chakras, which all subsequent authors have copied.

———. *Clairvoyance*. Adyar: Theosophical Publishing House, 1965 [1899]. Still the best discussion available on what clairvoyance means.

Powell, A.E. *The Etheric Double and Allied Phenomena*. Wheaton, IL: Quest, 1969 [1925]. Well-edited compilation of what trained clairvoyants had said on the subject,consisting mostly of quoted material from CWL and AB.

———. *The Astral Body*. Wheaton, IL: Quest, 1972 [1927]. Different subject, similar compilation.

Ritberger, Carol. *Your Personality, Your Health: Connecting Personality with the Human Energy System, Chakras, and Wellness*. Carlsbad, CA: Hay House, 1998. An excellent presentation of how to use the energy fields for physical and psychological healing.

White, John, ed. *Kundalini, Evolution, and Enlightenment*. New York: Paragon House,1990 [1979]. Essential reading for anyone interested in knowing about kundalini.

THE PHYSICAL REALITY OF THE MASTERS

Barborka, Geoffrey A. *The Mahatmas and Their Letters*. Adyar: Theosophical Publishing House, 1973. Documents the physical reality of the Masters through a thorough study of their letters and personal contacts with various people.

Olcott, Henry Steel. *Old Diary Leaves: The True Story of the Theosophical Society*, 6 vols. Adyar: Theosophical Publishing House, 1941-1975 [1895-1935]. Provides the closest thing to irrefutable evidence for the physical encounters the Masters had with Olcott and others, as corroborated through affidavits and other solid evidence. Those who deny the physical presence of the Masters in early Theosophical history never refer to this work, and with excellent reasons: The evidence provided by Olcott is nearly overwhelming.

Wachtmeister, Countess Constance. *Reminiscences of H.P. Blavatsky and the Secret Doctrine*. Wheaton, IL: Quest, 1976. Provides evidence of the Masters writing much of HPB's *Secret Doctrine*.

Index

Krohnen, Michael, *The Kitchen Chronicles: 1,001 Lunches with J. Krishnamurti*, vii
Kul, Djwal, Master, 121, 140
kundalini, 35-38, 46, 47, 60-61, 261-67, 263, 264
  definition of, 36-37, 46-47, 47-49
  spontaneous awakening of, 76-81
  yoga, 47, 56
Kunz, Dora van Gelder, 46, 52-53, 81
  CWL's clairvoyance, on, 52-53
  K's "discovery" by CWL, on, 52-53

language, limitations of, 243-47, 254-55, 260-61
Lao-tse, 9, 111
Latin American, 24
Leadbeater, Charles Webster (CWL), 8, 55, 57, 69, 73, 75, 77, 81-85, 87, 95, 114-16, 119-21, 123, 127, 131, 133, 141, 147, 156-67, 170, 181, 182, 256, 265
  clairvoyance, 40-53
  agrees with K's insights, 49
  development of by Masters, 120-23
  implies the observer is the observed, 49
  clairvoyant accuracy of, 41-43
  clairvoyant pioneer, 40-53
  declarations on Coming of the World Teacher, 57
  demythologizes field of subtle energies, 43-53
  hypnosis, on dangers of, 87
  declares K would be a greater speaker than AB, 51
  declares K would be the vehicle for the Lord Maitreya, 51
  discovers K, 50-53
  maintained that a Bodhisattva was to manifest, 185
  plays role in early development of K, 41, 50-53
  researches previous incarnations of K, 41, 51
  K's process, 160-62
  kundalini, on, 47-50
  metaphysical and clairvoyant teachings of, 52
  process, and K's, 47-50
  soul, on nature and primacy of, 44-45
  works cited or quoted:
    Chakras, The, 44, 47
    How Theosophy Came to Me, 120, 122
    Inner Life, The, vol. 2, 87
    Masters and the Path, The, 121, 127, 156
    Science of the Sacraments, The, 163, 164, 165
Leibniz, G.W., 243
Light on the Path, 226
limbic system, 66
Lincoln, Abraham, 7
logic, 228
  many-valued, 66, 174
  metaphysical implications of, 243-44, 245, 254-55
  two-valued, 172, 174, 175, 215-25, 243, 254, 255
  faith in, foundational for psychological and spiritual approaches, 215-22
  false safety in group identification, 222-25

Masters *(continued)*
 demythologized and deperson-
  alized by K and HPB, 241-43
 easy to assume one under-
  stands what HPB meant by,
  255
 examination of notion of,
  241-70
 explained by K, 262
 human beings with yogic abilities, 95, 257
 in charge of K's life, work, and
  death, 202-9
 in charge of process, 92-95, 99,
  139-41, 146, 166, 181-86
 in Theosophy, 262
 not nonphysical beings, 257
 physical bodies different, 171,
  175
 physical reality of, 6-11, 155-56
 started theosophical move
  ment, 147, 149, 156
 Tibetan tradition of, 262
maturity, 232-35, 238
Maya, 127
Mayan civilization, 252, 253
meditation, 229
medulla oblongata, 66
Mehta, Nandini, 5, 142-43, 146,
 179
memory, 247-48
Mendizza, Michael,
 *Krishnamurti: With a Silent
 Mind*, 95, 137
Mercavah, 19
Mesmerism, 188
Messiah, 62, 131, 133
metaphysics, 46, 207, 244, 254-55
 denied by HPB, 189-90
 denied by K, 46

denied by perennial schools, 46
 language, dependence on,
  243-47, 254-55, 260-61
 logical implications of, 243-44,
  254-55
 ludicrously false, 244
me, the *(see also* "I"; self, the),
 220, 223, 231, 232, 243, 245,
 248, 254
 examined, 243-51
 expects liberation by following
  algorithms, 220-22
 freedom from, the signature of
  wholeness, 222-25
 illusion, an, 232
 not me, and, 243, 245, 248,
  254-55
 subject-predicate grammar pro-
  motes illusion of, 245, 254
methods, psychological and spiritual, 216, 228, 232
 any, will yield results, 217-20
 expectations of, imply repetitive loops in the brain, 228
 require faith in logic, not transformation, 215-22
 still a place for, 228-31
mind, 221, 232
 analytical, 221, 232, 249-50,
  260
 conditioned, self-centered, 232
 dualism of mind-matter, 249
 philosophy of, 35
 unconditioned, 263
Mitchell, Edgar, 31
moksha (liberation), 251
Monad, 125
Montessori, 24, 112
Montreal, 248
morality, 212-15

Tathagata, 93

teachers
confusion about, 31-32
K's perspective on, 22-24

thalamus, 66

"that thing," 186, 192

that which is, 233

theology, 27

theosophical, 185, 252, 243

Theosophical, 135, 191

theosophical movement
started by the Masters, 138,
149, 151, 158

Theosophical Research Centre
Science Group, 41

Theosophical Society (T.S.), 4, 6,
7, 8, 15, 16, 22, 52, 56, 125,
148, 149, 193, 228, 237, 238,
258, 260, 266

theosophists, 16, 18, 39, 75, 85,
87, 136, 244

Theosophists, 52, 69, 70, 84, 103,
133-36, 151, 208, 209
accept CWL's work, but deny
him, 51-53
disagree with AB and CWL,
51-52
elitism of, 103

theosophy, xiv, xvi, 135, 146, 191,
238
cycles critical in twentieth
century, 68
distinction between Theosophy
and, 191-92
dying to the known central to,
70, 100
mutation of brain cells pivotal
to, 67-70
not a syncretistic system, 37

transformation at core of, 32

Theosophy, xiv, 10, 18, 70, 134,
148, 190, 191, 264

therapeutic fix, 223

therapy, 218, 219, 230-33
follows a logical algorithm
involving conditioning,
217-22

"things that matter," 111, 251,
262

thinker is the thought, the, 234

third eye, 169-77

Thompson, William Irwin, 250,
251

thought, 232

Tibet, 35, 265

Tibetan Book of the Dead, 113-15

time-bound algorithms and formulas, 234, 252

time-space, 232, 237

tradition, practice within a, 224

transformation (*see also* initiation; mutation; regeneration),
69, 70, 252
called for in twenty-first
century crises, 230
global, results from individual
mutation, 238
Heidegger's *authenticity* as part
of, 103
*mysterium tremendum et
fascinans*, akin to, 27, 62-63
perennial, 237-41
relationship, takes place only in
context of, 225-26
urgency of, given potential
global destruction, 231
within our reach, 227

323

QUEST BOOKS
are published by
The Theosophical Society in America,
Wheaton, Illinois 60189-0270,
a branch of a world fellowship,
a membership organization
dedicated to the promotion of the unity of
humanity and the encouragement of the study of
religion, philosophy, and science, to the end that
we may better understand ourselves and our place in
the universe. The Society stands for complete
freedom of individual search and belief.
For further information about its activities,
write, call 1-800-669-1571, e-mail olcott@theosophia.org,
or consult its Web page: http://www.theosophical.org

The Theosophical Publishing House
is aided by the generous support of
THE KERN FOUNDATION,
a trust established by Herbert A. Kern
and dedicated to Theosophical education.